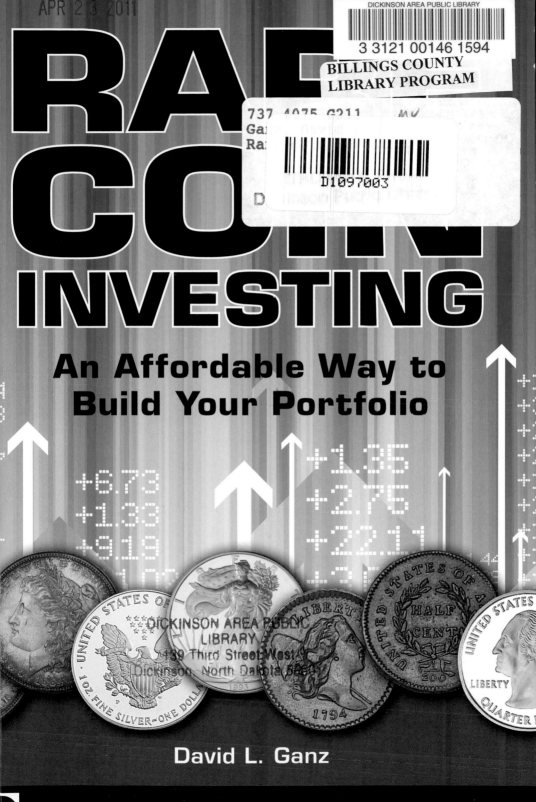

RARE COIN INVESTING

An Affordable Way to Build Your Portfolio

+673
+133
+919

+1.85
+2.76
+22.11

David L. Ganz

The World Authority on Coin Collecting

©2010 David L. Ganz

Published by

Krause Publications, a division of F+W Media, Inc.
700 East State Street • Iola, WI 54990-0001
715-445-2214 • 888-457-2873
www.krausebooks.com

To order books or other products call toll-free 1-800-258-0929
or visit us online at www.shopnumismaster.com

Library of Congress Control Number: 2010925010

ISBN-13: 978-1-4402-1358-8
ISBN-10: 1-4402-1358-5

Cover Design by Sharon Bartsch
Designed by Donna Mummery
Edited by Debbie Bradley

Printed in China

Dedication

To Kathy, who became an investor in numismatics through marriage and an astute partner in numismatic travel. Together we have planned our rare coin retirement, a cruise through life.

And for my friends John Jay Pittman, who persuaded me at Ben Stack's funeral that it was time to run for the ANA Board, and Reed Hawn, with whom I served two years on the Citizens Commemorative Coin Advisory Committee and from whom I continue to learn so much.

Kathy and David Ganz

Values

The charts in this book reflect the following "lock in" values reflected on April 18, 2010. (Unless otherwise noted.)

Gold	$1,136.30
Silver	$17.68
Platinum	$1,683.00
Coin Portfolio	$175,276.00
Portfolio Average	$8,956.30
Iowa Farmland	$4,371.00
Moodys AAA	5.31%
Dow Jones 30	11,018.20
CPI	217.61
S&P 500	1,182.25
NASDAQ	2,481.25

CONTENTS

Forword

By Hon. Jay W. Johnson

I first met author David Ganz, soon after I became the 36th U.S. Mint director in May 2000. As a former President of the America Numismatic Association, numismatic author and writer for a number of coin publications, he and his wife, Kathy, were some of the very first visitors to my new offices in Washington, D.C.

Kathy Ganz photo

And even though I was the director of the Mint, David was the one who, in our first visit, impressed me with his depth of knowledge of coins, and in particular United States coinage and the background to the beginning of the official U.S. Mint " 50 State Quarters" program.

In fact, as I found out from my predecessor, Phil Diehl, and other members of Congress, David not only knew a lot about the State Quarters program, he was the principal architect in the successful launching of the program. Yes, Congress passed the law authorizing it. And, in fact, I was a member of the 105th Congress that voted for the law (Public law 105-124 enacted Dec.1, 1997) creating the quarter program, as well as the golden dollar.

Jay W. Johnson

But, I know that I and many of my colleagues in Congress had no idea just what an innovative and successful coin collecting program we had created with the passage of this legislation. Even the U.S. Department of the Treasury, where some officials had their doubts and reservations about either the need or interest in this program, didn't have a full appreciation of just how successful this 50 State Quarter program would become.

In the fall of the first year of issuing State Quarters, a September 1999 U.S. Treasury report on "The Future of Money" had only one paragraph on the "Commemorative Quarter" program in which it stated: "Demand projections for this program are very tentative because no comparable, multi year circulating commemorative program has been attempted." Though it added "…initial estimates for the first half of 1999 suggest that the commemorative quarters are popular…"

Looking back, that was such an understatement! Through the rest of 2000 and 2001, as I gave speeches across the country launching many of the quarters in each state, I touted it as the "most successful collecting program ever … bigger than Beanie Babies and hula hoops!"

And though four Mint directors got to bask in the reflected glory of this amazingly successful coin collecting phenomenon, its creation goes back to the persistent and insistent personal persuasion of David Ganz as a creative numismatist and charter member of the U.S. Mint's new Citizen Commemorative Coin Advisory Commission.

He personally wrote an outstanding and lengthy "memo" to get the Department of Treasury and the U.S. Congress to authorize this legislation. It helped that the member of Congress who wrote the legislation, Congressman Mike Castle, also happened to be from the "First State" (first state to ratify the U.S. Constitution) of Delaware, and thus, the first state honored by the minting of its state quarter.

But, as I have said to many people in describing all that I learned of the most successful coin program ever in the history of U.S. coinage, it is to the author of this book and many others who I give the title to as father of the 50 State Quarter program.

Jay Worthington Johnson (1943-2009) was a member of the 105th Congress before serving as the 36th director of the United States Mint from May 2000 to August 2001. The Biographical Directory of Congress, 1774 to Present, has a more comprehensive biography at hhttp://bioguide.congress.gov.

THE UNDERLYING PREMISE

*Not every investment in rare coin is a collection, but
every collection of coins is an investment.*

— **Harvey G. Stack** [1]

Coin collecting and coin investing are not synonymous, but if you build a careful, systematic investment in affordable rare coins, you can simultaneously build a collection and plan for your rare coin retirement.

When I worked as an assistant editor of *Numismatic News* almost 40 years ago, we constantly took surveys of our readers to see why they collected coins, what attracted them to the field, and what we could do to pique their interest. Later, as a contributing editor to *COINage* magazine, Jim Miller, my friend and publisher, shared the results of similar polling that tried to quantify just why people bought (and sold) rare coins.

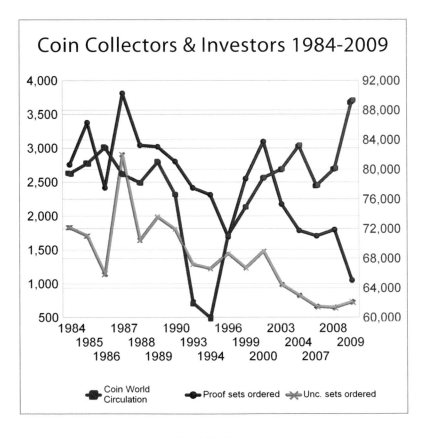

Later in my life, when I was already a practicing lawyer in New York City, I sought election to the board of governors of the American Numismatic Association, a national organization of coin collectors located in Colorado Springs, Colo., on the campus of The Colorado College on North Cascade Avenue. Its monthly journal, *The Numismatist*, was then nearly a century old, having started in 1888, a couple of years before the ANA itself was founded in 1891. In my decade on the ANA Board, first as a freshman member of the board, then as chairman of the Finance Committee, and finally as President (1993-1995), I watched as the organization (for itself, and its magazine) ran surveys trying to find the elusive principals of what defines a collector, and why they are attracted to coins.

During one other period, 1993-1996, I was a Clinton Administration appointee to the Citizens Commemorative Coin Advisory Committee, and for the two substantive years of membership, a majority of the members viewed it as their responsibility to try and find out the answers to the same question that had puzzled the newspaper and magazine publishers a generation earlier – because the response would undoubtedly make the programs that they endorsed more successful. Again surveys were taken, focus groups were sought and interviewed from within and without the collecting community.

Operating on the theory that there was simply a need for more potential members of the coin community, using the principal that a rising tide moves all the boats, the Citizens Advisory group recommended in its annual reports to Congress that circulating commemorative coins be struck to tap into the virgin territory of Americans with a proclivity to collect who either did not or had no opportunity that was interesting to do so.[2]

One other anecdote bears on the introductory nature of the subject – the commemorative coinage authorized by Congress to commemorate the centennial of the Statue of Liberty and to help shoulder the cost of repairs anticipated at more than $100 million. It was only the second modern commemorative (the Washington 250th anniversary was the first), and there was little to go by for statistical precedent.

I consulted with the Foundation that organized the remediation and made a recommendation to its executive director, Dr. Stephen Brigandi, that instead of focusing on expensive gold coins or even silver dollars, a better, more profitable approach and a better return on the Foundation's investment in successfully sponsoring the legislation would be to have a low-denomination, copper-nickel half dollar (available in uncirculated and proof), which would allow millions of Americans to enjoy collecting the coins but also make a greater profit on the surcharge allowed by Con-

1909 VDB cent.
Note the initials on reverse.
Heritage

How the bet was won
US Mint Photo

Vietnam Medals
US Mint

Vietnam Veterans Memorial
US Mint

gress to benefit the Statue of Liberty Foundation than with the precious metal counterpart alone.

A small bet was made with a steak dinner riding on it. The result with 6.9 million proof coins and 928,000 uncirculated specimen half dollars, was quite simply the most successful commemorative coin with the largest mintage in history (7,853,000 pieces that added over $22 million to the reconstruction costs of Lady Liberty).[3]

What my colleagues at *Numismatic News*, *COINage*, *The Numismatist*, *Coin World*, the Citizens Advisory Committee, and the Board of Governors of the American Numismatic Association found in their exhaustive studies of the psychology of collecting is that people collect coins because: they are fascinated with history; they love the brilliance of the design; they have an underlying fascination in the politics that created the coinage; they are gratified by the commemorative nature of what the Mints produce; and they like the ability to show off their knowledge about these things to their friends, neighbors, and fellow collectors.

Then each of the groups asked the follow-up question: what do you read in the newspaper or pe-

1906 Indian Head Cent

Legend:
- ■ 1906-1¢ VG
- ● Gold

riodical first. I always hoped that it would be "Under the Glass,"the column I started writing for a small monthly magazine in 1965, and which still runs in *Numismatic News*, a weekly periodical published by Krause Publications; or "Backgrounder," the column that I wrote in *Coin World* for almost 20 years; or "Coin Market Insider's Report," which *COINage* magazine has run since the early 1970s, or even "Coin Market Perspective," which had a decade run in *Coins* magazine.

No such luck. The answer was always the same: the price value guide that the periodical had showing its readers the state of the market. The people surveyed wanted to know what their coins were worth. And if you are reading this, so do you!

We'll get to what your coins are worth because you're probably already investing in coins – or thinking about it– even if you don't have a collection. My

1906 Circulated Indian Head Cent Obverse
Teletrade

1906 Circulated Indian Head Cent Reverse
Teletrade

Women in Military
US Mint Photo

mission is to tell you that there are affordable coins out there that you can collect – or invest in – that have a good future and pose a way that you can plan your rare coin retirement.

What attracted me to coin collecting (and ultimately coin investing) some 50 years ago was the ease of entry. No forms to fill out. No disclosure. Just sift through your pocket change and transform money into MONEY – real money. Perhaps my story is typical, but in 1960 I used to check my pocket change for things that were unusual. I found a well-worn, circulated 1906 Indian head cent in my pocket change, probably from a comic book or baseball card purchase. That wasn't unusual, because D.C. Comics charged 12¢ for a Superman comic, which meant tendering a dime and a nickel, with three cents change.

Thinking that I had been given a worthless foreign coin, I complained to the wise fountain of information, my mother, who took me to the Rockville Centre, N.Y., public library. A red-covered book by R.S. Yeoman set me straight at once: the coin was an Indian head cent, American issue, and was in very good condition (three letters of the word "Liberty" were visible). According to the Guidebook of United States Coins, then in its 14th edition, my pocket change investment was worth somewhere between 15 and 70 cents.[4] This wasn't rocket science; my allowance in those days was 25 cents a week in return for which I made my bed, cleared the dinner table, and dried the dishes. (This is so long ago there wasn't widespread use of dishwashers, except for the two hands of a child.)

For an investment of 1/25th of my weekly allowance I was hooked on coin collecting very quickly. Before long I was helping the local newspaper delivery boy go around each week to collect for the paper's subscription delivery costs. My fee: 25 cents, which I could apply toward buying any coins that I needed

*Circulated
2-Cent piece
Obverse & Reverse*
Teletrade

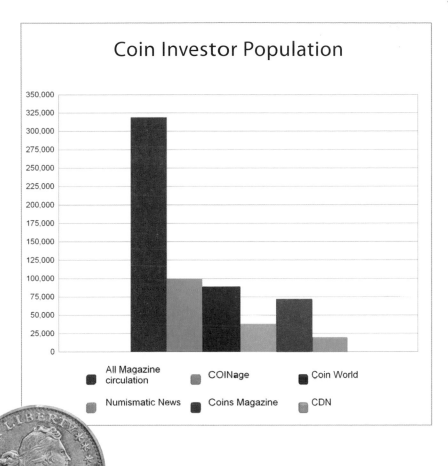

Coin Investor Population

Legend:
- All Magazine circulation
- Numismatic News
- COINage
- Coins Magazine
- Coin World
- CDN

1802 Half Dime Obverse & Reverse
David Lawrence Rare Coins

for my collection at double face value.

That started a lifetime of collecting, though in those days, I rarely bought anything more than an old, well-worn Shield nickel (cost by this "method," a whopping 10 cents), but still not a bad deal considering that the *Red Book* was quoting Shield nickels in good condition at $1.20 to $1.50 for the inexpensive common dates. I picked up some 2-cent pieces (4 cents cost) that way, too: the Guidebook listed inexpensive dates in good condition at 85 cents to $1.30.

Source: R.S. Yeoman, *A Guide Book of United States Coins*, Whitman Publishing (14th ed. 1961, 17th ed. 1964, 23rd ed. 1970, 32nd ed. 1979, 50th ed. 1997, 60th ed. 2007, 63rd ed, 2010). Gold prices annual average from Kitco, www.Kitco.com. 2010 price of gold estimated at $1,050/oz.

What is astonishing is to place this investment (the real start of a coin collection) in a very affordable coin from pocket change and to overlay on the same

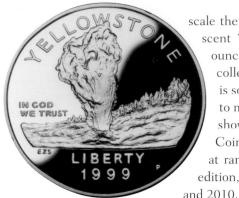

Yellowstone Old Faithful
US Mint

scale the price of gold, which in 1960 on the nascent "free" market averaged $36.50 per troy ounce, and to carry the returns over a 50-year collecting lifetime. Because the "investment" is so nominal, a convenient and practical way to measure the success is to borrow the price shown in the Guide Book of United States Coins (the Red Book) in seven years selected at random during the period: 1961 (the 14th edition, covering 1960), 1964, 1970, 1979, 1997 and 2010.

The overall gain is from the base cost of 1 cent. I measured it against the price quote in 2007, as well as 2010. Even as gold topped $1,000 per troy ounce in the late fall of 2009, the rare coin from pocket change had a better return when holding both for essentially a half century (see Chart 2).

Almost a dozen years ago, I wrote a book called *Planning Your Rare Coin Retirement*. It built a $10,000 portfolio and a $100,000 portfolio in 1997 and suggested reasons why these portfolios could grow over the long run. The results, in 2010 and beyond, exceeded my expectations and, I am assured, anyone who followed that advice. A more expanded view of the premise and results will be discussed in upcoming chapters.

This is not a book about 1804 silver dollars or 1913 Liberty head nickels.[5] It's a book of affordable rare coins that you can collect or invest in, or if you agree with Harvey Stack's theory – and I do – both.

Here are some of the statistics that form the basis of my underlying thoughts on the general topic of this book. It summarizes my experience as a writer for various coin magazines over the last 45 years and the experiences that were polled when I was on the board of (or legislative counsel to) the ANA, as the lawyer to the Professional Numismatists Guild, as a founding board member and counsel to the Industry Council for Tangible Assets, as a member of the Citizens Commemorative Coin Advisory Committee, and as a lawyer in New York City with a significant practice dependent on offering of advice that draws on this.

It's not the questions or answers from the surveys, but the impressions and trends that are the bulwark of my philosophy of collecting and investing. Each aspect of this counts in taking either a contrarian view, or one which you think will lead the herd.

So here is a summary of key analytical data and points from all the interchange with collecting investors:

- The average collector spends $2,500 annually maintaining and expanding his collection.

- Prior to 19996, most collectors (95%) were men
- Prior to 1999, there were about three million coin collectors in the United States.
- Prior to 1999, there were about 200,000 serious coin collectors in the U.S.
- Prior to 1999, there was a thin market for coin collecting items.
- Prior to 1999, the number of serious investors in rare coins was probably under 200,000.
- Post 1999 and the introduction of the state quarter program, the U.S. Mint says that between 120 million and 150 million people collect coins (most of them collecting state quarters)[7]
- Today there are probably more than 300,000 serious collector-investors, evidenced by the following periodic's circulation as reported in Library Trends magazine:[8]
- Bacon's 2008 Magazine Directory identifies the four largest North American magazines geared toward the hobby as *COINage* (circulation roughly 100,000), Coin World (circulation 89,000), Numismatic News (circulation 32,000) and Coins (circulation 72,000). Add to that The Numismatist (about 32,000) and the Coin Dealer Newsletter (about 20,000), and you have about 250,000 combined circulation.
- Median age of collector: 63[9]
- Average investment position: $380,000
- Average investment position excluding coins: $342,000
- Average value of numismatic collection: $39,100
- Collects popular series such as silver dollars (59%)[10]
- Collects other silver coins (50%)
- Collects gold coins (25%)
- Collects modern U.S. 1964-date (45%)
- Collects other things: antiques (28%), old books (12%), toys (11%); autographs (5%).
- Social and economic:
- Gender - Male (92%)
- Married (74%)
- Attended college (70%)
- Own my own home (89%)
- Average net worth (about $800,000)
- Average household income exceeds $100,000

Tax laws recognize three types of "collector" investors: those who pursue their hobby regardless of the profit or loss, investors who seek a long-term profit;and dealers. Some collectors become "vest-pocket" dealers; some dealers are also collectors. Some investors become collectors – but every collector is ultimately an investor, the longer that he or she holds on to the coins in their collection.

Over the next several pages, you are going to find out how to identify affordable rare coins, invest in them, use them to help assure your financial future and plan your rare coin retirement.

This book will look at some models of portfolio building as well as past performance as analyzed by Wall Street wizards of another generation – the Salomon Brothers survey that took a model portfolio for a dozen years starting in 1978 and showed how rare coins stood up against other investment entities. The method works so well, and is grandly illustrative, that you can compare how the extended Salomon charts look at the market of yesteryear and that of tomorrow. (I have extended some of the coins back 80 years, and carried all of the coins forward from the last time Salomon did the chart to the 21st century, now a generation later).

You'll also have the opportunity to look at the model portfolio of $10,000 that I suggested in the original 1998 edition of *Planning Your Rare Coin Retirement*, and the expanded $100,000 portfolio. This will give the opportunity to see how not only the portfolio as a whole made out, but selected individual coins as well. (There are too many coins to have extended analysis on each, but the typical specimens are included). Ditto on the $100,000 portfolio. At the end, I'll ask you the question, "How'd we do?" You can't hide from the printed recommendations. The answers will be black and white and may surprise you.

Please remember that past performance is not a guarantee or even a hint that a new portfolio – or the same one – will yield similar or identical results. Indeed, it could be the opposite. That's a hint to do your own research and draw your own conclusions.

We will also discuss how other collectors did. This will include John Jay Pittman and Harold Bareford. Both men have had their collections examined, but not from the standpoint of prior pedigrees and subsequent sales.

For example, Pittman's 1802 half dime in MS-61 (NGC) has an earlier and subsequent history:

Pittman's 1802 Half Dime in MS-61

Year	Auctioneer	Sale name	Price realized
1890	Banks	Parmelee	$205
1906	Chapman	Smith	$290
1941	Mehl	Dunham	$472.50
1947	Mehl	Will Neil	$630
1997	Akers	Pittman	$55,000
2008	DLRC		$345,000

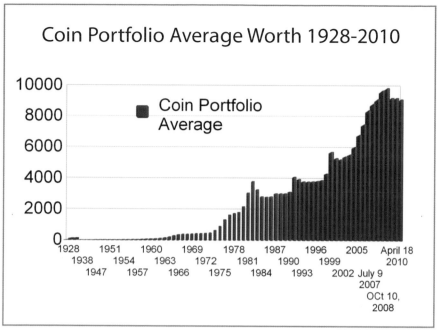

Coin Portfolio Average Worth 1928-2010

Formula @Average = [range of coins in portfolio]

This book takes on affordable rare coins, the gold standard and a lot more. If you want to know what makes a can't-miss coin, you'll find it here. The application of this is put into two new portfolios, one at $25,000 and one at $100,000.

You'll want to think about the *10 Steps Toward Financial Freedom* that are proposed as a means by which you can invest in affordable rare coins and plan your rare coin retirement. The book concludes with advise for post-retirement estate planning for coin collectors and investors.

Follow the premises of this book and I'm convinced that your rare coin retirement will be both pleasant and profitable.

Chapter 2

SALOMON I AND II:
THE BABY THAT ISN'T DIVIDED AT ALL

Part I. The explanation.

For collectors and investors of a certain age – and I am one of them, at the cusp – July 1st of each year was a time of caution, apprehension, and optimism as we waited to see what the annual edition of "A Guide Book of United States Coins," the ubiquitous Red Book, would say about the marketplace during the preceding 12-month period.

With great secrecy, the numbers were put together by Richard S. Yeo, whose pen name was R.S. Yeoman, and released in department stores, coin shops and major book chains across the country to the awe of those who were affected by it, which was exactly everyone who bought coins with an investment in mind (that, to my limited knowledge at the time, constituted the entire universe of people who collected or invested in coins).

1861 Dollar
Heritage Rare Coins

1862 3-Cent
Silver Obverse
Heritage Rare Coins

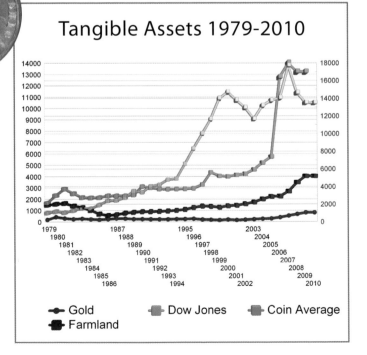

Tangible Assets 1979-2010

Gold • Dow Jones • Coin Average • Farmland

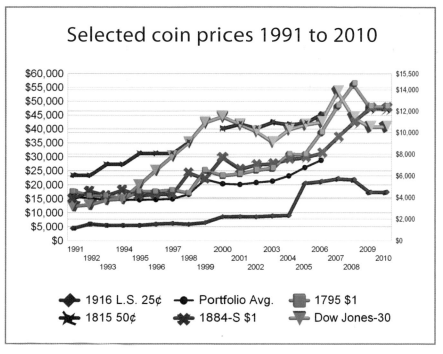

Selected coin prices 1991 to 2010

Left axis		Right axis
$60,000		$15,500
$55,000		$14,000
$50,000		
$45,000		$12,000
$40,000		$10,000
$35,000		
$30,000		$8,000
$25,000		$6,000
$20,000		
$15,000		$4,000
$10,000		$2,000
$5,000		
$0		$0

1991 1992 1993 1994 1995 1996 1997 1998 1999 2000 2001 2002 2003 2004 2005 2006 2007 2008 2009 2010

◆ 1916 L.S. 25¢   ● Portfolio Avg.   ■ 1795 $1
✕ 1815 50¢   ✖ 1884-S $1   ▼ Dow Jones-30

1862 3-Cent Reverse
Heritage Rare Coins

1866 5-Cent Obverse
Heritage Rare Coins

1866 5-Cent Reverse
Heritage Rare Coins

1881 50-Cent Obverse
Heritage Rare Coins

In 1960, when I began collecting coins, the way that you found out about a coin's value started with the "Red Book." The *Coin Dealer Newsletter* (a weekly price guide) was three years in the future. A weekly periodical devoted to the coin field was being conceived, but in the meanwhile, *Numismatic News* was a once a month hobby periodical, *Numismatic Scrapbook* was a monthly and *The Numismatist* (monthly publication of the American Numismatic Association) gave short reports on selected lots of auction results. *Coin World* began as a weekly, but not until mid-1960.

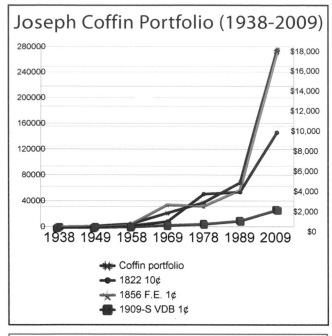

Joseph Coffin Portfolio (1938-2009)

Legend:
- Coffin portfolio
- 1822 10¢
- 1856 F.E. 1¢
- 1909-S VDB 1¢

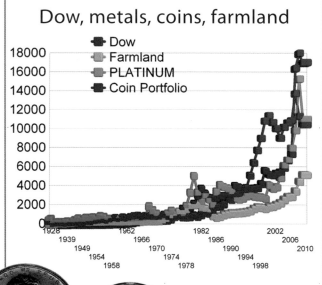

Dow, metals, coins, farmland

Legend:
- Dow
- Farmland
- PLATINUM
- Coin Portfolio

Dealers were using the teletype to communicate, but it was nothing at all like the Internet of today. It was a backwater time, though some books and newsletters had yet to populate the field. One of the oldest is John Kamin's "The Forecaster," now in its 47th year, but then but a distant glimmer.

There were some books; Joseph Coffin wrote "The Complete Book of Coin Collecting" and in the revised third edition (1959) he devotes a chapter to "Making a Profit from Coin Collecting," which suggests 38 coins, half cent to half dollar (no gold coins or silver dollars included) and, being very avant garde, lists prices in 1938, 1949 and 1958. (The accompanying chart that I have prepared lists these coins adding valuations in 1968, 1978, 1998 and 2009, and analyzes them along with the Salomon Brothers use of coin data.)

At right, are the coins that Coffin utilized and, comparing them with their 1938 cost, shows the annual compounded rate of return using December 2009 pricing.

The rare coin market was still flying high in the 1970s when Salmon Brothers decided to cover the rare coin field. Even as the *Wall Street Journal* and other financial periodicals reported that the art and auction

1909-S VDB
Obverse
Heritage Rare Coins

1909-S VDB
Reverse
Heritage Rare Coins

David L. Ganz

Joseph Coffin Portfolio Contents (1959)

Date	Denomination	Condition	1938	1949	1958	1969	1978	1989	2009	1938-2009 comp'd	1958-2009
1796	H¢	Fine	100	200	350	2350	400	7500	27500	8.23%	8.75%
1796	H¢	fine	150	300	500	3000	7300	20000	55000	8.67%	9.46%
1808/7	H¢	fine	15	20	35	185	125	175	575	5.27%	5.53%
1811	H¢	unc	30	50	100	600	1250	250	8750	8.32%	8.98%
1799	Lg1¢	Fine	50	100	225	1075	1300	2100	12250	8.06%	7.99%
1804	Lg1¢	Fine	20	75	150	45	1300	1100	400	4.31%	1.90%
1856	FE1¢	Unc	75	150	350	2250	2100	3700	17250	7.96%	7.78%
1857	FE1¢	Unc	8	18	24	115	475	200	450	5.84%	5.80%
1864	1¢	Unc	8	50	90	225	275	340	4250	9.24%	7.69%
1871	1¢	Unc	10	15	55	180	240	275	1200	6.98%	6.11%
1877	1¢	Unc	12	25	70	800	925	1500	3950	8.51%	8.06%
1909-S	1¢	Unc	4	20	80	285	300	400	1250	8.43%	5.43%
1909S VDB	1¢	Unc	2	12	75	220	340	650	1725	9.99%	6.22%
1914-D	1¢	unc	1	10	200	560	750	1650	2925	11.90%	5.29%
1923-S	1¢	unc	1	9	110	225	260	350	635	9.52%	3.43%
1864	2¢		15	40	95	275	475	1200	2550	7.50%	6.53%
1877	3¢	Proof	20	75	155	700	850	2000	3500	7.55%	6.18%
1877	3¢	Unc	2	8	30	420	445	1250	1200	9.43%	7.35%
1866	5¢	Unc	3	12	25	120	450	325	340	6.89%	5.15%
1867	5¢	Unc	3	16	70	160	525	425	2750	10.08%	7.31%
1871	5¢	Unc	5	40	100	200	270	300	520	6.76%	3.22%
1885	5¢	Unc	5	25	90	275	385	1200	2650	9.24%	6.72%
1912-D	5¢	Unc	2	25	80	220	250	275	340	7.50%	2.82%
1794	H10¢	vf	15	35	250	675	1100	2250	4125	8.23%	5.54%
1846	H10¢	xf	10	40	85	300	340	900	2675	8.19%	6.86%
1849-O	H10¢	unc	10	20	30	250	265	450	3675	8.68%	9.69%
1853-O	H10¢	unc	25	125	175	55	450	750	850	5.09%	3.09%
1822	10¢	unc	7.5	35	180	600	3300	3500	9350	10.56%	7.89%
1841	10¢	unc	45	150	250	47.5	400	350	1100	4.60%	2.89%
1856-S	10¢	xf	10	75	180	290	275	400	13500	10.69%	8.66%
1875-CC	20¢	unc	5	12	45	182.5	1000	1000	2625	9.22%	8.13%
1796	25¢	fine	25	65	350	2150	3100	5250	21500	9.98%	8.24%
1804	25¢	xf	10	30	200	650	3000	2200	26500	11.74%	9.85%
1822	25¢	unc	75	250	500	1750	2700	2100	29000	8.75%	8.12%
1805over4	50¢	xf	5	75	150	375	500	1000	1350	8.20%	4.32%
1806 over 9	50¢	xf	10	75	150	275	400	800	3050	8.39%	5.96%
1842-O	50¢	unc	12	60	175	300	450	575	900	6.27%	3.20%
										Average	
Total			805.5	2342	5779	22385	38270	68690	272160	8.24%	

Average compounded rate: 8.24%.

Note: Formula for calculating compounded is Rate (current value, former value, 71 years.)

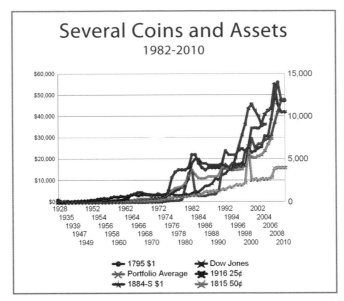

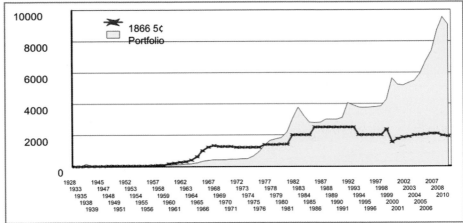

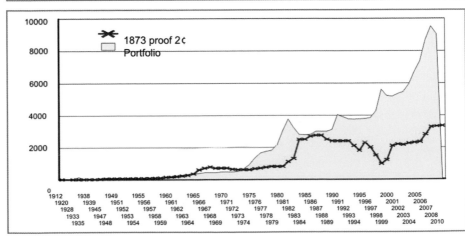

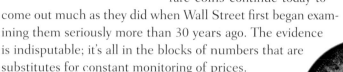

1807 Draped Bust
Dime
Heritage Rare Coins

field's sales moved the marketplace, and that gold, silver and platinum had significant activity as the stock market tanked and then recovered, Salomon Brothers noticed that there was still a bull market for collectibles.

Measuring tangible assets vs. the equities market, rare coins continue today to come out much as they did when Wall Street first began examining them seriously more than 30 years ago. The evidence is indisputable; it's all in the blocks of numbers that are substitutes for constant monitoring of prices.

1815 50-Cent Obverse
Heritage Rare Coins

Wall Street compared rare coins with many different kinds of assets before concluding that the market, while small, had a winning attitude. Researchers for the Salomon Brothers investment banking firm did a 10-year look back to many different classes of assets and specific examples.

The points of comparison included old master paintings, gold, diamonds, housing, farmland, Chinese ceramics, 90-day Treasury bills, bonds and stocks, foreign currency, oil, stamps, silver and rare coins. Each component had experts who provided data designed to be reliable, similar to the way a stock market analyst examines a company or an industry.

1847 $1 Reverse
Heritage Rare Coins

Pulling it all together was Salomon Brothers, a white shoe investment banking firm founded in 1910, which after mergers became a part of the Citigroup empire. It all began with Robert S. Salomon, who in 1978 commissioned a survey of all types of asset rates of return – he wanted a 10-year look back to 1968 – and published the results showing a superior performance of rare coins.

1928 Hawaiian
Commemorative Reverse
Heritage Rare Coins

For a dozen years afterwards – until 1991– Salomon Brothers annually published a listing of the assets and a point of comparison – the annual rates of return. This annual report, like the arrival of the "Red Book," was heralded by collectors and investors alike, even though there were by this time several weekly periodicals that covered the rare coin market

1932 $10 Obverse
Heritage Rare Coins

1794 Half Cent
Heritage

1807 Draped
Bust Dime
Heritage

1989
Salomon Survey

- Rare coins 30%
- Chinese ceramics
  40%

10 years rate of return
- Coins 13%
- Stocks 17%

20 years return
- Coins 17%
- Chinese ceramics
  13%
- Gold 12%
- Old masters 11%
- Diamonds 10%
- Inflation 6%

from every angle, as well as generalized coverage from the financial sector of the daily press.

Coins turned out to be a topnotch draw each year, though not always at the top. The reason is that a main line Wall Street firm was paying attention to rare coins as an alternative investment vehicle.

Salomon Brothers abruptly terminated coverage of rare coins and the survey itself after the Federal Trade Commission suggested the datum was being used by unscrupulous vendors to suggest that all coins had the posted rate of return, and probably because Salomon was having its own difficulty with federal regulators over its bond department's action.

Salomon's approach to looking at the coin market is similar to the way a market analyst looks at the Dow Jones Industrial Average (DJIA) in tracing market trends. The Dow today consists of 30 stocks that are widely diversified in terms of ownership and are well-capitalized. (The 30 stocks are broadly representative of the American economy.)

Components used by Salomon Brothers are set forth and examined so that the use of independent but collateral analysis involving points of comparison can be given a specific analysis that puts it all in context.

In my version, I have reached back farther than Salomon did, but using the same coins. I have done the same with other components, and in one case (farmland) reached out to an expert who guided me to the right location for valuation data, and has since helped fill in the blanks – including valuation of Iowa farmland per acre in early 2010.

Here's some general information about the components of the data charts that have been prepared by me and used throughout this book.

The Dow. Started in 1896, none of the original companies are still part of the Dow. It was published on May 26, 1896, and repre-

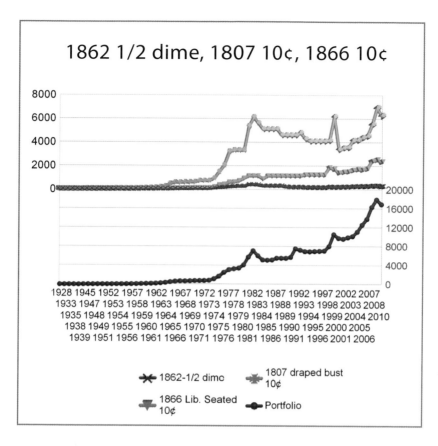

1862 1/2 dime, 1807 10¢, 1866 10¢

Legend:
- 1862-1/2 dime
- 1866 Lib. Seated 10¢
- 1807 draped bust 10¢
- Portfolio

sented the average of 12 stocks from important American industries.

The original components: American Cotton Oil Company (now part of Unilever), American Sugar Company (now Domino Foods, Inc.), American Tobacco Company (broken up in a 1911 antitrust action), Chicago Gas Company (today an operating subsidiary of Integrys Energy Group, Inc.) Distilling & Cattle Feeding Company (now Millennium Chemicals), Laclede Gas Light Company (removed in 1899), National Lead Company (removed in 1916); North American Company, (Edison electric company, broken up in the 1940s); Tennessee Coal, Iron and Railroad Company (a part of U.S. Steel since 1907), U.S. Leather Company (dissolved 1952), and United States Rubber Company (later known as Uniroyal, now a part of Michelin).

In a pre-computer age, this was an easy method to survey how the stock market behaved; the stocks were weighted so that they were representative not only of themselves but other similar stocks. Even today, when computers can tell precisely how all of the stocks are doing at any one time, the Dow Jones Industrial Average remains a valuable tool because it is so easy to find a reference point in the past.

All of the stocks in the original Dow have long been replaced, with three changes being made as recently 2009. Chevron was added in February 2008, Kraft Food was added September 2008, and on June 8, 2009, General Motors (GM) and Citigroup were replaced by insurance giant Travelers Companies and Cisco Systems.

Even with the ease that computers offer, the Dow market basket remains a measure that can be tagged against in any economic or investment analysis – and it looks great on graphs. By adding a hypothetical component, it becomes possible to bring the Dow back to 1888 – eight years before it started – to permit a look back of more than 120 years on coin prices and other components.

Gold. For more than 5,000 years, mankind has been fascinated with gold, and for good reason. If all of the gold mined since the dawn of time were melted in a crucible the size of the Washington Monument and poured inside as if it were a mold, it would not come even close to being half-filled. (It would go about a third of the way up).

Gold has industrial uses, investment possibilities, jewelry fabrication, and official reserve status between nations. In the 1830's, its value was set at $20.67 an ounce, and this fixed price formed the basis under which gold coinage became the international coin of the realm. Under this system, a 20 franc piece from whatever issuing authority – France, Italy (20 Lire), Switzerland (Vreneli) and others, all had .1867 troy ounces of precious metal.

Beyond that, gold's history is generally one of stability if you look at it from 1789 until 1933. There was talk of a 16:1 gold to silver price ratio at the time of the creation of a United States Mint in 1792, but the machinations of Alexander Hamilton were miscalculations – and the wrong price for the gold caused a major outflow of American gold coin.

Teletrade

Stack's

One of the major reasons today that early U.S. gold coin is so scarce is that very outflow; it went abroad and was recoined into less expensive (less metal) foreign coinage. (That is also why the gold and silver weights were changed so many times between then and 1837).

The Coinage Act of 1837 set the value of an ounce of gold at $20.67 and for nearly a century it was maintained at that level. Not until 1934 when the dollar was devalued was the price changed to $35 an ounce. Subsequently, during the Johnson years, gold was revalued officially to $38 an ounce, then under Nixon to $42.22 – still its official price.

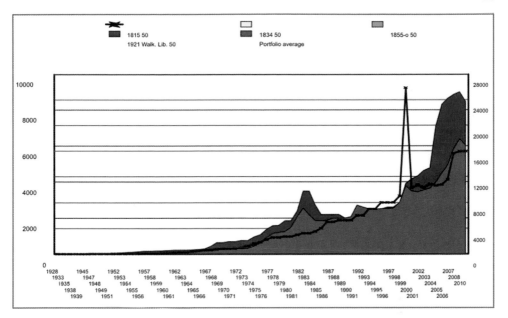

America's fortune and its world leader-
ship, its economic engine and its $11 billion
plus gold reserve (valued at the official price,
of course) have helped shape the 20th and
early 21st century Golden Age and Golden
Rules. (To get an idea of the real value of
America's gold reserve today, multiply it by
about 30 and you get an approximation of its
current value – $340 billion).

The most recent history of the price of
gold begins when the $20.67 price had to
be breached. On Oct. 22, 1933, FDR held a
"Fireside Chat," and speaking to the American people by radio from the White House,
he told them he planned to "establish a government market for gold in the United States
... (by) authorizing the Reconstruction Finance Corp.

FDR Fireside Chat
FDR Library

*"To buy gold newly mined in the United States at prices to be determined by the
Secretary of the Treasury . . ."*

The price of gold began to drift upward from $20.67, the level at which it
had been pegged during the preceding century.

On Jan. 30, 1934, the sham was ended. The Gold Reserve Act was signed
into law by Roosevelt, giving title of all gold coin and bullion to the U.S. government, ordering the withdrawal of all U.S. gold coin from circulation, and

mandating that any gold held by the government, including gold coin, be melted into ingots.

The next day, FDR formally devalued the dollar by raising the price of gold to $35 an ounce and by reducing the weight of the dollar to 15-5/21 grains of 9/10th fine gold. Previously, the dollar had been valued at 25.8 grains of gold, calibrated at the $20.67 an ounce rate.

Gold coins like the $20 gold piece (initially bearing $19.99 worth of gold) now had $34.86 in gold content. Small wonder that the President needed to mandate their recall.

Roosevelt's actions ultimately caused more than $1.59 billion in United States gold coins to be melted. Nearly $1.3 billion in double eagles ($20 gold pieces) alone were melted – 66.4 million coins. (See chart summarizing, Chapter 8).

Dates that had been very common became collector's items overnight, though a few abrogated their patriotic duty by becoming "golden" numismatists.

To some extent, FDR's inflationary policies worked, for the nation soon began to pull out of the Great Depression. Still, it was not until World War II's outbreak that the nation saw full economic recovery. (Look at those numbers and compare them to the recession of 2008-2009 and see a frightening comparison).

What though of the right to own gold, and the right to purchase gold coins of any date and denomination? Americans were denied this on the basis of the Gold Reserve Act and subsequent executive orders by six successive American presidents – Roosevelt, Truman, Eisenhower, Kennedy, LBJ, and Nixon.

In 1973, gold regulations were eased slightly to allow more gold coins minted between 1933 and 1961 to be admitted to the country as "rare and unusual" coins, however, a drive in Congress to reverse the action of four decades before failed when the House failed by a single vote to call for immediate ownership.

By early 1974, the President had gained the legal authority from Congress to allow private gold ownership at any time he felt it is in the best interests of the international economic situation of the United States.

In the early 1970s, I wrote that "Likelihood is that such action [to legalize private gold ownership] may come in 1974 or 1975, once the international monetary system has been successfully reformed – and gold removed as the linchpin of the system.

Little did I suspect that it would become legal in one of the most unusual unitings of interest of diverse political elements – the conservative "gold bugs" and the liberal Democrats.

Succinctly, the Democrats had a foreign aid package that was in need of passage; the conservative Republican "gold bugs," most of whom had voted against every foreign aid proposal that ever came before Congress, saw a golden opportunity.

They added a clause to the foreign aid bill that would simultaneously legalize private gold ownership by a day certain, but also retroactively repeal all of the regulations and laws that impeded holding the precious metal.

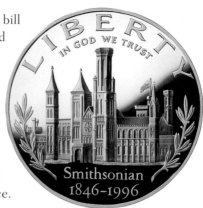

No doubt the process was assisted by the languishing role that gold had enjoyed in international trading. In fact, on Jan. 16, 1970, the price of gold actually declined below the official $35 an ounce price to a record low level in modern times of $34.95 an ounce. (The march to record prices came later).

The unusual political coalition held together, the foreign aid bill became law, and on Dec.

Smithsonian Castle 1996
US Mint

31, 1974, private gold ownership was again permissible for the first time in 40 years. Gold's historic role once again moved to preeminence.

What is clear from the history is that rare numismatic gold coins are considerably more scarce than previously suspected. The melting statistics that are referred to elsewhere lie in no single government source, but rather in many different locations.

Gold has had a wild and woolly ride since its legalization in 1975 (Dec. 31, 1974). That history – plus its reputation as an asset of last resort – caused it to rise to $834 an ounce in 1980, and then to descend into a lower, but stable, bliss. More recently, in 2008, gold topped $1,000 an ounce with pretenses to more. It reached $1,250 in 2009 and ended 2009 on the London gold fix at $1,104 an ounce. The fix in May 2010 was again over $1,200.

No wonder it is a valuable tracker in the Salomon survey; it is an asset of last resort with a modern future.

Silver, Platinum. Silver was included in the original study, platinum was not, but both have a long history that allows it to be utilized as a bellwether of things to come, and a mark-up of the past. Discovered by Italian scientist Julius Scaliger in 1557, large quantities of the metal were not available until about 1750, when the Spaniards found platinum in Peru. They named it platinum from their word "platino," which is Spanish for silver.

Until 1968, platinum had never exceeded $200 an ounce. By March 5, 2008, it was more than 10 times that number – to $2,276 an ounce. Coin investment products in bullion coins remain a relatively modest sum. Since then, it has receded to the $1,200-$1,400 level – but impressive for gain.

In 2007, the Philadelphia Mint sold about 35,000 platinum coins (uncirculated), or about 13,000 ounces. For 2008, under 2,500 ounces are involved for proof, as well as uncirculated issues (about a thousand for coin proof sets were ordered, for example).

1794 Half Cent
Heritage Rare Coins

Overall platinum bullion sales include, among others, American Eagles, Canadian Maples, Chinese Pandas, Australian Kangaroos, Australian Koalas, Australian Kookaburras, Austrian Philharmonics, Britannia, Canadian Maple Leafs, Isle of Man Cats, Gibraltar Dogs and Australian nuggets.

Source for the metal today remains largely South Africa (about two-thirds of the world annual production), with significant amounts also recovered in Russia and Canada as a by-product of nickel mining. Other notable areas of platinum production include the United States, Finland, Australia, and the Philippines, according to the CPM Group, which covers the field with paid newsletters and publications.

About 6.2 million ounces of platinum are utilized each year, according to Johnson Matthew, one of the oldest and largest dealers in the metal. In the early 1980s, about 17 percent of use was attributable to individual investment demand, mostly satisfied with coins and bars. Johnson Matthew says the rate now is less than 2 percent, or under 120,000 ounces annually.

U.S. production of platinum and palladium is presently limited to The Stillwater and East Boulder Mines in south-central Montana. Both are owned by Stillwater Mining Company. Combined, Stillwater and East Boulder Mines milled more than 1,200,000 metric tons of ore and recovered more than 18,400 kilograms of palladium and platinum in one recent year.

As scarce a metal as platinum is, it remains a metal that has been involved in contemporary coinage both for commemorative purposes and also as an investment vehicle, principally in one ounce and half and quarter ounce increments. Tenth and 20th of an ounce coins are generally intended for jewelry, though some find the allure of relatively inexpensive precious metals an invitation to collect.

Farmland. Some of the other relevant numbers used as a comparison or as a foil pertained to farmland. The farmland of charting choice is Iowa.

Locating data as far back as 1912 turned out to be providential. The U.S. Department of Agriculture Web site helped. But to go farther back, there was a paucity of data, especially as far back as 1888, part of the overview approach.

The *New York Times* Web site yielded an amazing article about what it cost to operate a farm in 1888 – and that the farmers were looking for an 8 percent return on investment. There was an obscure advertisement offering to sell land in Iowa. The ad did not give a price per acre, vital for modern comparison, but fostered an idea.

What was needed was advertisements for selling land in Iowa circa 1888. A commercial Web site offered the *Cedar Rapids Evening Gazette*. The Sept. 17, 1888, issue yielded ads offering to sell improved farmland at $25 an acre (more than my estimate for the average coin cost in the assembled portfolio).

According to Professor Mike Duffy, the chief analyst who measures farmland at Iowa State University, farmland was going for $3,500 an acre ("or more") in July 2007. A year later, on July 6, 2008, Duffy gave me an estimated figure of $4,500, a 26 percent annual increase. There has since been some backslide. The 2010 price for farmland, Duffy said in December 2009, is $4,500.

The Consumer Price Index: The Consumer Price Index (CPI) showed inflation averaging about 3.43 percent annually in 2007; it was at about 208 on the 1982=100 scale. It was at 216 in May, and on Sept. 16, 2008, edged still higher to 219.08, according to the Bureau of Labor Statistics. On a seasonally adjusted basis, the CPI was virtually unchanged (0.0 percent) in September following a 0.1 percent decrease in August 2008. In late December 2009, the November 2009 Labor Statistics release showed 216.33 (deflation). In April 2010, it stood at 217.61 (lower than 2008!)

If you look at the Bureau of Labor Statistics information (it has adjusted from a 1967=100 to 1982-4=100), the 1967 non-adjusted number in the year 2009 is equal to 648.02. The CPI uses a variety of measuring devices, but objectively measures the purchasing power of the dollar. The Federal Bureau of Labor Statistics has maintained CPI stats since 1913.

The portfolio. The Salomon Brothers original portfolio was intended to be like the Dow, its component parts interchangeable. It was intended to represent the market broadly, but included no gold coins (private gold ownership was still new and the thought was that gold coinage too closely mirrored the bullion market).

1. Neil Berman and Hans M.F. Schulman revealed the component parts in their 1986 book on the coin market. The complete list: 1794 Liberty Cap half cent, extremely fine; 1873 2-cent piece, brilliant proof; 1866 5-cent nickel with rays brilliant proof; 1862 3-cent silver brilliant uncirculated (BU); 1862 half dime BU; 1807 Draped Bust dime BU; 1866 Liberty Seated dime BU; 1876 20 cents BU; 1873 arrows quarter BU; 1886 Seated quarter BU; 1916 quarter BU; 1815 Bust half uncirculated; 1834 Bust half B.U.; 1855-O Seated half BU; 1921 Walking Liberty half BU; 1795 Draped Bust dollar BU; 1847 Seated dollar BU; 1884-S Morgan dollar BU; 1881 Trade dollar proof, and 1928 Hawaiian commemorative half dollar.

The 1881 proof Trade dollar was a choice that could easily be substituted; as a proof-only issue, an 1879 or 1880, or even 1882 or 1883 would work nicely as a substitute. The 1927 Hawaiian half dollar (mintage around 10,000 pieces) would substitute for many of the 144 commemorative halves; the modern era commemoratives were ignored because they were not yet a reality.

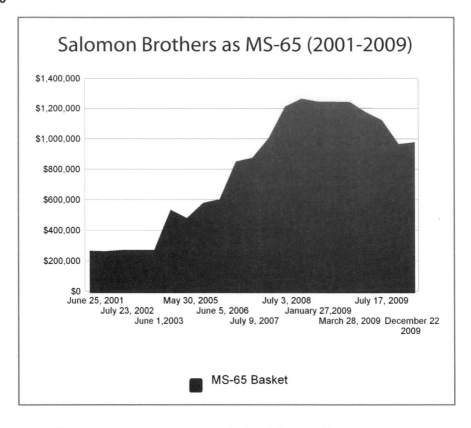

Salomon Brothers as MS-65 (2001-2009)

MS-65 Basket

Where Dow Jones statistics are calculated daily, and based on actual components and prices published in many periodicals, the coin list was first compiled by Salomon Brothers going back to 1978, and carried through 1990 was always done on an annualized basis. That is somewhat misleading in result, but still a useful analysis.

In the charts and analysis in my presentations, the Salomon Brothers raw data was not used. Instead, both back (older) and forward (subsequent) pricing was independently examined. Coin grading changes over the years are taken into account.

Coins, with the exception of a high-end circulated early American copper, are either choice uncirculated or proof (about MS-63 or Proof-63 on the numerical grading scale); if higher grades were utilized, such as a MS-65, the results (i.e., the return on investment) would be substantially higher.

In fact, Dennis Baker, whose NumisMedia has supplied me with working data for the past seven or eight years, has also included MS-65 data so I can compare the two. It is so off-the-chart as to make the comparisons ridiculous. A sample chart showing the recent returns since he began furnishing data is included.

Broad-based market purchases of MS-63 are possible; by their nature, MS-65 versions of many older rarities are either thinly traded or just not widely available.

chart and photos book published July 20, 2008, by Krause Publications ($19.99, available through the trade and through Amazon and Barnes & Noble).

For convenience, some of my data uses a conceit: the chart is so high now that I take the "average" price of a coin in it. For example, in 1978 (year one for Salomon), to assemble the model portfolio would have cost about $35,000; today (using Jan. 1, 2010, as a cutoff) it would run over $200,000. (The "average" cost of a coin is around $9,500).

There is also the issue of overweight coins. The 1795 silver dollar and the 1884-S Morgan dollar comprise more than 40 percent of the portfolio value today. Back in 1978, the 1884-S was a lot less important; but the 1795 dollar choice was a $15,000 choice in a $35,000 portfolio (42 percent).

Watching the Dow swing wildly today – hundreds of points in either direction – it is remarkable to watch the coin market displayed as an element of stability. The graphs that accompany compare rare coins with farmland, precious metals, and several other measuring devices.

Just on the chance that a claim might be made that the whole of the coin portfolio was a pretext, I took a genuinely rare coin – the 1794 dollar – in a collector grade condition (very fine) and matched it against the various index components. The coin has an extensive pedigree, and a number of sales. The earliest that I have documented being 1888, or 120 years ago.

Results are similar; a substantial rate of return with rare coins turning out to be a solid investment over the 19th, 20th and now 21st centuries. The same is true of the coins charted from the John Jay Pitman collection (Chapter 5), as well as those of Harold Bareford (Chapter 6). Some of those with extensive pedigrees before their charted sale have since been re-sold several times over. The result is a clear picture that can be measured against Salmon Brothers results – even though Pitman and Bareford were fanatics when it came to condition.

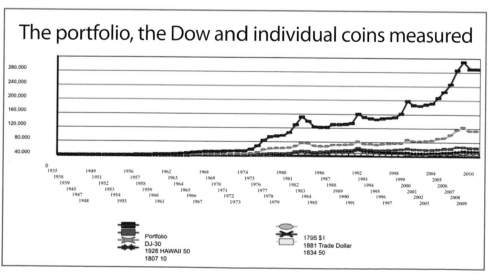

The portfolio, the Dow and individual coins measured

Portfolio
DJ-30
1928 HAWAII 50
1807 10

1795 $1
1881 Trade Dollar
1834 50

As active as farmland acquisition has been in this decade, and despite the explosion of the Consumer Price Index, the activity in the rare coin market has not yet been seriously affected by the recession that evidenced the collapse of Lehman Brothers and the stock market in the fall of 2008, and the greater economic calamity that affected much of the nation into 2010.

But for now, it suffices not to look to the future, but to look back to the past and prior years of the survey.

Part II.

Last year, 2009, was a bad year for the American economy, and coins proved to be no exception. The Dow Jones Industrial Average went up 63 percent or so from March 2009 to December 2009, which sounds impressive, but it had nowhere to go but in that direction. To slip further down the charts would have been unthinkable.

The easiest way to present what happened to coins and other measures of value, is to do it by benchmarks. For the coins in the Salomon Brothers survey, the easiest way to do that and maintain the dignity of the charting, is to take the average price at a given time of all of the components. Thus, you'll see that the market basket of coins declined from July 2008 to December 2009. But if you go back seven years to 2003, it's a different picture:

	2003	2010	Gain or loss	Compound
Farmland (Iowa)/acre	$2,275.00	$4,500.00	97.8022%	10.23%
Coin portfolio average	$5,468.00	$9,051.00	65.5267%	7.46%
Dow Jones Ind. Avg.	9,018.00	10,428.00	15.6354%	2.10%
Gold	$359.00	$1,104.00	207.5209%	17.41%
Silver	$4.52	$16.84	272.5664%	20.67%

Note: Uses year-end Dow Jones Industrial Average, year-end London Gold Fix, 12/22/09 Coin Portfolio Prices, courtesy of NumisMedia (Dennis Baker), and December 2009 farmland prices courtesy of Professor Michael Duffy, University of Iowa.

It is equally interesting to view coins as a long-term investment, to compare them with financial instruments of 10 years duration, and other elements that a typical investor might consider as an alternative to more conventional investments. Consider the portfolio since 2000 as a match against farmland, equities (Dow Industrial and Standard & Poors 500), the Consumer Price Index and precious metals (gold, silver, platinum), which show compound rates of gain or loss (2000-2009) as follows:

Portfolio

Date	Portfolio	Average	Gold	Silver	CPI	Pt	S&P	Farm	Dow Jones
2000	$102,656	$5,231.75	$325.00	$4.98	112.42	$552	1320.28	$1,857	11,357
2001	$101,035	$5,165.20	$271.19	$4.40	93.8	$505	1148.08	$1,926	10,646
2002	$104,231	$5,338.00	$310.07	$5.05	107.25	$525	879.80	$2,083	10,003
2003	$106,926	$5,468.75	$359.10	$4.52	124.21	$651	1111.90	$2,275	9,018
2004	$116,441	$5,943.50	$403.15	$6.63	139.45	$819	1203.20	$2,629	10,163
2005	$131,742	$6,707.50	$437.70	$7.31	151.4	$896	1216.00	$2,914	10,623
2006	$144,796	$7,372.25	$574.65	$9.09	198.77	$1,065	1273.46	$2,950	10,847
2007	$170,843	$8,688.50	$756.00	$12.69	214.7	$1,307	1531.85	$3,500	13,649
07/08	$187,351	$9,525.00	$931.00	$18.01	219.96	$2,022	1262.90	$4,500	11,288
12/22/09	$177,147	$9,051.40	$1,104.00	$17.02	216.33	$1,467.00	1114.65	$5,201	10,428

Compound Return

2000-09	5.6%	5.6%	13.01%	13.08%	6.76%	10.27%	-1.68%	10.85%	-0.85%

When looked at over a decade, the Dow gains in 2009 don't quite make up for the declines since 2001. Same with the Standard & Poor's 500. By contrast, consumer prices have gone up on average (compounded) nearly 7 percent annually. The biggest gain is for all of the precious metals (gold, silver, platinum), but coins are none too shabby at 5.6 percent.

How do coins do over the longer haul, from say 1928? That takes a span of 82 years (more than three quarters of a century). It is fair to have some other points of comparison, assuming for example that each was fully invested – what would the compounded rate of return be?

Because of the effects of long-term compounding, there is no clear advantage when you eyeball the numbers. Coins have cycles, and so do Standard & Poor's. Farmland goes up and down and all have sideways motions where there is neither gain nor loss.

One of the benefits that Wall Street always speaks of is that in any decade since (roughly) the 1920s, stocks have turned positive. But so, evidently, has the precious metals as a group.

Year	Gold	Silver	Platinum	Portfolio	CPI	Farm	Dow Jones
1928	$20.67	$0.58	$79	139.55	17.74	$96	300
1933	$35.00	$0.25	$31	134.75	13.42	$79	100
1935	$35.00	$0.58	$33	150	14.22	$71	144
1938	$35.00	$0.43	$33	8.61	14.60	$63	143
1939	$35.00	$0.39	$41	9.61	14.39	$59	121
1945	$35.00	$0.51	$35	20.4	18.24	$104	150
1947	$35.00	$1.00	$59	26.58	23.14	$115	179
1948	$35.00	$0.74	$84	28.4	24.94	$161	177
1949	$35.00	$0.72	$72	29.3	24.70	$218	199
1951	$41.00	$0.74	$93	30.15	14.18	$234	216
1952	$35.12	$0.89	$93	32.64	12.15	$234	290
1953	$35.11	$0.85	$100	34.24	12.14	$221	280
1954	$35.00	$0.85	$84	39.8	12.11	$229	394
1955	$34.95	$0.89	$117	45.35	12.09	$238	443
1956	$35.00	$0.91	$107	50.95	12.11	$243	499
1957	$35.01	$0.91	$80	57.75	12.11	$251	432
1958	$35.00	$0.89	$80	68.53	12.11	$269	577
1959	$35.00	$0.91	$80	86.58	12.11	$277	670
1960	$35.65	$0.91	$83	94.85	12.33	$261	618
1961	$36.79	$0.92	$84	109.78	12.73	$261	725
1962	$35.06	$1.09	$84	135.58	12.13	$267	652
1963	$35.00	$1.28	$81	170.99	12.11	$276	760
1964	$35.00	$1.29	$88	227.15	12.11	$291	867
1965	$35.15	$1.29	$98	310.73	12.16	$318	911
1966	$35.00	$1.29	$100	375.63	12.11	$354	792
1967	$35.00	$1.55	$110	411.43	12.11	$397	879
1968	$39.26	$2.14	$256	408.75	13.58	$409	906
1969	$41.51	$1.79	$202	422	14.36	$419	877
1970	$36.41	$1.77	$152	448.48	12.59	$419	831
1971	$40.25	$1.55	$110	460.13	13.92	$430	885
1972	$58.60	$1.68	$124	467.5	20.27	$482	1,020
1973	$97.81	$2.56	$154	491.13	33.83	$635	851
1974	$161.08	$4.71	$192	652.5	55.72	$834	605
1975	$161.49	$4.42	$150	918.25	55.86	$1,095	857
1976	$124.77	$4.35	$153	$1,347.50	43.16	$1,368	995
1977	$148.31	$4.62	$158	$1,647.25	51.30	$1,450	831
1978	$194.75	$5.40	$261	$1,743.00	67.36	$1,646	816
1979	$307.58	$11.09	$446	$1,816.25	106.39	$1,958	839
1980	$613.28	$20.63	$677	$2,180.00	212.13	$2,066	964
1981	$459.61	$10.51	$446	$3,042.50	158.98	$2,147	875
1982	$376.01	$7.94	$327	$3,763.75	130.06	$1,861	1,047

Year	Gold	Silver	Platinum	Portfolio	CPI	Farm	Dow Jones
1983	$423.68	$11.43	$424	$3,248.75	146.55	$1,691	1,259
1984	$360.68	$8.14	$357	$2,807.50	124.76	·$1,357	1,212
1985	$318.00	$6.13	$291	$2,780.00	110.00	$948	1,547
1986	$368.00	$5.46	$462	$2,805.00	127.29	$787	1,896
1987	$448.00	$7.02	$553	$2,995.00	154.96	$878	1,938
1988	$438.00	$6.53	$525	$2,996.25	151.50	$1,054	2,169
1989	$381.53	$5.50	$507	$2,997.50	131.97	$1,139	2,753
1990	$383.70	$4.83	$467	$3,105.00	132.72	$1,214	2,634
1991	$362.38	$4.05	$371	$4,047.50	125.35	$1,219	3,169
1992	$361.00	$3.94	$356	$3,903.75	124.87	$1,249	3,301
1993	$360.00	$4.31	$370	$3,758.75	124.52	$1,295	3,754
1994	$384.00	$5.28	$401	$3,747.50	132.83	$1,356	3,834
1995	$388.50	$5.40	$421	$3,763.00	134.38	$1,455	5,117
1996	$418.14	$4.35	$395	$3,785.50	144.64	$1,682	6,448
1997	$335.00	$4.94	$388	$3,843.00	115.88	$1,837	7,750
1998	$301.00	$6.38	$385	$4,258.75	104.12	$1,801	8,999
1999	$265.30	$4.90	$367	$5,624.35	91.77	$1,701	10,799
2000	$325.00	$4.98	$552	$5,231.75	112.42	$1,857	11,357
2001	$271.19	$4.40	$505	$5,165.20	93.80	$1,926	10,646
2002	$310.07	$5.05	$525	$5,338.00	107.25	$2,083	10,003
2003	$359.10	$4.52	$651	$5,468.75	124.21	$2,275	9,018
2004	$403.15	$6.63	$819	$5,943.50	139.45	$2,629	10,163
2005	$437.70	$7.31	$896	$6,707.50	151.40	$2,914	10,623
2006	$574.65	$9.09	$1,065	$7,372.25	198.77	$2,950	10,847
2007	$756.00	$12.69	$1,307	$8,688.50	214.70	$3,500	13,649
07/08	$931.00	$18.01	$2,022	$9,525.00	219.96	$4,500	11,288
12/09	$1,104.00	$17.02	$1,467.00	$9,051.40	216.33	$5,201	10,428
Compounded Growth	5.03%	4.26%	3.67%	5.29%	3.14%	5.05%	4.48%

Silver, for example, places as a better rate of return than inflation (measured in turn by the CPI at 3.14 percent compounded). Gold weighs in at a slightly over 5 percent gain. Platinum (3.67 percent), silver (4.26 percent) and gold (5.03 percent) have artifices because gold and silver were both nationalized during FDR's tenure.

What is clear enough is that the coin portfolio works well as a method of approximating a market investment and then measuring its return. And to no surprise for those who have actually done it, the investment in coins proves out that it can be a very wise one. Indeed, as Harvey G. Stack, the original compiler of the coins component of the Salomon Brothers survey has often said, while not every investment in coins is a collection, every collection – read here the components of the portfolio, and a whole lot more – is an investment.

Chapter 3

THE ORIGINAL PORTFOLIO, AND HOW'D WE DO?

When *Planning Your Rare Coin Retirement* was written in 1997, the world was a different place. Sept. 11 had not yet happened; the 1993 World Trade Center attack was already a distant memory. Precious metal was at an awkward stage; gold was $335 an ounce, silver weighed in at $4.54, and platinum was $388 an ounce. The coin prices reflected this reality.

The Dow Jones Industrial Average was 7,750, Standard and Poor's was 970, and farmland in Iowa averaged $1,835 an acre. The Consumer Price Index stood at around 160, and Treasury bills maturing in less than a month had a rate of 5.26 percent.

Into all this, the original *Planning Your Rare Coin Retirement* actually set up three portfolios. The first portfolio included a gold coin, and I suspected that I was going to be challenged on that, so I put together 100 gold coins that were then available for around $100 or less. Those coins turned into a separately listed portfolio themselves at around $9,000.

Because a number of collectors and investors who acquire gold coins also go for platinum coins, several of them are included. What they all have in common is that even though they mostly have modest mintages, they all are slavish to the precious metals market. When it goes up, so do they. As it declines, they do, too.

The average coin in the 1997 gold and platinum portfolio cost $86. (The prices for these coins were not done from catalog but from real advertisements in numismatic periodicals that included *World Coin News*, *Numismatic News*, *Coins* magazine and other periodicals that included magazines and newspapers). The individual gold and platinum pieces had a portfolio value of about $8,300. The value in January 2010 of this same portfolio was $24,400 – a gain of about threefold over the intervening dozen years – with results of simple interest of about 16 percent annually and a compounded rate of return of about 9.37 percent, not bad by any stretch of the imagination in the 1998 to 2010 time period.

In the $10,000 portfolio, the actual fleshed out value expended turned out to be about $12,600. The average cost per coin was just under $100. About 25 gold coins were included, mostly modern commemoratives, a few bullion coins, and about eight dated, circulated quarter eagles together with two gold $1 type coins (type

*Argentine
Argentino
Gold Coin*
Teletrade

Modern Proof Set
Teletrade

I and III). Other than that, no gold was included, but some silver Eagles (proofs) were, as were a number of sets of coins where the grades were an over-all impression, both assigned to each coin. The 2010 worth: about $36,750.

Canadian $5 Platinum Coin
Teletrade

There are a few gold and platinum pieces in that investment, but not many of the hundreds of coins involved (there were some uncirculated rolls involved). The compounded interest rate of return was 9.3 percent (not counting the gold and platinum portfolio within the portfolio).

Over 200 coins in the $50 to $195 price range (with the average price being just less than $100) were picked for the rare coin retirement portfolio. Some went up, some went down, some moved sideways – but overall it was good strategy that is evident not only in the buy recommendations, but in the results!

Here's how the portfolios did. First is the general portfolio with just a few gold coins, presented by way of a quick summary. They were part of a bigger chart that had various component parts. For example, one line read "proof sets" and covered the period 1950 to 1997; we can see how that line item in your rare coin retirement plan did in the accompanying chart.

They were easy to acquire and sold for $2,297, a mini-collection, the first of many from the earlier sale. It made a profit of about $700, as follows:

Proof Sets Values 1997 vs. 2010

Proof sets	May 97	Jan 10, 2010	Proof sets	May 97	Jan 10, 2010
1950	$610.00	$780.00	1975	$13.00	$7.75
1951	$480.00	$670.00	1976	$11.00	$6.35
1952	$250.00	$300.00	1977	$9.00	$66.25
1953	$220.00	$250.00	1978	$9.00	$7.50
1954	$99.00	$118.00	1979	$10.00	$6.35
1955	$96.00	$175.00	1980	$9.00	$5.35
1956	$59.00	$65.00	1981	$8.00	$6.65
1957	$25.00	$29.00	1982	$5	$3.52
1958	$47.00	$54.00	1983	$7.00	$5
1959	$27.00	$29.00	1984	$6.00	$5.60
1960	$21.00	$29.00	1985	$5	$4.45
1961	$14.00	$38.00	1986	$7.00	$4.45
1962	$14.00	$20.00	1987	$8.00	$3.75
1963	$14.00	$15.75	1988	$7.00	$5
1964	$14.00	$15.75	1989	$8.00	$6.50
1965	0*		1990	$8.00	$5.25
1966	0*		1991	$11.00	$9.65
1967	0*		1992	$7.00	$4.50
1968	$8.00	$5.85	1993	$12.00	$8.85
1969	$8.00	$6.75	1994	$12.00	$8.25
1970	$10.00	$7.25	1995	$35.00	$149.00
1971	$5	$5.10	1996	$14.00	$13.25
1972	$5	$6.15	1997	$28.00	$21.50
1973	$10.00	$7.25	Total	$2,297.00	$2,998.82
1974	$12.00	$7.25			2.25%

No proof sets were made from 1965-1967 (special mint sets were produced) because of the national coin shortage.

The overall proof set collection shows a gain of 44 percent, but a tougher view is the continually compounding rate of 2.25 percent annually. Some individual coins did better than others. The 1961 showed an annual compounded gain of 8.68 percent; then there is the 1995 proof set at a compounded return of 12.8 percent, and the 1977 weighing in at 18.1 percent annual, compounded rate of return. There are overall gains, but occasional losses; in general the 1950s were well taken care of.

A choice is also given to allow acquisition of a gold or platinum coin in the portfolio and to show that it was possible to create a portfolio of bargain gold and platinum coins, I searched far and wide among foreign coins and found over 100 that met the criteria of being appropriate for this particular collecting.

Here, most of the coins involved with the chart are of modest denomination or size. The average cost in 1997 for any of the coins involved in the rebirth of the chart is between $86-$99. The coins are all collectible, and in 1997, I checked out the many foreign coins and individually believe that all of the gold coins were advertised for sale in *World Coin News*, a monthly periodical from Krause Publications or other similar publications.

World Gold Coin Portfolio with Selected Platinum Issues

Australia	1896	Sovereign	Unc.	$110.00
Austria	1881A	8 Florin/20 Franc	XF	$87.00
Austria		1 Ducat	XF-AU	$43.95
Austria	1915	1 Ducat (restrike)	BU	$42.95
Bahamas	1974	$100	Proof	$130.00
Barbados	1975	$100	Proof	$60.00
Belgium		20 Francs	XF-AU	$70.00
Belize	1981	$100 national Independence	Pf	$125.00
Belize	1981	$50	Proof	$40.00
Belize	1985	$100	Proof	$45.00
Bermuda	1975	$100	Proof	$105.00
Bermuda	1977	$50	Proof	$75.00
Bolivia	1952	7 Gramos	BU	$95.00
Brit. Virgin Islands	1981	$50	Proof	$55.00
Brit. Virgin Islands	1975	$100	Proof	$100.00
Bulgaria	1894	10 Leva	VF	$100.00
Canada		1/15 oz Maple Leaf	BU or Pf	$57.50
Canada		1/10 oz Platinum Maple Leaf	BU	$52.65
Canada	1987	Olympic $100 proof		$99.00
Canada		1/10 oz Platinum Lynx	$30 proof	$109.95
Canada	1989	Indian		$102.00
Canada	1976	Olympic $100 unc		$94.00
Canada	1997	Maple leaf	1/4 oz	$96.50
Cayman Islands		$25	BU	$83.00
Columbia	1913	5 Pesos	AU	$105.00
Comoros	1976	10,000 Francs	Pf	$125.00
Cook Islands	1975	$100	Proof	$130.00
Cook Islands	1988	Bison	Proof	$45.00
Cuba	1916	2 Peso	BU	$119.00
Egypt	1930	100 Piastres	AU	$100.00
El Salvador	1971	50 Colones	Proof	$100.00
El Salvador	1971	25 Colones	Proof	$75.00

World Gold Coin Portfolio with Selected Platinum Issues

Equatorial Guinea	1970	250 Pesetas	Proof	$100.00
Finland	1882	100 Maarka	BU	$99.00
France	1801	(AN 12A) 20 Francs	VF	$125.00
France	1815	20 Fr Bordeaux Louis XVIII	VF	$115.00
France	1814	20 Francs	XF	$95.00
France	1886	20 Francs (3d Republic)	AU	$78.00
France		20 Francs	XF-AU	$70.00
France	(1899-1914)	20 Franc Rooster	BU	$79.95
France	1856	A 5 Francs	VF	$51.00
Germany		10 Marks	BU	$115.00
Germany		20 mark	XF/AU	$84.50
Gibralter	1997	Classical heads (set of 4)		$198.00
Great Britain	Sovereign	Eliz. II	XF-AU	$84.00
Great Britain	Sovereign	Old style	XF-AU	$87.00
Great Britain	1989	Sovereign	Proof	$100.00
Great Britain	1986	½ Sovereign	Proof	$61.00
Guernsey	1981	£1	Proof	$125.00
Guinea	1970	1000 Francs	Proof	$75.00
Guyana	1976	$100	Proof	$50.00
Haiti	1973	200 Gourdes	Proof	$75.00
Haiti	1973	100 Gourdes	Proof	$60.00
Hungary	1885	20 Fr/8 Florin	XF	$82.00
India	1918	Sovereign	BU	$105.00
Iran	AH1322	5000 Dinars	XF	$75.00
Iran	1342	AH ½ Toman	VF-XF	$39.00
Iran	1971	500 Rials (Fr 109)	Pf	$125.00
Italy		20 Lire	XF-AU	$68.00
Jamaica	1975	$100	Proof	$100.00
Japan	1835	2 Shu	XF	$52.00
Liberia	1977	$100	Proof	$125.00
Luxembourg	1953	20 Francs (KM #1M)	BU	$100.00
Malaysia	1976	200 Ringgit	Pf	$100.00
Malta	1974	20 Pounds	Proof	$90.00
Malta	1974	10 Pounds	Proof	$60.00
Mexico		2 Pesos	BU	$24.95
Mexico	1906	5 Pesos	Unc.	$55.00
Mexico	1946	2½ Pesos	BU	$42.00
Mexico	1905	10 Pesos	XF-AU	$99.00
Mexico		5 Pesos	BU	$43.00
Mexico		10 Pesos	BU	$82.50
Mexico		2½ pesos	BU	$32.95
Mexico	1985	250 Pesos	BU	$99.00

World Gold Coin Portfolio with Selected Platinum Issues

Netherlands		10 Guilder	XF-AU	$72.50
Netherlands	1988	2 Ducats	Proof	$120.00
Netherlands	1975	1 Ducat	Proof	$60.00
Netherlands Antilles	1979	50 Gulden	BU	$40.00
Panama	1975	100 Balboas	Proof	$90.00
Papua New Guinea	1975	100 Kina	Proof	$110.00
Peru	1965	100 Soles	BU	$65.00
Russia		5 Roubles Nicholas II	XF-AU	$47.95
S. Africa	1964	Proof Set	Proof	$135.00
South Africa		2 Rands (1961-83) 1/4 oz	BU	$88.00
South Africa	1894	½ Pond	VF	$75.00
South Africa	1982	Krugerrand 1/10 oz	BU	$42.95
Spain	1878	Alfonso XII (Fr 343R)	BU	$85.00
Sudan	1978	25 pounds (Fr 4)	Pf	$135.00
Switzerland		20 Francs	XF-AU	$70.00
Switzerland		10 Francs	XF-AU	$100.00
Turkey	1969	50 Kurish	MS64	$75.00
Turks & Caicos	1976	50 Crowns	Proof	$100.00
Turks & Caicos	1981	100 Crowns	Proof	$90.00
Turks & Caicos	1976	25 Crowns	Proof	$75.00
Venezuela	1905	20 Bolivares (Fr 6)	MS64	$100.00
Venice	1789	Zecchino (Fr. 1445)	VF-XF	$155.00
Yugoslavia	1982	5000 Dinara	Pf	$100.00

About $8,300

Average per coin: $86.56

To look at the bigger picture, it's necessary to see how much gold each issuing authority put in the coin. None of these gold coins is particularly heavy; the U.S. coins are all based on the gold Eagle (I have always remembered that the U.S. double Eagle or $20 gold piece coin has .9675 troy ounces of gold; everything feeds off that number.)

1998 Dolley Madison Obverse
US Mint Photo

The accompanying chart lists gold (and a few platinum) coins from nearly half the number of countries in the world. Gold's troy ounce market price that this chart is figured on is $1,179 an ounce, thus raising the tide of gold coins upward.

First Flight $10 Gold Obverse
US Mint Photo

The balance of the portfolio consists of some world coins, some sets, some American coins and some others that were in first rate collections in 1997; and some that weren't. As the earlier book *Planning Your Rare Coin Retirement* notes,

"We've identified coins whose average cost is [around] $100, spread over a portfolio of 100 coins — a $10,000 package to start. But there are many coins that meet these qualifications, and there are sets that deserve inclusion as well...

*1970-D
Kennedy Half*
Teletrade

There's a special list of 100 gold coins assembled at a total cost of about $10,000, which could well be your Golden Rare Coin Retirement. But there are many other coins that also could be satisfactorily added to your rare coin portfolio. That choice is yours."

From that, these were the general groups that were chosen for the overall portfolio that was utilized, and against which success or failure can be measured:

- Peace Dollar (MS-65)
- Barber Dime (MS-63)
- 1991 1/4 oz. $10 American Eagle (gold) (Unc.)
- 1970-D Kennedy Half Dollar (Unc.)
- 1970-S Kennedy Half Dollar (Proof)
- Complete Set of Kennedy Half Dollars
- 1989-D Congressional Half Dollar (Unc.)
- 1993 Madison 50-cent Commemorative (lettered edge) (Unc.)
- 100 Foreign Gold Coins Under $100 [separate chart] summarized in the whole.
- Vietnam War Memorial Commemorative $1 (Unc.)
- Thomas Jefferson Commemorative $1 (Unc.)
- 1995 Double Die Lincoln Cent (MS-65)
- 1988W Olympic $5 Gold (BU)
- 1903-O Morgan Silver Dollar (MS-60)
- U.S. Proof Set Collection 1950-1997 (complete) [separate chart summarized in the whole]
- 1997 Platinum 1/10th Ounce Bullion Coin
- 1881-S Morgan Silver Dollar (MS-65)
- 1994 ANA Commemorative Platinum Coin (Turks & Caicos)
- Roosevelt Dime Set 19946 - 1997 (Unc. and Proof)
- Indian Head Cents 1900-1909 (MS-65 and Proof-64)
- 1904-O Silver Dollar (MS-65)
- Lincoln Memorial Cent 1959 - 1997 (Proof) Including S-Mint Proofs
- Lincoln Cent 1934-1958 (Unc.)
- Jefferson Nickel 1938-1965 (Unc. set)

- Roosevelt Dimes 1965-1997 (Unc. and Proof)
- Eisenhower Dollars 1971-1978 (Unc. and Proof)
- Susan B. Anthony Dollar Set 1979-1981 PDS (Unc. and Proof)
- Washington Quarter Sets 1941-1964
- Washington Quarters 1965-1997 ((Unc. and Proof)
- Carson City Silver Dollar Set (Various)
- Silver Eagle Sets 1986-1996 (Gem Proof)
- Isle of Man 1/25 oz. Gold
- $5 Gold Pieces (about One Dozen Half Eagles)
- Modern Commemorative Coinage
- Classic U.S. Commemorative Coinage

A colorama of collectible coins
Ira & Larry Goldberg

All this is boiled down to a chart that neatly summarizes the whole *Planning Your Rare Coin Portfolio* of 1997:

1997 Retirement Portfolio

Date	Mintmark	Type	Cond.	Qty	Cost Each	Total	FMV	Gain	Return
1921	P	Peace $1	MS65	1	$130.00	$130	$1,980.00	$1,850.00	25.48%
1922	P	Peace $1	MS64	2	$40.00	$80	$141.00	$61.00	4.84%
1922	D	Peace $1	MS64	1	$70.00	$70	$513.00	$443.00	18.06%
1923	P	Peace $1	MS64	2	$40.00	$80	$141.00	$61.00	4.84%
1926	S	Peace $1	MS63	1	$57.00	$57	$960.00	$903.00	26.53%
1935	P	Peace $1	MS63	1	$68.00	$68	$680.00	$612.00	21.15%
1902	P	Barber 10¢	MS63	1	$100.00	$100	$140.00	$40.00	2.84%
1903	P	Barber 10¢	MS63	1	$100.00	$100	$165.00	$65.00	4.26%
1904	P	Barber 10¢	MS63	1	$100.00	$100	$150.00	$50.00	3.44%
1905	P	Barber 10¢	MS63	1	$100.00	$100	$150.00	$50.00	3.44%
1906	P	Barber 10¢	MS63	1	$100.00	$100	$140.00	$40.00	2.84%
1907	P	Barber 10¢	MS63	1	$100.00	$100	$140.00	$40.00	2.84%

Date	Mintmark	Type	Cond.	Qty	Cost Each	Total	FMV	Gain	Return
1908	P	Barber 10¢	MS63	1	$100.00	$100	$150.00	$50.00	3.44%
1909	P	Barber 10¢	MS63	1	$100.00	$100	$130.00	$30.00	2.21%
1910	P	Barber 10¢	MS63	1	$100.00	$100	$140.00	$40.00	2.84%
1911	P	Barber 10¢	MS63	1	$100.00	$100	$145.00	$45.00	3.14%
1912	P	Barber 10¢	MS63	1	$100.00	$100	$135.00	$35.00	2.53%
1913	P	Barber 10¢	MS63	1	$100.00	$100	$130.00	$30.00	2.21%
1914	P	Barber 10¢	MS63	1	$100.00	$100	$140.00	$40.00	2.84%
1915	P	Barber 10¢	MS63	1	$100.00	$100	$150.00	$50.00	3.44%
1916	P	Barber 10¢	MS63	1	$100.00	$100	$135.00	$35.00	2.53%
1908	D	Barber 10¢	MS63	1	$120.00	$120	$185.00	$65.00	3.67%
1911	D	Barber 10¢	MS63	1	$120.00	$120	$155.00	$35.00	2.16%
1912	D	Barber 10¢	MS63	1	$120.00	$120	$150.00	$30.00	1.88%
1911	S	Barber 10¢	MS63	1	$105.00	$105	$320.00	$215.00	9.73%
1916	S	Barber 10¢	MS63	1	$105.00	$105	$150.00	$45.00	3.02%
1991		1/4 oz ($10)	BU	1	$99.25	$99	$253.00	$153.75	8.11%
1970	D	Kennedy 50¢	MS63	9	$10.50	$95	$117.00	$22.50	1.80%
1970	S	Kennedy 50¢	PF65	9	$8.00	$72	$72.00	$0.00	0.00%
1964 to 1996		Kennedy Set	BU	1	$300.00	$300	$535.00	$235.00	4.94%
1989	D	Congress 50¢	BU	8	$12.00	$96	$160.00	$64.00	4.35%
1993		Madison 50¢	BU	2	$20.00	$40	$60.00	$20.00	3.44%
*Various sep. chart		Gold coins	Varies	1	$85.00	$8,336	$24,430.00	$16,094.25	9.37%
1994	P	Vietnam $1	BU	3	$27.00	$81	$147.00	$51.00	4.15%
1993	1994	Jefferson 1	BU	3	$31.00	$93	$75.00	-$18.00	-1.78%
1995		Double Die Cent	MS65	4	$25.00	$100	$172.00	$72.00	4.62%
1972		Double Die Cent	AU50	1	$145.00	$145	$300.00	$155.00	6.25%
1988	W	Olympic $5	Unc	1	$99.50	$100	$334.00	$234.50	10.62%
1903	O	Morgan $	MS60	1	$125.00	$125	$410.00	$285.00	10.41%
*1950 to 1997 per sep chart		Proof Sets	Proof	1	$1,300.00	$1,300	$2,998.92	$1,698.92	7.21%
1997	1/10 oz	Platinum Proof	Proof	1	$99.00	$99	$212.00	$113.00	6.55%
1881	S	Morgan $	MS63	3	$28.00	$84	$138.00	$54.00	4.22%
1878	CC	Morgan $	MS63	1	$82.00	$82	$318.00	$236.00	11.96%

Date	Mintmark	Type	Cond.	Qty	Cost Each	Total	FMV	Gain	Return
1879	CC	Morgan $	VF	1	$100.00	$100	$306.00	$206.00	9.77%
1880	CC	Morgan $	MS60	1	$130.00	$130	$526.00	$396.00	12.35%
1881	CC	Morgan $	MS60	1	$143.00	$143	$490.00	$347.00	10.81%
1882	CC	Morgan $	MS-64	1	$76.00	$76	$263.00	$187.00	10.90%
1883	CC	Morgan $	MS-64	1	$76.00	$76	$244.00	$168.00	10.21%
1884	CC	Morgan $	MS-64	1	$76.00	$76	$210.00	$134.00	8.84%
1885	CC	Morgan $	AU50	1	$155.00	$155	$570.00	$415.00	11.46%
1965 to date		Wash set	BU & Pf	1	$95.00	$95	$185.00	$90.00	5.71%
1941 to 1964		Wash set	BU & Pf	1	$260.00	$260	$675.00	$415.00	8.27%
1979 to 1981		Anthony $1	BU	1	$135.00	$135	$285.00	$150.00	6.42%
1981	P	Anthony $1	BU	20	$2.75	$55	$18.00	-$37.00	-8.89%
1981	D	Anthony $1	BU	20	$2.75	$55	$15.60	-$39.40	-9.97%
1981	S	Anthony $1	BU	20	$2.75	$55	$31.00	-$24.00	-4.67%
1971 to 1978		Ike dollars	BU & Pf	1	$105.00	$105	$175.00	$70.00	4.35%
1938 to 1965		Jeff. 5¢ set	BU	1	$130.00	$130	$290.00	$160.00	6.91%
1934 to 1958		Lincoln set	BU	1	$60.00	$60	$280.00	$220.00	13.70%
1959 to 1997		Lincoln set	BU & Pf	1	$120.00	$120	$135.00	$15.00	.99%
1904	O	Morgan $	MS65	1	$95.00	$95	$140.00	$45.00	3.28%
1904	P	Indian cent	MS65	1	$50.00	$50	$440.00	$390.00	19.87%
1904	P	Indian cent	Pf-64	1	$95.00	$95	$280.00	$185.00	9.43%
1946 to 1965		FDR set	BU	1	$100.00	$100	$180.00	$80.00	5.02%
1901	P	Indian cent	MS65	1	$50.00	$50	$440.00	$390.00	19.87%
1902	P	Indian cent	MS65	1	$50.00	$50	$440.00	$390.00	19.87%
1903	P	Indian cent	MS65	1	$50.00	$50	$440.00	$390.00	19.87%
1905	P	Indian cent	MS65	1	$50.00	$50	$440.00	$390.00	19.87%
1906	P	Indian cent	MS65	1	$50.00	$50	$440.00	$390.00	19.87%
1907	P	Indian cent	MS65	1	$50.00	$50	$440.00	$390.00	19.87%
1908	P	Indian cent	MS65	1	$50.00	$50	$440.00	$390.00	19.87%
1909	P	Indian cent	MS65	1	$50.00	$50	$440.00	$390.00	19.87%
1900	P	Indian cent	Pf-64	1	$95.00	$95	$280.00	$185.00	9.43%
1901	P	Indian cent	Pf-64	1	$95.00	$95	$280.00	$185.00	9.43%
1902	P	Indian cent	Pf-64	1	$95.00	$95	$280.00	$185.00	9.43%
1903	P	Indian cent	Pf-64	1	$95.00	$95	$280.00	$185.00	9.43%
1905	P	Indian cent	Pf-64	1	$95.00	$95	$280.00	$185.00	9.43%
1906	P	Indian cent	Pf-64	1	$95.00	$95	$280.00	$185.00	9.43%
1907	P	Indian cent	Pf-64	1	$95.00	$95	$280.00	$185.00	9.43%
1908	P	Indian cent	Pf-64	1	$95.00	$95	$280.00	$185.00	9.43%
1994		Turks & Caicos	Plat ANA	1	$50.00	$50	$240.00	$190.00	13.96%

Date	Mintmark	Type	Cond.	Qty	Cost Each	Total	FMV	Gain	Return
*1986-1996 Eagles		Sep.chart	Pf-65	1	$300.00	$300	$587.00	$287.00	5.75%
1989		1/25 crown Isle of Man	BU	1	$22.00	$22	$125.00	$103.00	15.58%
1996		1/25 crown Isle of Man`	BU	1	$22.00	$22	$125.00	$103.00	15.58%
1987		Constn $5	BU or Pf	1	$99.00	$99	$334.00	$235.00	10.66%
1997		Gold 1/10 oz Eagle	BU	1	$43.00	$43	$132.00	$89.00	9.80%
1997		Gold 1/10 oz Eagle	BU	1	$96.00	$96	$306.00	$210.00	10.14%
1988		Olympic $5	BU or Pf	1	$99.00	$99	$344.00	$245.00	10.94%
$1 Type 1 (1849-1854)			VF	1	$103.00	$103	$180.00	$77.00	4.76%
$1 Type 3 (1856-1889)			VF	1	$107.00	$107	$180.00	$73.00	4.43%
$2½ Indian (1908-1929)			VF	1	$119.00	$119	$205.00	$86.00	4.64%
1899		$5 Liberty	MS60	1	$144.00	$144	$450.00	$306.00	9.96%
1900		$5 Liberty	MS60	1	$144.00	$144	$450.00	$306.00	9.96%
1901	S	$5 Liberty	MS60	1	$144.00	$144	$450.00	$306.00	9.96%
1902	S	$5 Liberty	MS60	1	$144.00	$144	$450.00	$306.00	9.96%
1903		$5 Liberty	MS60	1	$144.00	$144	$450.00	$306.00	9.96%
1903	S	$5 Liberty	MS60	1	$144.00	$144	$450.00	$306.00	9.96%
1904		$5 Liberty	MS60	1	$144.00	$144	$450.00	$306.00	9.96%
1906		$5 Liberty	MS60	1	$144.00	$144	$450.00	$306.00	9.96%
1906	D	$5 Liberty	MS60	1	$144.00	$144	$450.00	$306.00	9.96%
1907		$5 Liberty	MS60	1	$144.00	$144	$450.00	$306.00	9.96%
1907	D	$5 Liberty	MS60	1	$144.00	$144	$450.00	$306.00	9.96%
1908		$5 Liberty	MS60	1	$144.00	$144	$450.00	$306.00	9.96%
1996		Community Service $1	BU	1	$144.00	$144	$138.00	-$6.00	-0.35%
1993		Madison $5	BU	1	$144.00	$144	$334.00	$190.00	7.26%
1994		World War II $5	BU	1	$144.00	$144	$334.00	$190.00	7.26%
1995		Olympic $1 (track)	BU	1	$35.00	$35	$45.00	$10.00	2.12%
1992		Columbus $5	BU	1	$144.00	$144	$334.00	$190.00	7.26%
1992		Olympic $5	BU	1	$144.00	$144	$334.00	$190.00	7.26%
1995		Olympic $1 Blind Runner	BU	1	$35.00	$35	$25.00	-$10.00	-2.76%
1996		Smithsonian $1	BU	1	$35.00	$35	$95.00	$60.00	8.68%

Date	Mintmark	Type	Cond.	Qty	Cost Each	Total	FMV	Gain	Return
1991		Mt Rushmore $5	BU	1	$144.00	$144	$334.00	$190.00	7.26%
1995		Olympic $1 - Gymnast	BU	1	$35.00	$35	$45.00	$10.00	2.12%
1989		Congressional $5	BU	1	$144.00	$144	$334.00	$190.00	7.26%
1996		Olympic $1 - Swimming	BU	1	$35.00	$35	$24.00	-$11.00	-3.10%
1996		Olympic $1 - Soccer	BU	1	$35.00	$35	$33.00	-$2.00	-0.49%
1995		Civil War Battles $1	BU	1	$35.00	$35	$26.00	-$9.00	-2.45%
1994		Women in Military $1	BU	1	$35.00	$35	$45.00	$10.00	2.12%
1994		POW $1	BU	1	$35.00	$35	$49.00	$14.00	2.84%
1994		Vietnam $1	BU	1	$35.00	$35	$45.00	$10.00	2.12%
1988		Olympic $5	BU	1	$144.00	$144	$334.00	$190.00	7.26%
1994		Capitol Bicentennial $1	BU	1	$35.00	$35	$21.00	-$14.00	-4.17%
1994		World Cup $1	BU	1	$35.00	$35	$23.00	-$12.00	-3.44%
1995		Special Olympics $1	BU	1	$35.00	$35	$55.00	$20.00	3.84%
1994		World War II $1	BU	1	$35.00	$35	$26.00	-$9.00	-2.45%
1986		Statue of Liberty $5	BU	1	$35.00	$35	$334.00	$299.00	20.68%
1993		Madison $1	BU	1	$35.00	$35	$21.00	-$14.00	-4.17%
Total					$12,640.50	$21,417	$61,172.52	$39,545.52	7.23%

The balance of the portfolio consists of some world coins, some sets, some American coins and some other coins that were in first rate collections in 1997.

There were winners and losers in this that are plain as day. The average rate of return with minimal gold and platinum is about 9.3 percent annually. When the gold coin portfolio is blended in – it really did well as a stand-alone – the numbers change dramatically.

How the calculations are done

Using Quattro pro for windows, the @RATE function is used to compute the periodic rate of interest is used to compound a lump sum (initial) investment to a targeted amount over a specified number of years. There are a dozen years involved (1998-2010), the "initial" investment is the cost and the targeted amount is the current selling price.

The formula: @RATE(target amount [or end amount], initial amount, term).

Overall, even with obvious mistakes – the set of Jefferson nickels that declined by 46 percent in a dozen years was merely fanciful, there were a number of winners.

Not surprising, at least to me, a number of individual commemorative coins did nicely, largely because of low mintage. Thus, the Vietnam Veterans Memorial, with just 57,290 coins in uncirculated (compared to five times as many proofs) turned out to be an outstanding winner.

To the same end, the Congressional 1989 half dollar in uncirculated (163,753 pieces in unc., compared to 767,897 produced as a proof) returned a solid 4.3 percent annually over the dozen years that the retirement compilation was measured. And one of my favorite designs, Elizabeth Jones's $5 gold piece (Nike design) for the 1988 Olympics at Seoul (62,913 uncirculated versus 281,465 proofs – almost a 5:1 ratio) gave a solid 7.2 percent annual return.

The ANA-Madison Foundation overstrike serial numbered edge is harder to calibrate; it's listed but not priced in the "Red Book," and on Dec.18, 2007 one was offered on eBay at $269 (the story behind the coins is fascinating and only 9,656 of them have serial numbers). The rate of return using a $30 (not $269) cost is about 3.44 percent annually.

Add in the component of the gold-platinum chart and it becomes a free-for-all. Even there, some of the coins are losers, despite the price-hog that gold has become. On average, the gold and platinum weighed in at 9.37 percent annually (compounded). Some of the above-average coins (in terms of rate of return) are modern in origin, others are older.

1876 25-Cent Obverse
Heritage Rare Coins

What is clear only is that these coins all are of a lower (smaller) sized coin – which is what made them attractive in the first place. Put differently, if you spend $1,300 today, you can acquire a one ounce gold coin, or for roughly the same amount, you can acquire four coins of lesser weight gold.

Some of the coins were made expressly for tourists and casual collectors, but most of them seem genuine gold coin issues that fall outside the traditional banking business. So a 1789 Venetian Zecchino in very fine condition (Friedberg 1445) fits the bill.

The big item is the tripling in value of gold coins, all of which were intentionally limited too around $100 or less. I admit it; it was a gimmick. My friend, the late Jim Miller, suggested to me that there would be a neat story in inexpensive gold coins, and using that as a hook, I set out to find them. All of those coins came from real advertisements in the numismatic trade press, and the price of gold then ($294-308 an ounce while the book was in progress), and the price now (over $1,136.30 an ounce) made a substantial difference. The numbers, in the end, are the numbers

Here's the summary: with all of the incantations and versions used, $12,640.50 would have been the cost for individual items; the extension (100 foreign gold coins, for exam-

1815 50-Cent Obverse
Heritage

ple; 10 1970-D JFK half dollars, and so forth) about $21,000. The value of the coins chosen (over the dozen years since original publication) amounts to a 7 percent rate of return, because the original investment jumped to a value exceeding $60,000. The actual numbers are

> New total value: $61,172.21
> Gain: $39,545.23
> Rate of return: 7.23% annually

1868 Shield
Reverse
Heritage Rare Coins

It is relevant that gold was valued at $1,124 an ounce for calculation purposes; platinum at $1,500. Silver did not use its price per ounce as the basis for any calculations other than Eagles, for which it was valued at $17.50 an ounce. It can be expected that if there is substantial movement in them, the overall portfolio and its objective would change. But regardless, even without any gold or platinum, this is one show with a good and long run.

The patterns in all of these (to be explored elsewhere in this book) are that you can identify what makes for a better investment – what is likely to grow and grow – and what is not. As the gold chart shows, with an average cost of under $100, it is quite affordable. Some of these coins are destined to be included again; others the same date, but better condition (the coins that make the grade have all of the pressure taken off them).

1873 25-Cent
Obverse
Heritage Rare Coins

So on balance, the picks were good ones, and some of the items here won't quite be recycles, but you may have heard their stories before as to why I picked them and, indeed, why they were picked in the past.

About $16,000 of the overall profit is attributable to golden choices, but at the end of the day, having looked at the picks, on balance the answer to the question, "How'd we do?" is a rousing, "Job well done!"

1873 25-Cent
Reverse
Heritage Rare Coins

First Flight $10
Reverse
US Mint Photo

For rates used in charts and graphs see page 3.

Chapter 4

HOW SOME OTHER COLLECTORS DID: JOHN JAY PITTMAN

(L to R) John Jay Pittman, then president of the ANA with the author, Rep Wright Patman D-Texas, chairman of the House Banking & Currency Committee, Rep. Leonor K. Sullivan, D-Mo. House subcommittee on Consumer Affairs chairman (handling coinage matters). The House Conference report on bicentennial coinage gives Pittman full credit for promoting a circulating commemorative that became the bicentennial quarter. Author's collection (1973)

John Jay Pittman was one of the world's truly great coin collectors, who epitomizes the credo of investing in affordable rare coins. He was a chemical engineer for Eastman Kodak while also living the life of an occasional "vest pocket" coin dealer – perhaps the greatest one of all time.

He had a good eye, an understanding wife, and the good fortune to be around at a time when coin investing was in its nascency. Collecting over a seven-decade period during the middle to late 20th century, he had a world class collection of coins, tokens, medals and paper money.

1819/18 Proof 1¢
Pittman

Value	Year
45000	
40000	
35000	
30000	
25000	
20000	
15000	
10000	
5000	
0	1923 1954 1997 2003 2003 2005

Unlike well-known great collections such as Eliasberg, containing the first complete set of U.S. coinage ever assembled; Garrett, replete with late 19th century proof sets purchased directly from the Mint; or the Norweb family collection, with significant holdings of American, British and Canadian coinage, this one truly spans the globe.

Its holdings of early American proof gold coinage is rivalled, perhaps, only by the exemplars in the Smithsonian national museum. The British proof patterns, and indeed, the overall United Kingdom coinage, is nearly the equal of the assemblage in the British Museum.

Japanese coinage in this collection is probably second only to the holdings of the Central Bank of Japan. Canadian coinage rarities include every major one, making it a clear second to the collection of the Bank of Canada and the Royal Canadian Mint. Its Mexican and South African holdings are legendary for their scope.

It is probably a fair assessment that no one national museum has trans-national numismatic holdings that are the equal of these magnificent pieces.

Significantly, over the last 60 years virtually all of the coins in the collection were placed on display at local coin clubs, regional and state shows, and the national conventions of the American Numismatic Association. Many of the holdings were actually written up in *The Numismatist* as part of the standard show-and-tell from coin club meetings.

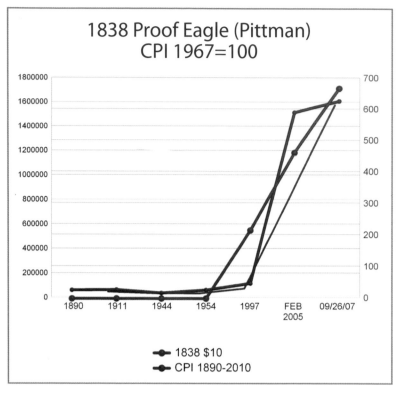

1838 Proof Eagle (Pittman)
CPI 1967=100

— 1838 $10
— CPI 1890-2010

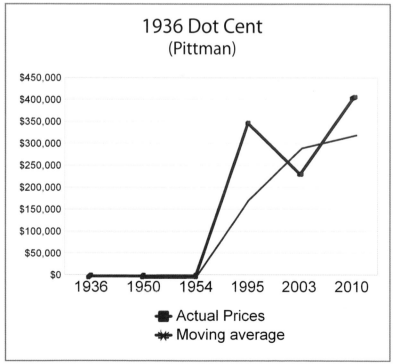

1936 Dot Cent
(Pittman)

■ Actual Prices
✳ Moving average

This extraordinary assemblage was put together over a lifetime by a remarkable individual whom, over a period of more than 20 years, I grew to know quite well.

John Jay Pittman, the late president of the American Numismatic Association, spent more than 30 years on the ANA board of governors (I served with him for 10 of those years) and was a distinguished collector who truly enjoyed an international hobby.

What makes the assemblage all the more remarkable is that Pittman, who died on the day before his 83rd birthday on Feb. 17, 1996, did not have the fabulous wealth of a Norweb, Eliasberg or Garrett. He worked as a salaried employee and bought his coins the way most collectors do, one at a time, over many years.

Collected over a course of an adult lifetime, from about 1940 until 1996, what ultimately constituted more than 12,000 items were sold at public auction by David W. Akers in 5,250 lots spread over three catalogues and over 1,000 printed pages.

The overall value of the collection was mere speculation before the sale, but several years before, knowledgeable dealers who were acquainted with some of the extraordinary gems in the Pittman holdings said that they would not be surprised if the collection were ever sold to see a price realized of more than $30 million. It brought a third more than that.

Akers, the well-known Florida dealer, is a specialist in gold coinage, and a very knowledgeable collector of Canadian coinage in his own right. He and others predicted that the Pittman collection sale would be talked about by future generations of collectors with the same reverential tones of the Jenks sale, the Grinnell paper money offering, Garrett's deaccession, and the other great ones. Akers began the sale in October 1997 in Baltimore.

Interestingly, Pittman's collection that does not have major American rarities such as an 1804 silver dollar (which was not produced by the Mint in the year it was dated) or a 1913 Liberty nickel (which was evidently manufactured by Mint employees and spirited out of the Mint).

He could not afford them, even years ago when prices were at relatively lesser levels than today. Generally, Pittman felt that he could husband his resources by buying rare, but under-appreciated coins instead.

Still, Pittman's is a collection whose early American proof gold and silver coinage is significantly more complete than that in the Smithsonian Institution's national coin collection.

It is some measure of Pittman's collecting acumen that of the collectible 1936 dot Canadian cents that are known, all three were in the Pittman collection. (Lot 1 of the estate sale starts with this rarity.)

1868 2-Cent Reverse
Heritage Rare Coins

Those made a good record, too. One, PCGS MS-66, has a relatively long history. It begins with coming from T. Roberts, an employee of the Royal Canadian Mint; from him, it went to his widow, Mrs. T. Robert. It passed then to John Jay Pittman in 1954, where it was sold as part of the 1936 Dot Specimen set for $250. Pittman held it for almost 45 years. When the John Jay Pittman Collection, Part Three (David Akers, August 1999) was sold, it appeared as Lot 2486a, and was uncertified, sold as part of the same set for $345,000. From there, it went to The Sid and Alicia Belzberg Collection of Canadian Coinage (Heritage, January 2003), certified as Specimen 66 Red by PCGS, Lot 15608, and was sold alone for $230,000.

The latest offering was the 2010 FUN sale (January 2010) where Heritage offered it alone and it brought an impressive $402,500.

An informal announcement made at the ANA 1996 Early Spring Convention in Tucson, Ariz., named Akers as auctioneer in a sale that every major house, and some smaller ones, wanted to sell. The catalog offering the first portion of the collection of a lifetime was released in September, 1997. The last was in August, 1999.

There isn't another collection like it, something that John Jay Pittman wasn't shy about telling others during his lifetime. He exhibited portions of his collection widely and regularly for others to appreciate and to learn from.

"He had a wonderful eye for quality," Akers said.

Those who saw him use a large loupe magnifying glass in examining a prospective addition to the collection certainly would have agreed.

Q. David Bowers, himself a past president of both the ANA and the Professional Numismatists Guild, remembers the ubiquitous tools of John Jay's trained eye: "His 'trademark' was a brass-rimmed, thick-lensed magnifying glass without a handle, about half the size of a roll of silver dollars."

Pittman was a native Tarheel who was born Feb. 18, 1913, and grew up near Rocky Mount, N.C. One of his daughters, Polly Edwards Pittman, wrote an appreciation of her father's life for volume one of the auction catalog.

"JJP" was the oldest of seven children. He was 10 years old before he had his first new pair of shoes. His father worked for the railroad, and later became a barber "to keep the family together." His mother was a school teacher.

At 13, Pittman caught a boxcar and rode the rails as far as Wyoming before returning home to school. The following summer, at age 14, he hitchhiked to New York City where he worked the docks, then in the garment district, and finally as a Wall Street runner.

Graduating high school at 17, with the help of an uncle who made a tuition loan, he went to and then graduated from the University of North Carolina.

"The school was founded in 1789," he once told me, "the same year as your school, Georgetown University. Whenever there are academic processions, our schools stand together."

He waited tables in college, worked as a soda jerk and after spending the summer following graduation at Princeton, had to honor the terms of his uncle's loan by helping to educate his next younger brother and sister. He evidently had hoped to become a doctor, but medical school was too long and costly so, Polly says, he settled on chemical engineering

He took a job with Kodak in January 1936 and moved to Rochester, N.Y. By 1940, he and has wife Gehring built a house on Acton Street, and raised three children, Jay, Betsy and Polly.

By 1943, Pittman had already been collecting with sufficient intensity that he felt it appropriate to join the American Numismatic Association. His membership application was signed by George Bauer, Floyd Newell and William Hutcheson, and published in the September 1943 issue of *The Numismatist*.

1921 Canadian Nickel

Membership number 9759 was give to Pittman (later converted to life member 152), who began a lifetime of membership in, and service to the organization. He ultimately served for 30 years on the Board of Governors, a record for longevity unlikely to ever be broken, since term limitations now set tenure at no more than 10 years.

A fairly comprehensive general listing of the numismatic acquisitions of Pittman can be found chronicled on the pages of *The Numismatist* under "Club News," a monthly feature designed to tell members what was transpiring at coin clubs across the nation.

It is remarkable that extraordinary rarities are described along side a common issue like the 1943 Salvadorean 25 centavos coin, all part of the John Jay Pittman collection.

It's interesting to look back at the pages of *The Numismatist* because they reveal as much of the man as a collector as it shows what was brought to show-and-tell at various numismatic organizations that he belonged to.

In June 1944, the 724th meeting of the Rochester Numismatic Association was held, and Pittman was in attendance. He was just 30 years old. The March 10, 1945, was the first at which Pittman brought coins for show and tell.

At that meeting, he brought only two uncirculated sets for display, both Canadian – symbolic since he later went on to become the only American president of the Canadian Numismatic Association. (He was also, at the same time, president of the ANA, and was made honorary president of the Sociedad Numismatica de Mexico). The sets so casually shown: a complete set of Canadian coinage of 1921 and 1936.

Included in those sets are major rarities: the 1921 half dollar (75 to 100 pieces known), and the 1921 silver 5-cent piece (only 460 pieces known). The *2011 Standard Catalog of World Coins 1901-2000* lists this set at $120,000.

In the 1936 uncirculated set, the dot cent is a rarity, but the key is the dot dime with just four specimens known; that set is valued at $400,000 in the latest catalog.

Stack's

Heritage

The auction catalog, Lot 1, also confirms that Pittman's Canadian collection was a world-class one. There are only three confirmed collectible examples known of the 1936 dot cent. All three are in Pittman's collection. The first, a gem matte proof, was in the 1997 sale; the other two were sold in 1999.

At the March 3, 1945, meeting of the Rochester Numismatic Association, Pittman seconded the motion to purchase a $100 war bond during the seventh war bond drive, and showed a collection of Trade dollars, all uncirculated.

He was well traveled, visiting mints around the world and making lifelong friends in the process. At the November 1945 meeting of the RNA, he showed some 200 Kodachrome color slides of Germany, France, Britain, Austria and Italy, and had been elected secretary of the club.

In December 1945, Pittman exhibited 15 silver dollars in fine to uncirculated condition from 1795 to 1803; a set of 45 proof silver dollars, 1858 to 1921; a set of proof Trade dollars 1873-1883, and a set of 24 Peace dollars in uncirculated containing all dates and mintmarks.

Three of those proof Trade dollars were auctioned individually. The 1873, nearly choice proof, bought from Barney Bluestone in 1946 for $9, sold for $1,870. The 1882 proof (one of just 1,097 minted) cost JJP $72 at an auction that Akers could never determine. No mind, it realized $1,870. The last one, an 1883 proof (one of just 970 coined), was bought out of the Robert Herdegen collection sold by Hans M.F. Schulman in December 1973. The then-ANA president paid $625 for the coin that resold for $1,210.

At the 755th meeting of the Rochester group, reported in January 1946, a complete set of Panamanian coins 1904-1944 were placed on display by Pittman. Included in the complete set: the 1918 2½ centesimos, of which only seven examples are known today; a 1904 10 and 50 centesimos proof (of which only 12 pieces are known); a 1930 1/10 and 1/4 Balboa (of which only 20 pieces are known); and a 1931 Balboa (one of only 20 pieces known).

The matte proof one Balboa was Lot 3626 (KM-13). Purchased from Philadelphia dealer Catherine Bullowa for $12.50 in 1953, the reward reaped for this coin was $3,910.

The 757th meeting for the Rochester Numismatic Association saw Pittman exhibit a complete set of Lincoln cents (lacking five mintmarked coins), all red uncirculated and proof, a complete set of proof 3-cent nickels (the 1865 in uncirculated), and a "perfect b.u. 1924 double eagle." (Lot 1221 offers a "subdued medium orange gold color" double eagle with "some marks on the figure, but not many in the fields.")

One of the coins was a 1921-S in uncirculated, full mint luster with reddish gold toning. Pittman had acquired it from New Netherlands in 1943 for $5. It reappeared in 1997 as Lot 323, which rang in at $467.50; from there it appeared at the Heritage Auctions September 2006 sale (as PCGS MS-65) at $920.

Showing that his interest was not just limited to U.S. coins or rarities, the March 1946 issue of *The Numismatist* saw Pittman exhibit an uncirculated silver and copper coins set of Outer Mongolia and two 5 franc pieces of France in aluminum for 1945.

For the 761st meeting, Pittman exhibited a complete set of small cents 1857 to 1909 in uncirculated and proof and 50 uncirculated Indian Head nickels. For the 768th meeting reported in July, Pittman exhibited half dollars from 1807 to 1814, and 1916 to 1945.

What was described as a complete set of proof Liberty head nickels was shown at the 770th meeting (the 1912-D and S were uncirculated); Pittman never did acquire, or even try to acquire,

1792 Half Disme Obverse & Reverse
David Lawrence Rare Coins

a 1913 Liberty head nickel. In November 1946, Pittman showed a complete set of BU Mercury dimes (including the 1942 over 1, the report states) with a complete set of proof dimes 1858-1915, and most dates of dimes from 1796 to 1858 in uncirculated. Included were proofs of 1831, 1843, 1845, 1846, 1847 and 1850.

The 1831 was later upgraded, for in 1957 JJP took top honors in B. Max's Will W. Neil auction in June of that year. (The cost was $20.) The 1997 resale price: $10,450.

The 1843 also was a recent acquisition, a very choice proof from Kosoff & Kriesberg's Numismatic Gallery's ANA sale for $17. The 1997 resale price: $26,400. Only eight to 10 proofs of this date are known. (Pittman had a back-up specimen, since he also had an original 1843 proof set that included the dime).

At the 776th meeting of the Rochester Numismatic Association, Pittman showed a 1799 silver dollar and 1874 $3 gold piece together

1881 3-Cent
Heritage Rare Coins

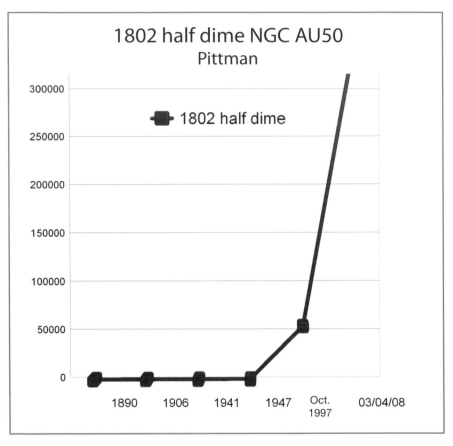

with a complete uncirculated set of Barber dimes and quarters from the Denver Mint, and some other coins.

In April 1947, *The Numismatist* reported the 779th meeting of the Rochester group, and John Jay Pittman, appointed by President Truman as a member of the 1947 Assay Commission, displayed the 1947 Assay Commission medal.

Later, in May 1950, he would display 13 assay medals from 1921 to 1933, and still later, in 1957, he would display 50 different medals from 1860 to 1947. This holding remains one of the most complete collections ever put together. I know he had duplicates, for I bought one or two of them from him for my own collection.

At the 785th meeting of the Rochester Numismatic Association, Pittman's show-and-tell consisted of just a few gold coins. These included the South Australian Adelaide pound of 1852 (one of between 20 and 50 pieces known, KM-2, Friedberg 3.), which was put out together with a British 2 pound (£2) proof of 1893 (one of only 793 pieces produced by the British Royal Mint).

1847 $1
R *everse*
Heritage

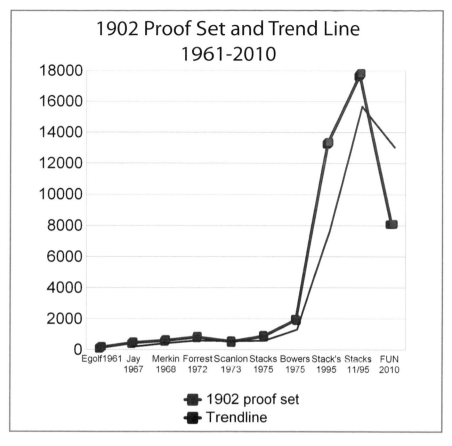

1902 Proof Set and Trend Line 1961-2010

Pittman lost the 1852 South Australia (Adelaide) pound in a 1964 robbery; he acquired another at James Charlton's 1964 Canadian Numismatic Association sale for $115CDN ($107 US). The 1999 auction sale result: $13,800.

In the August 1947 issue of *The Numismatist*, it was reported that Pittman exhibited "a complete set of quarter eagles in proof and uncirculated" condition while at the Sept. 2, 1947, meeting of the RNA he put out a set of 20-cent pieces, complete except for the 1876-CC.

November 1947 saw a complete set of bronze 2-cent pieces in proof and 3-cent silver mostly in proof (1855-1873), with the rest in uncirculated.

His interests continued to be worldwide, as "recent" acquisitions showed. In January 1948, a 1787 Brazilian 6000 reis gold coin was shown, and at the 798th meeting in March, a 1939 Vatican set through 100 lire gold (one of only 2,700 sets produced) was displayed.

For the Rochester club's 800th anniversary, Pittman took out a major rarity: the 1907 $20 flat edge high relief, while the following month uncirculated U.S. quarters were brought out, complete except for the 1823 and 1827.

The 1907 $20 high relief with the wire rim was purchased by Pittman on Sept. 5, 1947, for just $100. Its resale at auction in 1997: $8,800.

July 1948 reports on the 806th and 807th meetings of the club report that Pittman showed a Russian rouble of 1776 and a 10-piece South African proof set of 1923 (one of 655 sets known, KM# PS-1). His South African collection was also outstanding.

October 1948 saw a complete proof set for the year 1876, cent through double eagle offered, while the 810th meeting saw a display of half cent through dollar in proof for 1856, and complete proof sets of 1854, 1855 and 1857.

An 1856 large cent appeared as Lot 278 in the estate sale. Pittman purchased the large cent at the 1952 ANA auction sale for $67.50. It realized $5,500. The 1856 half dime is Lot 504, and was purchased in July 1947 for a mere $15. The 1997 auction re-sale: $7,150.

At the 812th meeting, the rare half disme of 1792 was displayed, but not further described. The rarity was better described when Pittman showed it again at the 881st meeting as an uncirculated specimen. Pittman bought the half disme at the 1948 ANA sale for $100.

At the 814th meeting, he displayed a complete set of U.S. commemorative half dollars, small cents and 3-cent pieces. Another time, in May 1949, a complete set of Cuban one and two gold pesos was put on display.

At the 831st meeting of the RNA, Pittman showed an original set of gold, silver and copper coins in the original leather box of issue for proof coins of 1846 (half cent through double eagle), one of four original sets that he would ultimately own of different dates. The astonishing auction price in his estate sale: $522,500. (Pittman had purchased it for $750 on July 20, 1949, from Abe Kosoff and Abner Kreisberg's Numismatic Gallery. Incredibly, he bought another 1846 proof set from Spink in London in April 1951 for $210. (He later traded it for proof double eagles.)

December 1949 brought out an 1837 silver proof set (six pieces, with both the half dime types of large and small 5), the half dime rarity (mintage 3,060) from the Dunham Collection sold by B. Max Mehl, and an 1846 proof silver dollar.

The 1802 half dime had an illustrious and long pedigree. Pittman acquired it out of the Will W. Neil collection (sold by B. Max Mehl in 1947) at $630. It harkened back to the 1890 Parmelee collection ($205 price realized), with some famous inbetweens.

(Pittman maintained more than one collection of coins, so that in addition to the original proof set, there was also an individual coin in this instance).

At the start of 1950, the six-piece gold proof set of 1886 was displayed together with proof dollars of 1852 and 1845, an uncirculated 1812 large cent, an 1820/19 overdate large cent, and an 1849 proof large cent. The 1886 original gold proof set is lot 835 in the Akers sale. (Pittman purchased the coins in four consecutive lots of New Netherland's 28th sale in 1949 for a total of $463.50.)

Rarities in the collection go onward. The Cuban gold 10 pesos of 1916 was displayed at the 838th meeting together with the rare proof sovereign of Britain dated 1826.

There were two Cuban 1 peso coins in the Pittman sale; one catalogued as "very choice proof" was part of a 1916 proof set that JJP bought from New Netherlands Coin Co. in 1957 for $1,600. The other (both catalog as KM-16, Friedberg 7) was "choice proof" and also was bought from New Netherlands in 1955 for $25.

Price realized was $2,300 for the very choice proof, and $1,265 for the choice proof. Heritage's Long Beach September 2006 sale saw one of the coins on the re-sale, a decade after the original sale.

The catalog described it as: "Republic gold Peso 1916, Ex: Pittman Collection, Proof 67 Ultra Cameo NGC, a spectacular coin which would surely enhance even the finest collection – the contrast between the frosted cameo bust and the sparkling reflective surfaces is a wonder to behold." The price realized: $7,475.

At the 885th meeting, he revealed he also had the £5 proof of 1826, just as a year earlier he had shown that he had the £2 specimen of 1826. At the 838th meeting, British proof sets of 1902 and 1911 (pence to £5 pound) were also shown. The 1916 Cuban 10 peso coin was also shown; the companion Cuban 1915 gold proof was shown in January, 1951.

For the 840th meeting, reported on in the January 1950 issue of *The Numismatist*, 1902 and 1911 British proof sets £5 to 1 pence (one of 2812 sets) were shown.

The next month, for the Rochester Numismatic Association's 841st meeting, a Vatican proof set dated 1947 (one of just 1,000 sets produced) consisting of 1, 2-, 5- and 10-lire coins was on display.

For the 844th meeting, Pittman brought out a real treat; rarities like $10 gold eagles of 1842 and 1933. But he also showed coins from Tunis, the 5, 10 and 20 francs (Tunis) 1939.

At the 845th meeting John Jay Pittman became the president of the Rochester Numismat-

Classic 19th Century Reverses
Bowers & Merena

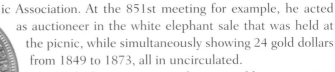

1855 50-Cent Reverse
Heritage

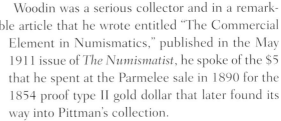

1855 With Arrows
Heritage

ic Association. At the 851st meeting for example, he acted as auctioneer in the white elephant sale that was held at the picnic, while simultaneously showing 24 gold dollars from 1849 to 1873, all in uncirculated.

He had not yet acquired a prize addition: an 1854 type II proof gold dollar with a lineage as impressive as its condition, which in the Lorin G. Parmelee auction sale of June 1890 had been called a "sharp perfect proof."

The buyer at that sale was Bill Woodin, who would later write a book on pattern coinage and become FDR's first Secretary of the Treasury. Then 22 years of age, Woodin was on the verge becoming president of one of the largest railroad freight car builders in the United States.

Woodin was a serious collector and in a remarkable article that he wrote entitled "The Commercial Element in Numismatics," published in the May 1911 issue of *The Numismatist*, he spoke of the $5 that he spent at the Parmelee sale in 1890 for the 1854 proof type II gold dollar that later found its way into Pittman's collection.

"Now was the last chance to complete your series – to replace your 'good' coins with proofs"; he then lists dozens of acquitions of gold dollars and quarter eagles.

These prices, Woodin says, "will show how United States gold went begging during the years 1888 to 1898. It seemed to us at that time as if United States gold coins would never be appreciated." Then the clincher:

"I firmly believe that many of these pieces will prove to be most profitable investments to the purchaser."[12] Look how they did:

1854 Type II Gold Dollar

Date	Price Realized	Sale
1890	$5	Lorin G. Parmelee Sale (1890), lot 1244;
1911	$65	William H. Woodin Collection Sale (1911), lot 851; March 2-3 1911
1956	$525	Thomas Melish Collection Sale (Abe Kosoff, 4/1956), lot 1742
1997	$176,000	John Jay Pittman Collection (David W. Akers, 10/1997), lot 864
2009	$218,500	ANA Money Show (Bowers & Merena) Los Angeles, March 2009

The 1600 8,4, and 1 reals struck by the British for India were shown at the 856th meeting, and for the 860th meeting in February 1951, a 1746 British four-piece proof set was on display. So were the George IV half crowns of 1820, 1821, 1825 and 1826.

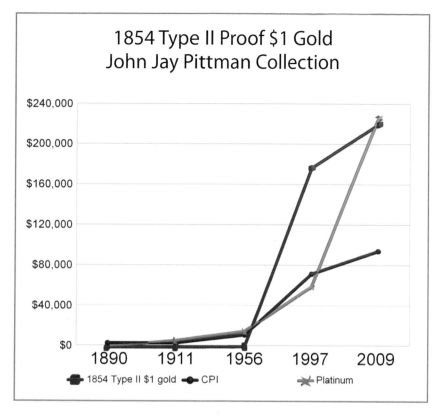

Pittman's English collection has coins in it that are simply otherwise unavailable. Included: a 2 guineas of 1687 (King James II), a triple unite of Charles I of Oxford dated 1643 and a half sovereign of Edward VI.

For the 879th meeting, Pittman brought out two major rarities: an 1803 proof silver dollar (restrike) and an 1839 proof half dollar pattern. At the 881st meeting, the 1792 half disme, uncirculated, went on display.

In February 1954, Pittman traveled to Egypt for the auction of the coin collection formerly owned by King Farouk, which had been seized by the Egyptian government, nationalized, and then offered for public auction sale by Sotheby's.

Abe Kosoff, the late *Coin World* columnist, co-founder of the Professional Numismatists Guild, and well-known coin dealer, chronicled some of the coins that Pittman garnered at the sale that was attended by noted numismatists the world over.

But 20 years before Kosoff revealed them to the

1862 3-Cent
Obverse & Reverse
Heritage

1850 $1 Reverse
Heritage Rare Coins

1862 $2.50 Obverse
Heritage Rare Coins

1884-S $1 Reverse
Heritage Rare Coins

1886 5-Cent Reverse
Heritage Rare Coins

1903 10-Cent Proof Reverse
Heritage Rare Coins

public at large, Pittman brought the coins for show- and-tell to the Rochester Numismatic Association, which had a summary duly reported on the pages of *The Numismatist*.

The 921st meeting on April 6, 1954, featured coins from the Palace collection. Among them, a U.S. $10 gold piece in proof dated 1838, labeled unique at the time but actually one of four known. (One is in the Smithsonian, an impaired one was in the Eliasberg collection, and a third was in the collection of Francis Cardinal Spellman). The Pittman piece traces its pedigree to Lorin Parmelee, whose collection was auctioned in 1890, where it brought $45.

From there it went to William Woodin, whose collection was sold in 1911 at $200, then to Waldo Newcomer, Colonel E.H.R. ("Ned") Green, J.F. Bell (Jake Shapiro) sold by Stack's (in December 1944 at $90) and on to King Farouk. No precise price can be ascertained (see chart on page 66).

Pittman recognized that the Farouk sale was the opportunity of a lifetime, and was astonished to see the cataloging done by Fred Baldwin. Baldwin lotted rarities with common coins, so the 1838 proof eagle came with an 1839 (type of 1838), the 1839 type of 1840 and the 1840 in XF.

Total price for the lot was $562 plus a 5 percent government tax or about $590 for all four coins combined. The 1998 resale was spectacular: the 1838 ($550,000), 1839 type of '38 ($3,575), the 1839 type of '40 ($143,000), and the 1840 ($3,300). The less-than-$600 investment realized a total of over $700,000.

There's always a post-script, as the chart and graph show:

1838 Proof Eagle

Lorin Parmelee	1890	Bangs	$45
William Woodin	1911	ELDER	$200
J.F. Bell	1944	Stack's	$90
Farouk	1954	Sotheby's	$148
John Jay Pittman	1997	Akers	$550,000
Private Sale	Feb. 2005	David Albanese	$1,177,000
Private Sale	Sept. 26, 2007	David Albanese	$1,700,000

1889 $20 Obverse
Heritage Rare Coins

That wasn't the only bargain of rare gold Pittman got at the Farouk sale. He also acquired Lot 248 with the 1835 proof, the 1836 large 5D and small 5D in proof, the 1837 and 1838 proof and the 1838-C and 1838-D in unc. For $510, Pittman acquired 18 proof gold coins, including the 1842 small letters in brilliant proof, Kosoff wrote.

Others could reach into inheritance for this unique instance; Pittman took out a second mortgage on his residence at 4 Acton St., Rochester, N.Y. – a mortgage which remained in effect until the mid-1960s – to afford these rarities.

In the early 1950s, Pittman's collection evidenced substantial completeness in several areas. At the 909th meeting of the Rochester club, he exhibited a complete set of proof half dollars and proof quarters from 1858 to 1915, as well as a complete date set of halves from 1807 to 1836.

At the 944th meeting, he showed an 1870-S $1 gold piece, an 1802 quarter eagle, a 1920-S and 1933 $10 gold piece, and some other contemporary gold coins. A half year later at the 950th meeting, out came gold proof sets of 1908, 1909 and 1911. A proof 1953 Cuban peso, and others.

At the 971st meeting of the Rochester Numismatic Association, Pittman

1903 Nickel Proof Obverse
Heritage Rare Coins

laid out his collection of proof quarter eagles, starting with 1834, 1835 and 1836, and then 1840, 1843, 1844, 1845, 1846, and 1848. Almost incidentally, he then added a run of proof quarter eagles complete from 1880 to 1915, an amazing holding not duplicated by Garrett (whose 1893 was uncirculated).

Many of these proof quarter eagles remained with the collection and are found in the Akers catalog, starting around Lot 936.

In 1958, *The Numismatist* changed its narrative form of club meetings, making extractions of individual show and tells much more difficult. Nonetheless, in January 1958, Pittman attended the nearby Buffalo Numismatic Association meeting and exhibited Dahlonega gold coins of half eagle denomination, 1838-1860 (complete) and Charlotte mint from 1838 to 1861. These are found in the catalog starting at lot 943.

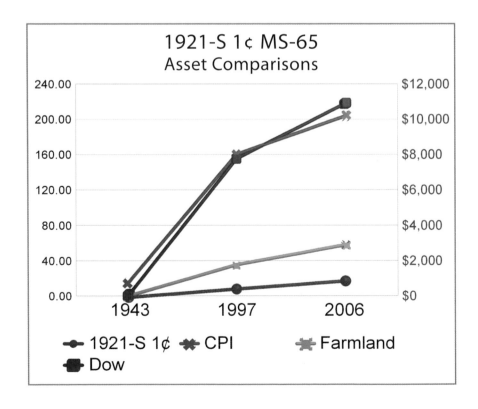

Pittman learned that I was a collector of Hawaiian coinage, and thereafter discussed rarities and that particular series with me many times. Then one day he casually mentioned that some would be placed out in his next exhibit. They were the same coins that he exhibited in January 1958.

In February of that year, his collection of dimes, complete from 1796 to 1829, was placed on exhibit at the Rochester club together with an 1883 Hawaiian proof set including the eighth of a dollar.

Later years saw Pittman exhibit "selected rarities" at the annual convention of the American Numismatic Association, usually with cards typed by his wife, Gehring on a manual typewriter that gave useful historical information about incredibly rare coins.

1855 50-Cent Obverse & Reverse
Heritage Rare Coins

Some of these are listed in reference books that make casual notations about collectors and their holdings. Walter Breen, for example, attributes a number of major rarities to John Jay Pittman. Among them: an 1843 original cased proof set sold by B. Max Mehl from the Will W. Neil collection for $1,250 to Amon Carter Sr. (and later to Pittman); a complete 1844 proof set as well as those of 1845 and 1846, and a 1836 $5 half eagle.

The 1844 proof set, including gold with the original case, was offered as a set as Lot 833 by Akers. A lot earlier, the 1843 original proof set hit the auction block.

Selected Early Pitman Proof Sets

1845	Half cent to eagle, 10 coins, assembled	$756,250
1846	Half cent to eagle, 10 coins, original X-Numismatic Gallery (Kosoff-Kriesberg) July 20, 1949 @ $750 Possibly x-Frossard Nov. 4, 1892	$522,500
1868	Cent to dollar, 10 coins (original)	$26,400

1862 Half Dime Reverse
Heritage Rare Coins

1862 Half Dime Obverse
Heritage Rare Coins

Pittman's emphasis changed somewhat in 1959 when he was first elected to the Board of Governors of the ANA. He became immersed in the politics of the ANA, and ultimately served on its board for more than 30 years, longer than any individual before, or since.

His last term of office coincided with my term as President, 1993-1995. It was at his instigation in 1985 that I first ran for the ANA Board, and at my request, it was he who swore me into office as President.

During his own term as President, 1971-73, the hobby was in the midst of excitement over the coming bicentennial, and the initial proposal of the United States Mint to commemorate the occasion with a half dollar and dollar bearing the dual date 1776-1976.

As ANA President, Pittman testified before Congress in 1973 that the half dollar and dollar didn't circulate and that the tribute was inadequate. Specifically, he suggested a solution: adding the quarter as a circulating bicentennial commemorative.

His role in creating the bicentennial quarter dollar is acknowledged in the official House of Representatives report on Public Law 93-127 in which Rep. Leonor K. Sullivan, D-Mo., gave him credit for the proposal.

Mrs. Sullivan wrote that she was "impressed by Mr. Pittman's plea for inclusion of the quarter, the subcommittee urged the Treasury to restudy the feasibility... Mrs. Brooks [the Mint director] subsequently reported that it would be possible ..."

Pittman, a life member, is one of the most honored members of the American Numismatic Association. He was also instrumental in working with Congress for the passage of the Hobby Protection Act in 1973.

For more than two decades following his early retirement from Eastman Kodak in Rochester, N.Y., in 1971, Pittman reached out to enrich the hobby

1862 $2.50 Reverse
Heritage Rare Coins

with his background in chemical engineering and metallurgy, and wealth of historical and political knowledge.

Pittman was honored repeatedly by the ANA. His numismatic service led to receipt of the ANA Medal of Merit in 1962; the Farran Zerbe Memorial Award for Distinguished Service in 1980; Honorary Life Membership in 1991; the Lifetime Achievement Award in 1994; and the Glenn Smedley Memorial Award in 1995. In 1992 he was inducted into the ANA's Numismatic Hall of Fame.

At the time of his demise, some of the Pittman collection was no longer extant, having been traded for other coins (such as the 1933 $10), or lost in a 1964 robbery. Nonetheless, as Akers acknowledges, "it's unlikely that anyone will ever be able to put together a collection like it again."

Yet, there are few classic rarities, except for the 1802 half dime. The reason: they were overpriced relative to the cost of other coins not recognized as classic rarities, but nonetheless scarce. That is a strong lesson for readers to remember.

John Jay Pittman in his half century of collecting bought affordable rare coins that were undervalued because he researched them and new more about them than their owner, even if that was a professional numismatist. He planned his job retirement from Eastman Kodak at age 58 and spent the next quarter century involved in his rare coin retirement, serving as ANA president and adding value to his collection, which ultimately realized over $40-million.

HOW SOME OTHER COLLECTORS DID: HAROLD S. BAREFORD

Harold S. Bareford's application for membership in the American Numismatic Association was published in the December 1946 issue of *The Numismatist*. He listed his address as 321 West 44th St., in New York City, the corporate headquarters for Warner Brothers. The publication also noted his collecting specialty as "U.S. and English Coins." He had been seriously buying American gold coins for a little over two years, and at age 52 must have considered that his collecting had risen to another level.

A 1916 graduate of Cornell Law School, he was commissioned in the field artillary in November 1917, serving 13 months until his discharge. By 1918, he joined the law firm of Thomas & Friedman, became a partner and eventually, in 1920, went to work for the firm's star client, moviemaker Warner Bros. He became assistant secretary and general counsel of Warner Bros., and a Warner director.

He was a litigator, an appellate brief writer, and in one memorable moment a witness that U.S. Supreme Court Justice Felix Frankfurter sat in by designation, as Bareford was cross-examined about the musical power in "talkies" of baritone Walter Wolfe. He also led the defense for the proxy battles that plagued Warner Brothers in the pre-war years.

By 1943 the firm had become Friedman, Bareford & Hazen, of New York City, and Capt. Bareford took a leave of absence to serve in the Coast Guard, from which he returned a major in 1945. Back to Warners he went until he turned 65 in 1959 and retired back into private practice, which he continued until his death on April 10, 1978, (age 84) after spending a typical day in the New York law office.

In the mid-1940s, after enlisting, he began buying gold coins. His name was published in *The Numismatist* and he became member No. 13375 of the American Numismatic Association effective January 1947.

Bareford was a collector's collector. In his lifetime, he owned an 1804 silver dollar and a host of other rarities. But he

Harold S. Bareford

also epitomizes the strategies of investing in affordable coins – researching the coins that would meet his standards, acquiring them, and then setting them aside to watch their value increase.

He understood the intricacies of coin grading, speaking about "The Minting and Grading of Coins" before the New York Numismatic Club on April 10, 1953. The paper he read was reprinted in *The Numismatist* of June 1953. A summary of his position: "The attempt to grade a coin better than it actually is, is one of our worst faults".

"This attempt to boost grades of coins has resulted in all kinds of minutely differing descriptions," he said.

"The introduction of the point system of grading was a commendable effort to make grading a more exact science. However, both dealers and collectors exaggerate condition with the point system as much as they do with the descriptive system."

Amazingly, Bareford saw that it was a problem for low grade as well as high grade coins. He essentially concluded that "no two people will agree unless a coin is a gem uncirculated specimen." Then, he didn't say but could have, the real arguments begin as to what grade the gem is in points: 65 or some number between there and a mint state 70.

Bareford's collection of gold coins, assembled and cataloged in 242 lots by Stack's, was put up for public auction on Dec. 1, 1978, about a half year after his death. (The silver coinage, the 1804 dollar and the English coinage would be sold over the next seven years, also by Stack's; the record is similar, but not as spectacular.)

Meticulous records were kept by Bareford, so we know that the 242-lot offering (24 coins were eagles and double eagles – over 200 were lower-denomination coins) cost him $13,832.15 for all of the purchases combined. All of the coin purchases were made from dealers or at auctions between 1944 and 1954. The 1978 resale price brought an incredible $1,207,215 or $4,988 per lot, an 8,627 percent increase in total. The numbers are so substantial as to make it difficult to offer analysis or commentary.

And no wonder. He wrote in 1947 that "I collect only the very finest specimens ... and am not interested in any coin which is not perfect."

His son William J. Bareford said in 1978 that his father's collection of half eagles, "will show that no collection ... has ever come on the market in which the average conditions of the coins has been higher."

1872
$1 Gold

Because of these exacting standards, and the fact that they were individually purchased, it is much easier to break the success down individually. Since the Bareford auction sale took place more than 30 years ago, it is useful to take some selected examples and see where they have gone since. (Appendix 1 lists all of the Bareford gold coins, their acquisition cost, selling price and gain. Appendix 2 manipulates the data to see the best performing result.)

Looking at it in 1978, the results were impressive. Every single coin in the catalog experienced substantial growth, some as much as 100 times what Bareford paid for it less than 30 years earlier. (From the perspective of what those coins bring now, more than a half century later, coins were well worth Bareford's investment).

Most of the coins were in uncirculated condition, or were choice proofs, and the 275 people in attendance, as well as the many mail bidders, were evidently impressed with quality. All were described by cataloger Norman Stack.

Typical of the gains was an 1872 $1 gold piece, one of 30 specimens struck, which Bareford acquired out of B. Max Mehl's Will W. Neil collection (Lot 2321 on June 17, 1947) for $52.50. Mehl cataloged the coin "perfect brilliant proof with wire edge," adding that it was "a real rarity in this beautiful condition." He noted that the Atwater (1945) specimen was only very fine and then quoted (1947) catalogs at $45. (The first year of publication of R.S. Yeoman's *Guide Book of United States Coins* listed it at $37.50.)

Stack's noted the pedigree, used the coin's photo, and spent three lines describing Lot 57: "1872 brilliant proof. 30 specimens struck. An extremely rare item with only three records of sale in about 10 years (our [Charles]Jay, [George] Scanlon, and [John Work] Garrett [1976] specimens."

The "Red Book," according to my catalog notes made prior to attending the sale, priced the coin at $2,500. It opened at $1,700 and in quite extensive bidding action was hammered down at $4,750 to "EJH," according to my catalog notes.

By 2007, the coin hit the auction block at the Heritage Auction's Central State Sale in St. Louis. The catalog reveals a surprise: the proof coin is actually the "Finest Known Business Strike 1872 Gold Dollar, MS68 PL" as graded by Numismatic Guaranty Corporation (NGC). It's proof-like, which is what fooled earlier catalogers.

Here's the rest of the description:

1872 G$1 MS68 Prooflike NGC. Ex: Bareford. There is no question that this is the single finest existing business strike of the date and among the best of the design type. Both sides are fully brilliant with rich yellow and orange-gold color. It is a sharply struck example with deeply mirrored fields and fully lustrous and frosty devices. Offered as a "brilliant proof" in Stack's catalog of the Bareford collection. However, this piece does not have quite the necessary depth of field or sharpness of strike that should exist on proofs. Ex: Will W. Neil (B. Max Mehl, 6/1947), lot 2321; Harold Bareford (Stack's, 12/1978), lot 57.

With a regular mintage of just 3,500 pieces, the coin is a super rarity, regardless. There are two or three others that are around in MS-68 or MS-69; Heritage offered them in 2003 and in May 2009 (they did not sell). The Bareford pedigree did. The price realized: $18,975. The gain was over $14,000 from the Bareford price or 299.47 percent, which is roughly (uncompounded) 10 percent annually.

Another Bareford treasure with an extensive pedigree is a Proof-65 double eagle graded today by PCGS as Proof-65 deep cameo. Akers estimates that just 12 or 13 pieces exist. Bareford's standards were so exacting that only 16 double eagles were in the auctioned collection. It came out of the November 1954 Davis-Graves Sale (Stack's) at $575 on April 9, 1954, and went, according to my notes to "DK" for $25,000. Its next appearance was as Lot 370 in Auction '79 (Paramount's session) where it sold for $28,000 – and then disappeared into someone's collection.

Harold Bareford continued to work at his job as a high-powered lawyer literally until the day that he died. He could have enjoyed a rare coin retirement, but he never retired. Like others who "coin" successfully, Bareford had an eye for quality and acted on it. He did not overpay for coins and was in a position to buy rarities (an 1804 dollar was in his collection). But in buying gold coins over a 10-year period (1944-1954) he identified a section of the market that was mispriced, relatively speaking, and underrated by others; it obviously bounced back in a big way.

His son, William J. Bareford, whom I met and interviewed at the Dec. 1, 1978, auction sale, was surprised by the results that showed his father's $13,000 investment yield over $1 million. "If it had gem on it," he said, "the prices went through the roof."

And his last tip: "Dad never could justify paying more for the common ones over the uncommon ones."

A good rule to collect by.

HOW SOME OTHER COLLECTORS DID: LOUIS ELIASBERG

Life magazine called Louis Eliasberg the "King of Coins" in the April 27, 1953, issue – the one with young Queen Elizabeth on the cover. That's also the title that one of his sons asked Q. David Bowers to put in his then-untitled manuscript designed to explain how Louis Eliasberg formed his fabulous coin collection that was a virtual duplicate of the *A Guide Book of United States Coins*, by R.S. Yeoman, more commonly known as the "Red Book."

One of the reasons that *Life* magazine gave for the nomenclature is that Eliasberg accomplished the impossible. He updated the collection of gold, silver and copper coins to a high point. *Life* said the collection would one-up anyone else who tried to duplicate it.

The collection was the work of one man who spent about 25 years (1925-1950) and approximately $400,000 assembling it. Yet when it was sold, (the gold part of the collection in October 1982, and the silver and copper portion a generation later in 1996 and 1997), the initial sale gave no public hint as to whose collection was being sold.

The division was part of prudent estate planning on the part of Eliasberg; the gold portion was consigned by the Gold Coin Corporation of Arizona, which was part of more prudent tax planning. See the following chapters on this point, and how it can benefit our rare coin retirement.

At the time, it was simply a mystery – except when you knew who had acquired all of the pedigree items in the collection. Later, all of the coins from the entire collection became a pedigree on their own– with special markings by both PCGS and NGC when the coins are encapsulated.

Eliasberg's collection was magnificent, of that there is no doubt. But those who follow stories like this closely know that Eliasberg did not quite succeed in his task; one coin evidently escaped. My notes say that when the family turned the collection over for auction by Bowers & Merena in the early 1980s, he was one coin down: an 1866 No Motto $20 gold piece. Neil S. Berman sold the deficient coin to the estate. But this did not come out until years later.

The King of Coins was by then deceased and his estate or heir was offering the gold coin collection anonymously through Bowers & Merena. From my perspective, there was a mystery to be solved as to who was selling the Eliasberg coins without calling them such.

One good thing about being a collector is that you collect. I keep the old auction catalogs and cross-reference them. Well, five years after Eliasberg, Bowers & Merena conducted the "The King of Siam" sale in New York on Oct. 14, 1987.

I was reading the catalog for Lot 2043 for an 1866-S No Motto $20 gold piece in EF-40, described as "finer" than the Eliasberg coin. There was a paragraph added in small type (it looks like six-point type, but at the time, I could read it easily).

"When the cataloguer studied the Eliasberg Collection prior to presenting it at auction in 1982," Bowers wrote, "it was discovered that the collection had no 1866 No Motto double eagle. Whether Louis Eliasberg overlooked the variety or whether he considered his collection complete because he had an 1866-S with motto is not known. However, in the interest of completeness the Eliasberg family purchased one through us, and we acquired it from dealer Neil Berman. So as a footnote to numismatic history, the Eliasberg Collection was 'completed' in 1982 with Neil Berman furnishing the missing piece!"

1815 50-Cent Obverse
Heritage Rare Coins

Eliasberg was born in 1896 in Selma, Ala., and lived a full life into the bicentennial year of 1976. He moved to Baltimore around 1907 and, according to his son, Richard, in 1925 he began to collect "methodically." Starting the

1815 50-Cent Reverse
Heritage Rare Coins

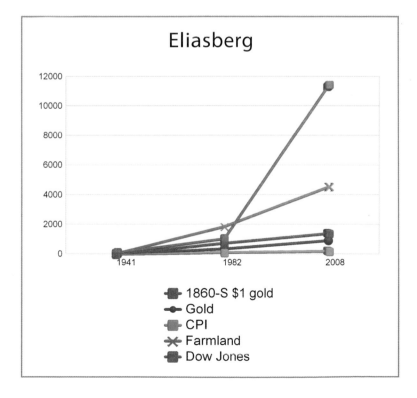

following year, he began to buy systematically from the leading dealers of the day. He recorded his purchases in Ben Green's "The Numismatists' Reference and Checkbook" where many familiar names (or initials) appear: "BB" for Barney Bluestone, "Gut" for the Guttag brothers, "HC" for Henry Chapman, "MM" for B. Max Mehl and others.

Initially, the collection was silver and copper coinage – little gold at the time. He started acquiring more and more expensive coins, but not until 1933 did he understand the importance of being a "numismatist," who held a sort of exemption from the government's seizure orders that called in gold bullion and gold coin.

Eliasberg, who by this time was running The Finance Company of America in Baltimore, lost confidence in the U.S. dollar and wanted to buy gold, but couldn't. That's because of the nationalization order by FDR. (See Chapter 8.)

"Feeling as I did about gold, I realized that the only way I could legally acquire gold was by becoming a numismatist," Eliasberg said. That's because FDR's seizure order exempted "rare and unusual coin." A collector was allowed to maintain up to four of each date, mintmark, variety and type – though there was a premium of that over its gold content.

"I started buying gold coins at as close to their bullion value as I found them offered," he said. At first it was disorganized, but by 1939 it became system-

1838 Proof $10
Obverse
Heritage Rare Coins

ized with checklists. In 1939 he bought a proof 1890 eagle from Stack's, along with a 1915 matte proof double eagle and an un-circulated 1922 $20.

But Eliasberg was in it for the long haul, and was not above admitting that he had made mistakes in his purchases. None of these three 1939 purchases were in the U.S. gold coin collection when it was sold in 1982; the 1915 matte proof had been replaced by one that he acquired in the 1942 purchase of the John H. Clapp collection, which had a gem matte proof-67 example. The proof eagle was nowhere to be found (an AU-50 coin was its placeholder). The 1922 was described as choice AU-55 obverse, MS-60 reverse. Eliasberg was always looking for completeness and better condition.

Eliasberg began to buy at auction, and as Q. David Bowers records in his *King of Coins* book, Eliasberg was a major player in the June 1941 William F. Dunham sale by B. Max Mehl, a mail bid auction sale. Among the pieces were a 1796 without stars quarter eagle; two overdate $2.50 gold pieces, 1802 over 1 and 1806 over 4; and an 1807 quarter eagle. He also obtained the 1796 over 5 half eagle, 1805, 1810 large date half eagles and both the curved and square variety of 1820 $5 gold piece, an 1830 5D (small) and an 1861-0 double eagle.

These were all relatively speaking inexpensive coins, even the double eagle, which Bowers today refers to as an elusive coin. Some of these coins stayed in the collection until it was sold, and we'll look briefly at three of them:

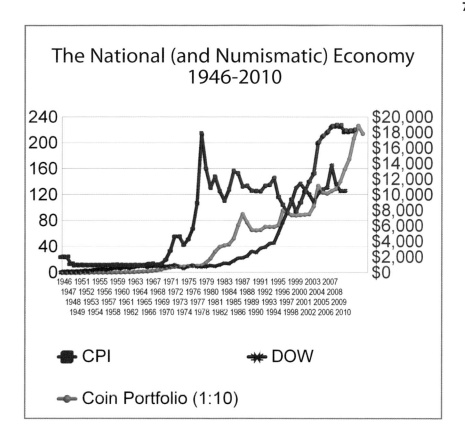

The National (and Numismatic) Economy
1946-2010

CPI   DOW   Coin Portfolio (1:10)

Date	Type	Eliasberg Grade	1941 Dunham	Eliasberg Open	Eliasberg Hammer	Cumulative %
1796 without stars	$2.5	XF-40	$81.50	$10,000.00	$24,000.00	14.50%
1806 over 4	$2.5	XF-45	$55.25	$2,000.00	$4,200.00	1.83%
1861-O	$20	AU-50	$40.25	$1,550.00	$4,250.00	2.49%

The no stars 1796 represented good quality, nice condition, and a significant compounded gain-rate profit. The whopping cost to Mr. Eliasberg: less than $82.

These early date coins are elusive but also hard to pinpoint because the grading standards have changed on them. Consider if you will "The Little Princess," a fabled proof issue quarter eagle from 1841. The Eliasberg coin had an impressive pedigreed history, which allows us to see how it did over protracted periods of time.

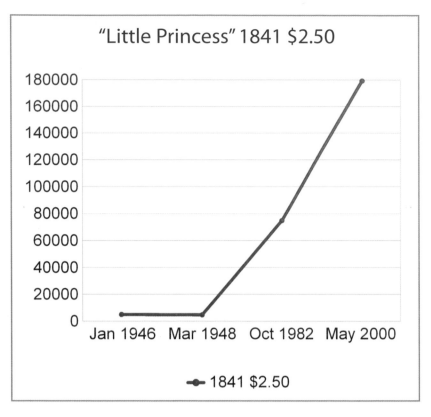

"Little Princess" 1841 $2.50

(Chart showing value rising from near $6,000 at Jan 1946 and Mar 1948, to $75,000 at Oct 1982, to approximately $178,250 at May 2000)

Legend: 1841 $2.50

1841 Little Princess

Jan 1946	FCC Boyd	WGC Lot 208	$6,000	
Mar 1948	JF Bell	Memorable Lot 101	$5,750	-0.24%
Oct 1982	Eliasberg	Gold Coin Lot 227	$75,000	15.34%
May 2000	Harry Bass	Lot 105	$178,250	4.93%

1841 $2.50 Little Princess Obverse & Reverse
Stack's Rare Coins

This particular analysis starts with the collection of Fred (F.C.C.) Boyd, an executive with the Union News Company, whose collection Abe Kosoff sold in 1946 ("The World's Greatest Collection"). The collection included "The Little Princess," where it brought $6,000 and was bought by Jacob Shapiro, whose pseudonym, "Jake Bell" or J.F. Bell, was involved in many transactions. (He later was a partner in RAR-

COA of Chicago). The price realized for his specimen declined when Bell's hold-ings were put up to auction in the "Memorable Collection," and the coin went into hiding.

The buyer at the Memorable sale in early 1948 "shopped" the coin; eventu-ally only Eliasberg went through enough due diligence to acquire it. He held it until his death in 1976. When the collection was put on the market in 1982, the catalog said nothing about Eliasberg being the owner, but his acquisition of the "Little Princess" having been published in *Life* and *Look* magazine made it obvi-ous as to whose collection was being offered.

The "Little Princess" acquisition, and its price history, also show a truism about buying coins as an investment: you need to allow time for the investment to develop. When FCC Boyd sold his collection, the 1841 quarter eagle brought $6,000; two years later, on resale, the price went down. There are a number of reasons that can account for this; the economy was in the toilet, discretionary spending was nationally reduced, and there was a general malaise in what was then perceived as a rich man's hobby (especially on high ticket items). But on the long-term Eliasberg holding, it compounded nicely, about 15 percent annually from 1948 to 1982. The successor purchaser at the Eliasberg estate sale, Harry Bass, saw a return of about 5 percent annually over the 18 years that he had the coin.

My catalog notes for the Eliasberg sale show that bidding commenced at $25,000 and progressed in $5,000 increments rapidly. There were multiple bidders; my catalog notes say that Numismatic Investments of Florida (Marty Haber) and Fred Weinberg were among them. Auctioneer William Hawfield handled the bidding and the offers. His last cry was $75,000, which went to bid-der 121, which my catalog identifies as Harry Bass.

Bass was in attendance (He didn't always represent himself at auctions – he frequently used agents.) and was an active bidder on this. He had another 1841 "Little Princess," which was Proof-60 and not nearly as nice as this one. But soon, as we joked at the time, he could have made a pair of cufflinks.

Fortunately, Bass was a skilled numismatist and

1881 50-Cent Obverse
Heritage Rare Coins

1881 5-Cent Obverse
Heritage Rare Coins

1873 2-Cent Obverse
Heritage

1873 2-Cent Reverse
Heritage

1873 25-Cent
Obverse
Heritage

1881-S Dollar
Heritage

enjoyed the research and challenge of the chase. His rate of return, by the time his collection was sold a decade ago, wasn't bad, but also wasn't great. (The line using the @ Rate formula shows 14 percent for Eliasberg and more than 4 percent for Bass).

Eliasberg's one big purchase had a significant impact on the overall strength of his collection, turning it from a numismatic investment that was as close to the price of gold bullion as he could make it, to a truly world class collection comprised of world-class coins. He paid $100,000 to acquire intact the Clapp collection. Brokers for the collection were J.B. and Morton Stack, the patriarchs of the Stack's coin firm of New York.

Numerous stories in future years would peg the Eliasberg investment in his collection as being in the millions – largely because the commentators and writers, looking at their notes, could simply not believe their eyes. The Clapp collection brought many rarities, and common coins, too, at a "mere" $100,000 cost.

But even the scarcest coins, such as the unique 1870-S $3 gold piece, were not all that expensive by today's standards. The late Arthur Kagin of the Hollinbeck Coin Company (later ANA vice president and father of one of today's famous dealers, Dr. Donald Kagin) wrote to Eliasberg on July 5, 1944, offering a very fine example – the only example known – at $8,500. It was sent to Baltimore, but returned.

But in December 1945 Eliasberg was ready, and the Celina Coin Company offered it at $12,500. He had Stack's negotiate the acquisition; he bagged it for $11,000 plus a 5 percent commission ($11,550 total), which was invoiced on Jan. 28, 1946. (Its earlier history showed it in the 1911 William Woodin sale at $1,450).

Years later, in 1982, with CBS-TV news national cameras twirling, Jane Bryant Quinn reported bidding on the coin started at $100,000, jumped to $325,000 and then it was off to the races. Harvey G. Stack was bidding against the "book" to $475,000, when the book came back with a half million dollars. Lester Merkin, a respected dealer, came back with a floor bid of $525,000, and the book answered with $575,000. Harvey Stack, on the floor, answered with $625,000. And it was over (with buyer's premium, $687,000). The return on investment, compounded, averaged 11.7 percent annually over the 36 years that Eliasberg and his estate held the coin.

1870-S $3

Woodin	1911		$1,450	
Stacks	1946		$11,500	0*
Eliasberg	1982	XF-40	$625,000	11.74%

*Not calculated because of intermediate holdings

Eliasberg had rarity after rarity. The unique 1870-S $3 was followed by another choice morsel, an original (class I) 1804 silver dollar. Another case showing that rarities can always make a nice return if held long enough. (But, as the charts show, Eliasberg had common coins, semi-scarce pieces, rarities – the whole shooting match; he was a collector.)

1804 Silver Dollar

Collection	Holding period	Sale	Price	Gain
Stickney	1907		$3,600	Annual gain
Col. Ellsworth	1907-1923			
Wayte Raymond				
Wm. Cutler Atwater	1923-1946	1946	$10,500	2.78%
ELIASBERG				
ELIASBERG Estate	PCGS Proof-65	1997	$1,815,000	13.39%

There aren't too many people that you can do this with, but you can compare the acumen of holding an 1804 dollar with that of a 1913 Liberty nickel. The two coin stories are similar in that there are unchronicled moments of each.

This historic 1913 Liberty nickel has a long and involved history that dates back some 90 years to the time in December 1919 when a former Mint employee, Samuel Brown, advertised in the ANA's monthly periodical, *The Numismatist*, that he was willing to buy an example of the coin for $500. In 1920, he raised the price to $600 a coin.

Evidence points to the fact that Brown had produced the coins, on Mint machinery, using government dies, on government planchets that awaited the decision of the Treasury chief to change the design to the Indian head and Bison reverse.

Eventually, it would come out that there were five specimens produced, all tracing their pedigree to Brown. In the 1920s, they were acquired by Col. Ned Green and in 1941, they came into possession of Eric P. Newman and Burdette Johnson, in settling the Green estate. By late 1941, all five went to Newman and then began to be broadly disbursed.

In the early 1930s, Fort Worth dealer B. Max Mehl organized a national campaign to find the so-called "sixth" 1913 Liberty nickel, offering to pay $50 for it (big money in the Depression) – and popularizing his mail order business.

The advertisement offered: "Old Money Wanted. Will pay Fifty Dollars for

1884-S $1 Reverse
Heritage

1913 Liberty Nickel
Heritage

Nickels of 1913 with Liberty head (no Buffalo)." None, of course, were ever turned in – but Mehl reaped publicity in print and on the radio and went on to become the biggest coin dealer in the world.

Eliasberg bought his out of the Atwater sale (1946).

All research on the 1804 silver dollar, at least in modern times, inevitably returns to the seminal volume on *The Fantastic 1804 Silver Dollar* by Eric P. Newman and Kenneth E. Bressett (1962), recently revised and reissued. They quote, as do many successive catalogers, from a letter dated Nov. 11, 1834, from U.S. Secretary of State John Forsyth of Georgia, directed to Dr. Samuel Moore, director of the United States Mint. Forsyth, confirmed June 27, 1834, and serving until the change of administrations on March 4, 1841, stated that President Andrew Jackson "has directed that a complete set of the coins of the United States be sent to the King of Siam and another to the Sultan of Muscat."

There are other provisos, but what is clear from the results is that the Mint director caused a "complete" set to be produced for both commercial treaties, the result of which is two more coins today called the King of Siam specimen, whose ownership is set to music in the Broadway show "The King and I" story about Mrs. Anna Leonowens, and the Watters-Childs specimen, whose provenance includes the Iman of Muscat. Sets prepared for the Emperor of Japan and the King of Cochin China (Indochina) were evidently returned to the Mint after their deaths.

Two other versions of the 1804 dollar were produced well into the late 1850s. Newman and Bressett weave the fascinating tale of deceit, nepotism, and fraud. The newspapers have been fascinated from the time that the coin began to sell at auction at multiples of the then-living wage.

Colonel Ellsworth was the buyer in 1907 – only the second owner since 1843– and he held it until Wayte Raymond purchased his entire collection for $100,000 in 1923. Raymond in turn sold it to William Cutler Atwater, who owned it from 1923 to 1946 when his collection was cataloged and sold by numismatic promoter B. Max Mehl of Fort Worth, Texas.

Mehl auctioned off the Atwater collection in a sale that numismatic literature cataloger John Adams grades "A+." The coin was acquired by a dealer for a customer at $10,500. The ultimate buyer's name: Louis Eliasberg, who just happened to be starting on acquiring one of every United States coin. (He eventually completed this task). When his estate finally sold off the coin in 1996, the price realized for the coin was an incredible $1,815,000. (The coin was graded Proof-63).

Rate of Return for 1913 Liberty Head Nickel

Newman & Johnson	A. Kosoff	1948		$2,350	
Abe Kosoff	Louis ELiasberg	1949		$2,468	5.00%
Eliasberg Estate	Jay Parrino	1996	PCGS PF-66	$1,485,000	13.95%
Jay Parrino	Dwight Manley	2001	PCGS PF-66	$1,840,000	4.38%
Dwight Manley	Ed Lee	2003	PCGS PF-66	$3,000,000	27.69%
Ed Lee	Legend Numismatics	2005	PCGS PF-66	$4,150,000	17.62%
Legend Numismatics	Ron Gillio for Cal. Collector	2007	PCGS PF-66	$5,000,000	9.76%

Eliasberg loved to go to local Baltimore coin shows and show off portions of his collection. It always had a good response. Not just the rarities, the "salt of the earth" coins in very fine condition that other collectors of lesser means tried to acquire. People responded to this.

The editors of *Life* told him that they had the highest letters to the editor in recent memory in response to the "King of Coins" article. More than 7,500 individuals wrote to Eliasberg to talk "coins" and he read and followed their objective response. And then, *Life* editors say, he answered every one of them!

In 2008, Scotsman Coin's auction firm, Scotsman Auction Co. of St. Louis, had more than 80 gold coins with Eliasberg pedigrees offered for sale at public auction. There were some rarities included (like an 1880 Stella and a 1931-S double eagle), but most were coins that had a moderate price in 1982 and a decent track record since. Many are the type of coin that could go into a rare coin retirement portfolio.

In reproducing the chart that follows, there has been some editing. An example is shown of a couple of eagles and none of the $20 gold pieces. The double eagles so mirror the bullion market for non-rarities that it is not worthwhile utilizing them; it throws off the message and the profit. A couple of eagles with 48 troy ounces of gold have a similar problem.

Date	Value	Scotsman Grade	Eliasberg Grade	Eliasberg Oct. 1982	Scotsman Sale Oct. 17, 2008	Compounded Gain/Loss
1855-O	$1	NGC AU-58	XF-45	$1,000	$4,100.00	5.58%
1857-C	$1	NGC AU-58	XF-40	$700	$5,250.00	8.06%
1857-S	$1	NGC AU-55	XF-40	$900	$1,500.00	1.98%
1860-S	$1	NGC AU-58	XF-40	$750	$1,400.00	2.43%
1862	$1	NGC PF-67* Ultra Cameo	PF-67	$8,000	$45,000.00	6.87%
1840-O (large O)	$2.50	NGC AU-58	AU-55	$1,000	$4,500.00	5.96%
1842-O (large O)	$2.50	NGC AU-55	VF-30	$550	$3,300.00	7.13%
1843-O small date	$2.50	NGC AU-58	AU-50	$750	$1,300.00	2.14%
1847	$2.50	NGC AU-58	VF-30	$425	$1,350.00	4.55%
1848-C	$2.50	NGC AU-58	XF-45	$1,000	$5,500.00	6.78%

Date	Value	Scotsman Grade	Eliasberg Grade	Eliasberg Oct. 1982	Scotsman Sale Oct. 17, 2008	Compounded Gain/Loss
1850-C	$2.50	NGC AU-58	XF-40	$750	$8,750.00	9.91%
1850-O, Breen-1,	$2.50	NCS scratched cleaned	XF-45	$525	$650.00	0.82%
1851	$2.50	NGC MS-67*	MS67	$6,750	$25,000.00	5.16%
1852-C	$2.50	NGC AU-58	XF-40	$950	$7,000.00	7.98%
1855	$2.50	NGC MS-62	MS60/63	$550	$1,050.00	2.52%
1856-S	$2.50	NGC MS-61	AU-55	$500	$4,000.00	8.33%
1859-S	$2.50	NGC AU-58	XF-45/AU-50	$450	$4,750.00	9.49%
1865-S	$2.50	NCS cleaned	AU50/60	$750	$1,450.00	2.57%
1867-S	$2.50	NGC MS-61	au50/55	$850	$3,750.00	5.87%
1877-S	$2.50	NCS polished, AU Details	XF-45	$500	$300.00	-1.95%
1925-D Indian Head	$2.50	NGC MS-64	BU65/60	$600	$2,500.00	5.64%
1927 Indian Head	$2.50	NGC MS-63	MS-60	$350	$825.00	3.35%
1928 Indian Head	$2.50	NGC MS-63	AU55	$550	$925.00	2.02%
1929 Indian Head	$2.50	NGC MS-64	65rx60	$750	$1,500.00	2.70%
1880 Flowing Hair	$4	NGC PF-66	PF-67	$50,000	$430,000.00	8.63%
1808 (normal date, wide 5 D)	$5		XF-40	$2,600	$4,400.00	2.04%
1847-C	$5		VF-30	$550	$4,000.00	7.93%
1855-C	$5		XF-45	$850	$5,250.00	7.25%
1857-S	$5		VF-30	$1,400	$850.00	-1.90%
1858-C	$5			$850	$5,000.00	7.05%
1866-S	$5	No Motto. NGC	VF-25	$750	$2,100.00	4.04%
1870-S	$5		VF-30	$800	$6,750.00	8.55%
1872-S	$5		VF-20	$400	$350.00	-0.51%
1874-S	$5		VG-8	$300	$600.00	2.70%
1876-S	$5		VG-30	$950	$2,400.00	3.63%
1879-S	$5		AU-58	$450	$565.00	0.88%
1881-CC	$5		AU-53	$450	$5,100.00	9.79%
1881-S	$5		XF-45	$850	$1,350.00	1.80%
1883-CC	$5	cleaned		$550	$1,950.00	4.99%
1883-S	$5		XF-45	$350	$390.00	0.42%
1884-CC	$5		XF-45	$850	$10,000.00	9.95%
1884-S	$5			$550	$500.00	-0.37%
1888-S	$5			$550	$425.00	-0.99%
1909-D Indian Head	$5	NGC MS-62	AU-55	$800	$1,350.00	7.93%

Date	Value	Scotsman Grade	Eliasberg Grade	Eliasberg Oct. 1982	Scotsman Sale Oct. 17, 2008	Compounded Gain/Loss
1911-S Indian Head	$5	NGC AU-58	AU50/55	$700	$650.00	-0.28%
1914-S Indian Head	$5	NGC XF-45		$400	$360.00	-0.40%
1842 large date	$10			$650	$675.00	0.15%
1850 small date	$10			$500	$3,000.00	7.13%

Amazingly, some of the Eliasberg coins brought less in 2008 than they did in 1982. The 1911-S Indian Head (incused) $5 half eagle is one; the 1914-S half eagle is another. The 1914-S received $360 in Scotman's 2008 sale, while at Eliasberg's 1982 offering it brought $400. (The rate of return is negative).

With the negatives and the positives of these 47 coins, whose randomness is simply that Scotsman put together an auction sale that allowed their comprehensive study, the average rate of return is 4.2 percent annually.[13] Something else to look at is how grading has changed over the past generation.

1884-S Obverse
Heritage

One example that is typical is a quarter eagle, the 1842-O (large O) $2.50, which Bowers in 1982 cataloged as VF-30 (very fine condition). The 2008 sale had the coins encapsulated by NGC and the identical coin improved in condition, being graded NGC AU-55 (about uncirculated).

Two $1 gold pieces that were both graded extremely fine in the original Eliasberg sale also improved to about uncirculated:

| 1855-O | $1 | NGC AU-58 | XF-45 |
| 1857-C | $1 | NGC AU-58 | XF-40 |

It's not just small-sized coins like the gold dollar or difficult to grade coins like the incused-surface Indian head eagle that have suffered gradeflation. The easy to grade double eagle had it, too. Take the 1930-S $20, a major rarity with a low mintage (74,000) called "brilliant uncirculated" and graded MS-60 in Eliasberg (1982). The 2008 verdict by one of the grading services: "1930-S Saint-Gaudens double-eagle, NGC MS-65 Eliasberg." (The price it received in 2008, which was $170,000, was fully reflective of the new grade.)

Here's the other thing, every one of the 47 Eliasberg coins could easily be placed into a new rare coin retirement program. If you take the scratched or poorly cleaned and very expensive coins out of the mix, here is what you are left with, which could well be called the Eliasberg retirement portfolio, with 2010 prices supplied by Dennis Baker's *NumisMedia*.

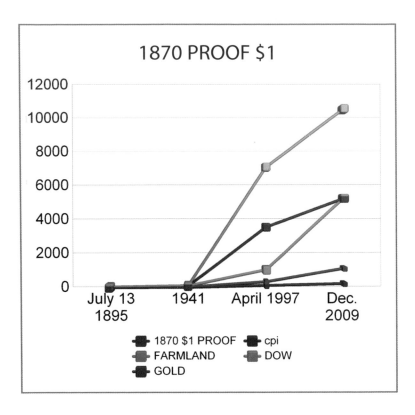

Coin	Type	Scotsman Grade	Eliasberg Grade	Eliasberg Oct 1982	Scotsman Oct 17 2008	Compounded Gain/Loss	Numis Media 2010 Price
1855-O	$1	NGC AU-58	XF-45	$1,000	$4,100.00	5.58%	$5,220
1857-C	$1	NGC AU-58	XF-40	$700	$5,250.00	8.06%	$7,840
1857-S	$1	NGC AU-55	XF-40	$900	$1,500.00	1.98%	$1,880
1860-S	$1	NGC AU-58 xDunham	XF-40	$750	$1,400.00	2.43%	$930
1840-O (large O)	$2.50	NGC AU-58	AU-55	$1,000	$4,500.00	5.96%	$6,190
1842-O (large O)	$2.50	NGC AU-55	VF-30	$550	$3,300.00	7.13%	$7,160
1843-O small date	$2.50	NGC AU-58	AU-50	$750	$1,300.00	2.14%	$830
1847	$2.50	NGC AU-58	VF-30	$425	$1,350.00	4.55%	$1,970
1848-C	$2.50	NGC AU-58	XF-45	$1,000	$5,500.00	6.78%	$5,780
1852-C	$2.50	NGC AU-58	XF-40	$950	$7,000.00	7.98%	$8,410
1855	$2.50	NGC MS-62	MS-60/63	$550	$1,050.00	2.52%	$710
1856-S	$2.50	NGC MS-61 xclapp, michelson	AU-55	$500	$4,000.00	8.33%	$5,820

Coin	Type	Scotsman Grade	Eliasberg Grade	Eliasberg Oct 1982	Scotsman Oct 17 2008	Compounded Gain/Loss	Numis Media 2010 Price
1859-S	$2.50	NGC AU-58	XF-45/AU-50	$450	$4,750.00	9.49%	$3,060
1867-S	$2.50	NGC MS-61 xclapp, frossard	AU-50/55	$850	$3,750.00	5.87%	$2,590
1925-D Indian Head	$2.50	NGC MS-64	BU-65/60	$600	$2,500.00	5.64%	$1,400
1927 Indian Head	$2.50	NGC MS-63	MS-60	$350	$825.00	3.35%	$950
1928 Indian Head	$2.50	NGC MS-63	AU-55	$550	$925.00	2.02%	$950
1929 Indian Head	$2.50	NGC MS-64	MS-65 MS-60 (Rev)	$750	$1,500.00	2.70%	$1,400
1808 (wide 5 D)	$5		XF-40	$2,600	$4,400.00	2.04%	$5,500
1847-C	$5		VF-30	$550	$4,000.00	7.93%	$2,130
1855-C	$5		XF-45	$850	$5,250.00	7.25%	$2,030
1858-C	$5			$850	$5,000.00	7.05%	$2,030
1866-S	$5, No Motto.	NGC VF-25		$750	$2,100.00	4.04%	$1,810
1870-S	$5		VF-30	$800	$6,750.00	8.55%	$810
1874-S	$5		VG-8	$300	$600.00	2.70%	$690
1876-S	$5		VG-30	$950	$2,400.00	3.63%	$1,780
1879-S	$5		AU-58	$450	$565.00	0.88%	$1,260
1881-CC	$5		AU-53	$450	$5,100.00	9.79%	$2,060
1881-S	$5		XF-45	$850	$1,350.00	1.80%	$388
1883-CC	$5		cleaned	$550	$1,950.00	4.99%	$1,450
1883-S	$5		XF-45	$350	$390.00	0.42%	$480
1909-D Indian Head	$5	NGC MS-62	AU-55	$800	$1,350.00	7.93%	$980
1842 large date	$10		AU-58	$650	$675.00	0.15%	$1,190
1850 small date	$10		MS-61	$500	$3,000.00	7.13%	$2,440
Total				$24,875	$99,380	4.69%	$90,118

This portfolio would be a $90,000 component, utilizing any (or all) of these coins (except the badly cleaned ones, which are already marked).

A few additional comments about the Eliasberg collection are in order. First, he was cognizant that he had created something special, but was always on the lookout for an upgrade. Second, to appreciate what he acquired, a look at many other catals is in order. Consider just one coin (acquired for less than $10 by Eliasberg), an 1860-S gold dollar:

Date	Denomination	Condition	Collection	Date	Price Realized	Gain/Loss
1860-S	$1 gold	XF	Dunham	1941	$9.75	
1860-S	$1 gold	XF-40	Eliasberg	1982	$750.00	11.17%
1860-S	$1 gold	AU58	Scotsman	2008	$1,400.00	2.43%

Eliasberg's gain was over 11 percent annually in the 41 years since the Dunham sale; even since then, the rate is almost 2½ percent each year. Considering that some banks are paying less than a half a percent, the rate of return, while not high, is still impressive. Finally, the comparison any of these selected coins with other tangible assets shows that coins remain a player.

Eliasberg, in buying the Clapp collection, had acquired a collection that, in scope, was similar to his own. He sold off duplicates in the October 1947 H.R. Lee auction conducted by Stack's (2,054 lots), and again at a New Netherlands Coin Co. Auction, the 49th catalog of June 12, 1957, which was acknowledged as "Duplicates from the Louis Eliasberg Collection," 1,425 lots spread over 73 pages and six plates.

Thus, a number of rarities that were originally in the collection were given up. One that was given up in an entirely different way was the 1933 $20 gold piece. Eliasberg had one, and when the Secret Service began prosecuting to obtain the coins back – there were famous cases against L.G. Barnard, James Aloysius Stack, J.F. Bell, Col. Flanagan, and others – Eliasberg simply deposited his example with the Secret Service without a fight. (The coin cost him the equivalent of around $2,000, and like all the rest of them, his had the fin-

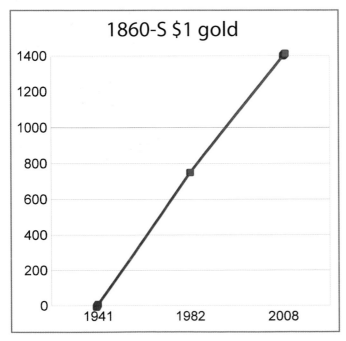

gerprints of Israel Swilt not literally on it, but figuratively.)

According to the Secret Service, "Eliasberg of Baltimore, Maryland, had purchased the Double Eagle in 1944 from one of the three collectors who had bought 1933 Double Eagles from Israel Switt in 1937."

Here's what happened to that: "Eliasberg learned when he was preparing to display his coin collection publicly that there was a cloud on the 1933 Double Eagle. When Eliasberg learned that there was a question about his right to possess the 1933 Double Eagle, he sent it to the Mint of his own initiative."

After his death in 1976, some pre- and post-mortem estate planning is obvious. The gold coins were placed into 1,074 lots and auctioned as "The U.S. Gold Coin Collection" by Bowers & Ruddy; it yielded $12.4 million. In May, 1996, Bowers & Merena (a successor firm) sold a portion of the silver and copper coins in 1,348 lots that yielded about $11.5 million. Finally, in April, 1997, about 2,000 lots were offered by Bowers & Merena bringing in $20.9 million, and the Eliasberg collection passed into history to become a pedigree quoted even today.

All told, about $45 million was made from the sale of the remaining collection, making it one of the highest yielding collections of all time.

But for the collector or investor who is unlikely to acquire thousands of lots and major rarities, the Eliasberg collection shows that even minor items like a common uncirculated Washington quarter benefits from the star power of an Eliasberg sale:

Coin	Condition	Sale	Eliasberg	Current	Gain
1904-O 25¢	NGC MS-66	Aug. 7, 2009	$4,630.00	$5,290.00	1.12%
1850-O $1	PCGS AU-53	Aug. 7, 2009	$1,320.00	$3,832.95	9.29%
1859-S	PCGS AU-50	Aug. 7, 2009	$2,310.00	$2,853.15	1.78%
1870 $1	PCGS PF-64	Aug. 7, 2009	$3,520.00	$6,049.00	4.62%
1875-CC Trade $1	PCGS PF-64	Aug. 7, 2009	$5,930.00	$10,638.65	4.99%
1833 50¢	PCGS MS-66	April 2009	$3,410.00	$9,200.00	8.62%
1952 25¢	PCGS MS-66	Jan. 8, 2007	n/a	$345.00	n/a
1861 25¢	PCGS PR-62	Oct. 24, 2009	$880.00	$891.25	0.11%

Sources: Aug. 7, 2009, sale by David Lawrence Rare Coin Auctions. Other prices from Heritage Auctions.

What turns out to be the value of the Eliasberg pedigree? Well, consider the 1952 MS-66 Washington quarter, probably a $100 item maximum as this is written. The proof, as they say, is in the pudding.

HOW SOME OTHER COLLECTORS DID: REED HAWN

Name a rare coin – a really rare one – and Reed Hawn has probably owned it. He has also bought and sold many thousands of rare coins where his profit was $200 or $300 a coin – making up in volume what some other rarities can only do by going for the moon. He figured out early that 100 percent profit on a $500 coin brought its selling price to $1,000, but the same percentage on a $500,000 acquisition requires a million dollar baby.

Reed Hawn's family money comes from oil and Arabian horses; his numismatic glory comes from the stellar array of rarities he has owned. But with five major "named" sales under his belt, and some others that few know anything about, his profits have come from working men's coins – generic, uncirculated half dollars whose eye appeal was spectacular, and whose price potential was the sky.

Hawn's 1838-O 50-Cent
Stack's Rare Coins

Because his career as a coin investor stretches from the 1960s until today, he has been buying "collector coins" in each of the six decades since he began collecting. In fact, my writing about coins nicely parallels his time in building and selling multiple collections of coins, taking thousands of coins to market.

His first sale – which I learned about almost 40 years after the fact – came at the 1971 ANA convention in Washington, D.C. "My first sale was the big ANA in D.C. in 1971, without my name on it, I was maintaining as much anonymity as possible," Hawn said in a 2010 text message to me. "Those were my half duplicates."

His 1804 silver dollar had a pedigree dating back to Joseph Mickley, one of America's first coin collectors. The 1913 Liberty nickel that he owned until 1993 was re-auctioned in 2010 for over $3.7 million. An 1876-CC 20-cent piece, or an 1827 restrike proof quarter, or an 1838-O half dollar? Yes, each of them was once part of the Reed Hawn collection.

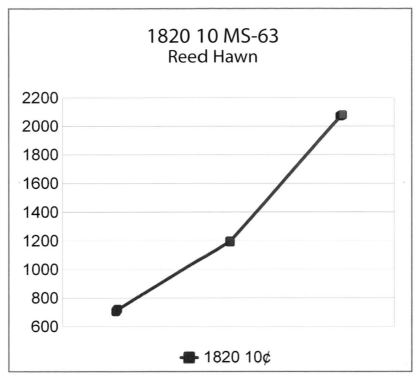

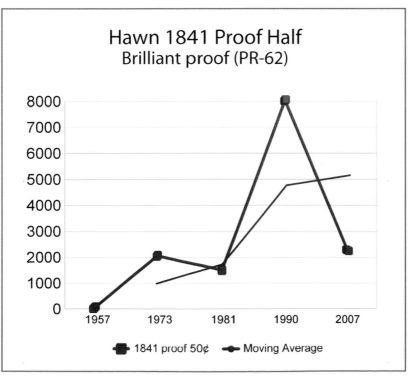

His name burst onto the public consciousness two years after the ANA sale in Washington in August 1973, just before his 24th birthday, when Stack's sold the Reed Hawn Collection, the first of no less than five catalogs that the mavens of East 57th Street in New York put out bearing his name. That first sale, which focused mostly on half dollars, left other former fine half dollar collections in the dust, not only for its completeness, but for the spectacular condition in which many of his coins found themselves.

Stack's, in those days, did not use numbers to grade coins, only adjectives, except for early large coppers which subscribed to Dr. Sheldon's numerical system. So the description was typically "brilliant uncirculated, a gem" – we know what it translates to because so many of the Hawn coins still make the rounds with the pedigree, this time slapped with an Numismatic Guaranty Corporation or Professional Coin Grading Service slabs.

What is remarkable about Reed Hawn, who has been my friend for nearly 20 years, is that his first "name" catalog at Stacks, Aug. 28-29, 1973, took place when he was just 23 years old; the collection was some 15 years in the making, and besides the major rarities, had a number of quality conditioned coins that Stack's then termed amazing, and which still stand the test of time. If you have done the calculations, he started building that collection at age 8!

I got to know Reed and saw him frequently when we both served as charter members of the Citizens Commemorative Coin Advisory Committee, which Congress created in the early 1990s to help resolve the mess that contemporary commemorative coin issues had evolved into. We saw each other, mostly in Washington, and spent a lot of talking time chatting up the coin market. Hawn turns out to be a marketing genius in the buying, building and auctioning of collections.

Looking first to the catalogs, he has eight separate listings in Martin Gengerke's Guide to American Numismatic Auctions:

- Hawn, Reed Stack's 08/28/1973, 815 lots
- Hawn, Reed Stack's 03/11/1977
- Hawn, Reed Stack's 10/13/1993, 1,298 lots
- Hawn, Reed Stack's 12/01/1993,
- Hawn, Reed Stack's 05/05/1998
- Hawn, Reed George F. Kolbe #73 06/11/1998
- Hawn, Reed Stack's 10/16/2003,
- Hawn, Reed Heritage/CAA 09/09/2004

The Kolbe (1998) auction was books and Heritage (2004) was for Texas paper currency. The rest were coin auctions with Stack's.

Born in Corpus Christi on Aug. 20, 1949, he was encouraged by his father, Bill Hawn, who (a Stack's catalog reports) gave him a circulated Metric gold dollar as a present. By the mid-1960s, Hawn was doing business by mail with

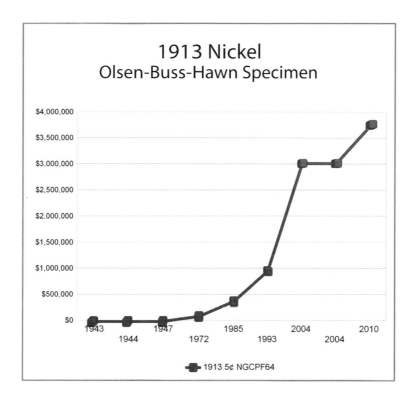

1913 Nickel
Olsen-Buss-Hawn Specimen

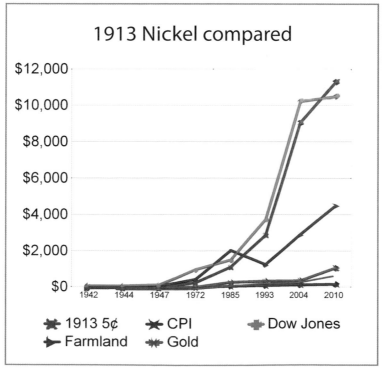

1913 Nickel compared

dealers all over the country. His first visit to Stack's came on a family trip to New York City where he met Harvey, Norman and Ben Stack. Hawn was all of 14 or 15 years old. (The Stack family presumed him two or three generations older– in his 70s).

He made a deal with Ben Stack: if he would help him build a collection to the "best possible" within his scope, he would commission Stack's to sell it at auction. It "must have sounded pretty arrogant of me, at my age," he said, but it was the start of a 40 year friendship.

Elsie Sterling Howard (from left) David Pickens and Reed Hawn converse at a Citizens Advisory Committee meeting in 1995.
Author's Photo

He made good on the second half of the promise in 1973 when he sold off a highly focused collection of half dollars that contained many key rarities. At least 10 of them were "killer" coins – to die for – in 474 lots of half dollars. The action then shifted to an 1802 half dime in XF condition and a magnificent listing of 18 early dimes.

Reed Hawn may be known for the rarities he kept – in the October 1993 sale he had both an 1804 silver dollar and a 1913 Liberty head nickel – and others.

Date	Pedigree	Sale
1804 silver dollar	Type 1 original	Oct. 13-14, 1993
1913 Liberty nickel	Olsen-Buss	Oct. 13-14, 1993
1842 small date 25¢	James A Stack est	Oct. 13-14, 1993
1876-cc 20 ¢	Superior 1991	Oct. 16, 2003
1838-0 50¢	Atwater 1946	Aug. 28-29, 1973
1794 50¢ BU		Aug. 28-29, 1973
1795 double date 50¢ b.u.	Merkin 1971	Aug. 28-29, 1973
1796 16 stars 50¢	Proof	Aug. 28-29, 1973
1921S Liberty 50¢		Aug. 28-29, 1973
1802 half dime	XF Geo Hall (Stack)	Aug. 28-29, 1973
1859 10¢ transitional	BU	Aug. 28-29, 1973
1836 Gobrecht dollar proof		Aug. 28-29, 1973

But that was a fraction of the 1,298 lot sale. Hawn looked at much lower-value coins as his bread and butter.

He said in an interview with *Numismatic News* editor David Harper that he had "resolved as a teen-ager to make money in numismatics."

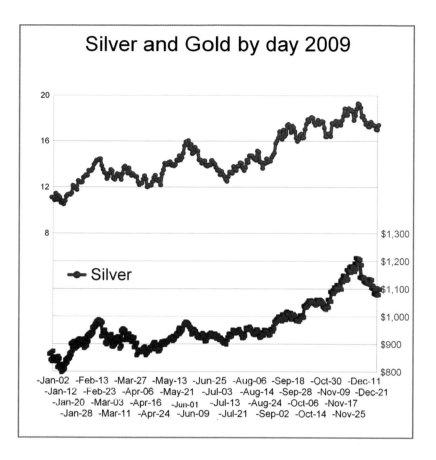

Silver and Gold by day 2009

-Jan-02 -Feb-13 -Mar-27 -May-13 -Jun-25 -Aug-06 -Sep-18 -Oct-30 -Dec-11
-Jan-12 -Feb-23 -Apr-06 -May-21 -Jul-03 -Aug-14 -Sep-28 -Nov-09 -Dec-21
-Jan-20 -Mar-03 -Apr-16 -Jun-01 -Jul-13 -Aug-24 -Oct-06 -Nov-17
-Jan-28 -Mar-11 -Apr-24 -Jun-09 -Jul-21 -Sep-02 -Oct-14 -Nov-25

"It was an investment for me," he declared. This commitment led to major hobby success for him.

"I made my money on the $600 coins," he said to me in early 2010 when we discussed the number of "name" collections that he had started from scratch. On the 1973 collection, the number was even lower: "I always made my money on the bread and butter coins, like most of the half dollars sold in 1973, many of them purchased for around $65."

In his view, "The great rarities, a real honor to own, were basically calling cards to get bidders interested in the auction sale." What he meant was a $65 coin that sold on auction for $650 – a ten-fold increase– was hard to equal in percentage terms on a $2,500 coin or even a $100,000 coin (which would have to jump to a million dollars to give the same rate of return).

Let's look at one of the rarities from the 1973 sale – the 1838-O half dollar, which is a major rarity and a real auction flag.

It's a coin whose very existence is denied by the Mint reports. Yet records show that on April 11, 1838, two pair of dies were shipped from the Philadelphia Mint to the U.S. Mint at New Orleans on the muddy, mighty Mississippi Rive in the French Quarter. They arrived on May 3, 1838, and were used in January 1839 to "test the press" at the New Orleans Mint for a production run. The obverse dies were defaced on June 21, 1839; the reverse dies were still good and held over for striking.

Some believe that the coin's mintmark was added in celebration of the opening of the first branch Mint of the United States to commence operations. Regardless, the coins struck were in very limited quantity– probably as few as 20 – and have the unusual feature (for the time) of depicting the mintmark on the obverse of the coin, above the date.

For many years, no one was quite sure about half dollars bearing that early mintmark. The story was published in *The Numismatist* in 1894, but few paid attention, and even into the 1950s, no one was able to nail the mintage or number of coins that survived.

The Smithsonian Institution's national coin collection has a specimen that came from the coiner at the Mint, Rufus Tyler. In an Ed Frossard sale of 1894 selling the Friesner collection, the buyer, Augustus G. Heaton, found an explanatory letter with the lot: "The enclosed specimen coin of the U.S. branch Mint at New Orleans presented to Pres. [Alexander] Bache [of Girard College, Philadelphia] by Rufus Tyler, the Coiner. It may be proper to state that not more than 20 pieces were struck with the half dollar dies of 1838." Bache was the grandson of Benjamin Franklin and had become president of Girard College in 1836.

Reed Hawn's buy-in was for a coin whose pedigree traces back to at least the Atwater collection sold by B. Max Mehl in 1936. The chart accompanying shows what a winner some great rarities can be:

1838-O Half Dollar

Seller	Auctioneer	Year	Price
William C. Atwater	B. Max Mehl	June 1946	$2,200
Reed Hawn	Stack's	August 1973	$41,000
Auction '79	Superior	August 1979	$62,500
James Pryor	Bowers & Merena	Jan. 1996	$104,500
Sid and Alicia Belzberg	Heritage	August 2008	$632,500

Hawn's point is that the profit is in the small workmen-like coins, not the rarities. That can be seen in this example. The 1916-D Walking Liberty half (Lot 416) cost $65 and realized $170 in BU. The simple gain is 161 percent. On a coin that cost $2,500, the same 161 percent has to go up to over $4,000. That's a valuable lesson that Reed Hawn still takes to heart.

You can also see it in the early years of the 1913 Liberty nickel:

1913 Liberty Nickel

Seller	Buyer	Year	Price	%Gain
Est. Col. E.H.R. Green	Johnson & Newman	1942	$400	
Fred Olsen	King Farouk	1944	$3,750	206.19%
Will W. Neil	Edwin Hydeman	1947	$3,750	0.00%
Abe Kosoff	World Wide Coin Investments	1972	$100,000	14.04%
Dr. Jerry Buss	Reed Hawn	1985	$385,000	10.93%
Reed Hawn	Dwight Manley	1993	$962,500	12.14%
Legend Numismatics	Blanchard	2004	$3,000,000	10.89%
FUN 2010		2010	$3,737,500	3.73%

Hawn's gain from an acquisition cost of $385,000 (sold at $962,000) averaged over 21 percent compounded in the eight years he held the coin. By contrast, Legend's resale made more dollars but a smaller percentage.

The 1804 silver dollar rarity that bears Hawn's names is a Class I original with a neat story and a number of homes over the past 150 years. Besides the Hawn coin, about 15 other specimens are known, evidently produced on three separate occasions using different dies. The Mint report for the year 1804, and succeeding mint reports, show 19,570 silver dollars being struck. The following year, 1805, weighs in with 321 dollars produced.

1794 Dollar
Heritage Rare Coins

Serious collectors today know that no silver dollars were produced from late 1803 until 1836, but the records say something else. In fact, as late as 1966, the annual report of the Director of the Mint in table C19 ("Annual Silver Coinage, Philadelphia Mint, number of pieces") still carries the same information, long since proven false.

1795 Dollar Draped Bust Reverse
Heritage Rare Coins

Probable origins of the physical coin, a silver dollar dated 1804, comes from a diplomatic mission in the 1830s to open up Siam (modern day Thailand) and Muscat (today part of the United Gulf Emirates) to the west. On June 20, 1834, President Andrew Jackson, having previously made a recess appointment, formally nominated Roger Taney to be Secretary of the Treasury.

At around the same time, the Senate acted on two separate treaties, as its executive journals disclose: "Resolved (two-thirds of the Senators present concurring), That the Senate do advise and consent to the ratification of the treaty of amity and commerce between the United States of America and His Majesty

Seyed Syeed Bin, Sultan of Muscat, made at the city of Muscat, in the Kingdom of Aman, the twenty-first day of September, in the year of our Lord, one thousand eight hundred and thirty-three."

Then, "The treaty with the King of Siam was read the second time and considered as in Committee of the Whole; no amendment having been made thereto, it was reported to the Senate accordingly. Mr. Wilkins submitted the following resolution for consideration: Resolved (two-thirds of the Senators present concurring), That the Senate do advise and consent to the ratification of the treaty between the United States of America and His Majesty the King of Siam, concluded at the royal city of Siayuthia (commonly called Bangkok), the twentieth day of March, in the year of our Lord one thousand eight hundred and thirty-three."

On Dec 6, 1836, in his last annual address to Congress, President Andrew Jackson reported, "Commercial treaties, promising great advantages to our enterprising merchants and navigators, have been formed with the distant governments of Muscat and Siam. The ratifications have been exchanged, but have not reached the Department of State. Copies of the treaties will be transmitted to you, if received before, or published, if arriving after, the close of the present session of Congress".

All research on the 1804 silver dollar, at least in modern times, inevitably returns to the seminal volume on *The Fantastic 1804 Silver Dollar*, by Eric P. Newman and Kenneth E. Bressett (1962). They quote, as do many successive catalogers, from a letter dated Nov. 11, 1834, from U.S. Secretary of State John Forsyth of Georgia, directed to Dr. Samuel Moore, director of the United States Mint who evidently directed that a "complete" set be produced for both commercial treaties.

Two other versions of the 1804 dollar were produced well into the late 1850s. Newman and Bressett weave the fascinating tale of deceit, nepotism, and fraud. The newspapers have been fascinated from the time that the coin began to sell at auction at multiples of the then-living wage.

Just as during the Vietnam War, GI's on R&R in Thailand were offered the "$50 special," a counterfeit 1804 silver dollar with an amazing story. When my wife Kathy and I visited Muscat on a cruise from Dubia to Istanbul two years ago, we looked for the counterfeit specials, but they had long since vanished from the local marketplaces, replaced by trade dollars with chop marks.

Hawn acquired his Class I specimen of the 1804 silver dollar by "private treaty," meaning a bill of sale. Ben Stack made the sale in January 1974, and the coin stayed in the Hawn collection until it was auctioned in October 1993. Here's a brief history of some of the public auction records of the coin, which starts with Joseph Mickley, probably the father of modern American coin collecting.

The Mickley - Reed Hawn Specimen 1804 Silver Dollar

William A Lillienthal		1868	$750
William Summner Appleton		1905	gift
Massachusettes Historical Society	Lot 5625	1970	$77,500
Chicago Private Collector	Sold via Stack's treaty to RH	1974	
Reed Hawn	Sold via Stack's	1993	$475,000
Heritage Apr 16 2008 NGC PR62	David Queller; Queller Family Collection	2008	$3,737,500

This was clearly intended to be a show stopper – the 1804 silver dollar always is – an abbreviation of owners showing the price level of the coin market along the way. It of course was a spectacular coin, and remained so when in April 2008 the David Queller family collection re-sold it through Heritage Auctions at the Central States Numismatics Society convention for more than $3.7 million.

Hawn had so many more neat coins, common and rare, that all work nicely into an examination of price philosophy. Consider the 1839 no drapery half dollar, a Proof-64 coin that might have pretenses to being from the 1946 World's Greatest collection. When Hawn's half dollar collection burst on the scene in 1973, the coin was believed unique in proof (another was sold in January 2010 at the FUN sale by Heritage for $74,500 as Lot 2554).

Proof examples of the 1839 half dollar are believed to have been struck on Aug. 13, 1839. Modern research believes that fewer than six exist, perhaps as few as three to four pieces. One proof and one business strike were evidently sent by Mint Director Patterson to the Secretary of Treasury and were distinguished as special strikings in a letter between the two officials even though the word "proof" was not used.

The pedigreed Hawn coin (sold out of his collection in 1973 for $10,500) brought $172,500 at the 2007 Florida FUN sale.

Heritage's List of Census 1920-S Double Eagles

1. MS-66 PCGS. Louis Eliasberg; The United States Gold Coin Collection (Bowers and Ruddy, 10/1982), Lot 1051, not certified at the time, graded Select Brilliant Uncirculated by the cataloger; Dr. Steven Duckor; Phillip H. Morse; The Phillip H. Morse Collection (Heritage, 11/2005), Lot 6641 (realized $517,500).
2. MS-66 PCGS. A coin with an unknown pedigree sold by Todd Imhof of Heritage Auction Galleries to Dr. Steven Duckor in early 2006.
3. MS-65 PCGS. Jeff Browning; The "Dallas Bank" Collection (Sotheby's/Stack's, 10/2001), Lot 185, not certified at the time, graded Gem Brilliant Uncirculated by the cataloger; Pittsburgh ANA (Heritage, 8/2004), Lot 7782; "Dr. EJC" PCGS Registry Set Collection; (the Akers and Bowers plate coin).
4. MS-65 PCGS. Milwaukee ANA (Heritage, 8/2007), Lot 2074, (realized $264,500).
5. MS-64 PCGS. Reed Hawn Collection (Stack's, 10/1993), Lot 1118, not certified at the time, graded Choice Brilliant Uncirculated by the cataloger; Long Beach Signature Sale (Heritage, 6/2000), Lot 7702; Philadelphia ANA (Heritage, 8/2000), Lot 7599; Benson Part II (Goldberg, 2/2002), Lot 2271; Dallas Signature Sale (Heritage, 10/2008), Lot 2486; Los Angeles ANA (Heritage, 7/2009), Lot 1128.
6. MS-64 PCGS. Dr. Thaine B. Price Collection (Akers, 5/1998), ILot 100, not certified at the time, graded Very Choice Uncirculated by the cataloger; Dr. Richard Arraign Collection (Goldberg, 5/1999), Lot 895; FUN Signature Auction (Heritage,1/2003), Lot 9326; San Francisco ANA (Heritage, 7/2005), Lot 10428; Long Beach Signature Sale (Heritage, 9/2009), Lot 1129.7. MS-64 PCGS. Phillip H. Morse Collection (Heritage, 11/2005), Lot 6642; Pre-Long Beach Auction (Goldberg, 9/2007), Lot 3523.
8. MS-64 PCGS. FUN Signature Auction (Heritage, 1/2007), Lot 3287.
9. MS-64 PCGS. The Rarities Sale (Bowers and Merena, 10/2004), Lot 940.
10. Very Choice Uncirculated 64. Auction '90 (Akers, 8/1990), Lot 1988.

Other Known Specimens:

A. A coin in the collection of the American Numismatic Society, reported as a Superb Gem by Jeff Garrett and Ron Guth.
B. A coin in the National Numismatic Collection, Smithsonian Institution, reported to grade at least MS-64 by Garrett and Guth.

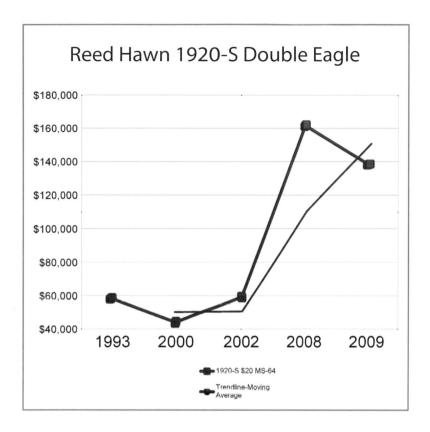

Another is the 1920-S $20 originally offered in the Reed Hawn Collection (Stack's, October 1993), Lot 1118, not certified at the time, but described as being Choice Brilliant Uncirculated by the cataloger. It realized $59,000 and then had an up and down history that shows a strong trend line:

1920-S $20

Date	Description/lot	Price Realized
1993	Reed Hawn (Stacks 10/93) Lot 1118	$59,000
2000	Philadelphia ANA (Heritage, 8/2000) Lot 7599	$44,800
2002	Benson Part II (Goldberg, 2/2002) Lot 2271	$59,800
2008	Dallas Signature Sale (Heritage, 10/2008) Lot 2486	$161,000
2009	Los Angeles ANA (Heritage, 7/2009) Lot 1128	$138,000

The price is an upward trend line (see graph page 101), but clearly does not go up identically each year; sometimes it advances, sometimes it declines. Two similar (but not identical) 1920-S double eagles, each PCGS MS-64, were sold Jan. 10, 2010, in the Heritage FUN auction as consecutive lots to disparate prices: $133,975 and $161,000.

In 2010, Heritage compiled a list of known 1920-S double eagles in MS-64 or better condition. With better resources than when Hawn's collection was sold, we now know the condition census (ranking Hawn's coin fifth on the all-time list). Then look at the trend line which acknowledges the thrill, the chase, and the need to evaluate. Hawn also knew when to sell – and allow the next owner to obtain his profit, too.

He did it with proof coins, too. Take the 1841 proof half dollar. This is truly a scarce coin that is absent from many of the most sophisticated collections. Consider this census (which has been modified for this book) that shows fewer than a dozen specimens exist:

1) Smithsonian Institution.

2) Very Choice Proof. James Kelly privately 1946; John Jay Pittman Collection (David Akers, May 1998, Lot 1522 for $44,000).

3) Choice Proof. John G. Mills (Samuel H. and Henry C. Chapman, April 1904); Louis Eliasberg Collection (Bowers and Merena/Stack's, April 1997, Lot 1,919 at $18,700).

4) Dr. Wilson Collection (New Netherlands, August 1952, Lot 310 at $60); Elliot Landau Collection (New Netherlands, December 1958, Lot 575); New York Specialist. Breen's plate coin in his Proof Encyclopedia.

5) Charles A. Cass "Empire" Collection (Stack's, November 1957, Lot 1,352 at $110); Reed Hawn Collection (Stack's, August 1973, Lot 137) at $2,100; RARCOA's Session of Auction '81, Lot 137 at $1,550; Stack's Session of Auction '90, Lot 210 at $8,000. Stack's, March 2007 ($2,300) (as Proof-60).

6) Impaired Proof "Extremely Fine" Golding Collection (Stack's, June 1952, Lot 232).

Taking a closer look at the Hawn coin (described as Brilliant Proof) it has since been called by some "1841 PR-62 Half Dollar." Here's how the 1841 proof half looks from the standpoint of Reed Hawn's collection:

Charles A. Cass, Empire Collection (Stack's, 11/1957), Lot 1352, $110
Reed Hawn (Stack's, 8/1973), Lot 137; $2,100
Auction '81 (RARCOA), Lot 137; $1,550
Auction '90 (Stack's), Lot 210; $8,000
Stack's (3/2007), Lot 849, as Proof-60, $2,300.

The Empire collection (1957) was a major auction; its catalog prices realized were actually printed inside the catalog, lot-by-lot, page by page, in red. (This is no longer done because of expense). Reed Hawn was not into the 1841 proof half for very much, but he received a magnificent price of $2,100 for the

Cass coin. Next it went to Auction '81, the conglomerate that Stack's, RAR-COA, Paramount and Superior ran from 1979 to 1990. The coin appears in the 500 lot section of the Rare Coin Company of America (RARCOA) at $1,550. From there, it next appears in Auction '90 (this time in the Stack's section) and an $8,000 price. In 2007, the coin was termed Proof-60 (it had previously been called Proof-62), and as a result of thata $2,300 price was received (see graph contrasting actual price versus baseline.)

On this one, the marketplace was looking at condition and failed to see what it thought was warranted. The buyer at the March 2007 sale caught a bargain!

For more than 50 years, Reed Hawn has collected coins for fun and profit. He is a Renaissance man. From Arabian horses and uncirculated common-date older half dollars he also is in the record books for rarities. His erudite comments helped reshape modern commemorative coinage, and the coins he bought, in at least five major auction sales, helped reshape the American numismatic scene.

GOLD AND BULLION COINS

Nothing is as exciting, shows as much promise or has as much potential for growth as gold. Long before modern times, the Egyptians and the Greeks made jewelry from gold. Roman armies were merciless in their search for gold for Rome's greater glory. The age of Exploration starting in the 1450s was a search for gold, first from the Aztecs, later from South and Central American natives.

That means gold coins have a future that, if the past is any guide, will parallel the path of the precious metal, even with a starting price of over $1,200 an ounce – a new all-time high reached just before Dec. 2-3, 2009. It becomes a great place to begin when "the limit" (as in "the sky's the limit") becomes the new starting point.

Gold has had many lives, a tangled history, and many price cycles. From ancient times, the lure of the golden metal has driven man mad. It caused Queen Isabel and King Ferdinand to give Columbus a mandate to travel to the west in search of alluvial metal and mines beneath the ground. The signing of the Treaty of Tordesillas between Spain and Portugal in 1492 was as much about dividing gold as it was the Portuguese and Spanish view of who controlled the colonial new world.

By 1536, a Casa de Moneda or Mint was already built and operating in Mexico City, operated by the viceroys for the Spanish crown. It turned out silver coin first, and by late in the 17th century, gold Escudos that moved millions of dollars across the Atlantic, giving back a portion to pirates, the weather, and shipwrecks that yield precious metal coins half a millennium later.

One of the earliest references to precious metals is in the holy Bible (Genesis 2:11) which notes "that is it which compasseth the whole land of Havilah, where there is gold."

From ancient texts we know that there is gold in the Holy Land, in modern Egypt and Israel. It is from

President Franklin Delano Roosevelt
FDR Library

David L. Ganz

the Mesopotamia region in Lydia around 750 B.C. that electrum – a natural alloy of gold with at least 20 percent silver and perhaps traces of copper – became the first crude coinage. King Croesus (d. 546 B.C.) is widely credited with creating the first gold (electrum) coinage; his name was a symbol of wealth in the ancient world ("as rich as Croesus").

The alluvial deposits of western Turkey in Antiquity were well known for the river Pactolus and it is here that King Midas is alleged to have been "cured" of his golden touch to the benefit of those who washed or searched in the river.

In its January 2009 issue, *National Geographics* magazine puts gold and its lustrous history into perspective: "In all of history, only 161,000 tons of gold have been mined, barely enough to fill two Olympic-size swimming pools." If that visual image doesn't provide a clue toward scarcity, then consider an analogy that the World Gold Council has utilized for years: all of the gold mined from the beginning of history until the present, if melted and poured in a mold the size and shape of the Washington Monument, would not be even two-thirds full.

Which is heavier, a pound of gold or a pound of feathers?

Gold is measured under a system of troy weight (31.1035 grams in a troy ounce), 12 troy ounces in a troy pound. The avoirdupois pound, on the other hand, contains 16 ounces. There are other subdivisions:

1 avoirdupois ounce = 437.5 grains, or 28.35 grams. 1 avoirdupois pound contains 16 (avoirdupois) ounces. This makes an Avoirdupois pound equal to about 453.6 grams, or the equivalent of 14.583 "troy ounces".

One troy ounce = 480 grains, or 31.10 grams. There are also 20 pennyweights to a troy ounce. A troy pound contains 12 troy ounces (over 13 avoirdupois ounces) and is equivalent to 373.24 grams. 32.15 troy ounces = 1 kilogram.

Thus, a "grocery store" pound contains about 14.6 troy ounces, and the proverbial (avoirdupois) pound of feathers is about 10 percent heavier than the troy pound of gold. Price is another story. Turkey feathers are about $35 a pound; gold has not been lower than $35 an ounce for more than 40 years (Jan. 16, 1970).

Gold's price cycle is such that in 1998, when *Planning Your Rare Coin Retirement* had yet to be published, a question arose as to whether gold coins in general, and any in specific, could (or should) be in the model portfolio. In the end, I created a model portfolio of gold coins, nearly all foreign, though some contemporary U.S. commemoratives were strategically included.

I selected about 100 gold coins with an average cost of $100 each to create a portfolio of about $10,000 in acquisition cost. (There were actually 104 gold coins from Australia to Yugoslavia that were slated for acquisition using prices in   as a basis – the total price was $9,001.75 – for an average cost of about $87 a coin.)

Most of the coins did not have a heavy weight. In 1998, the average price of gold per ounce was $301. But there was no problem accommodating a 10 or 20 Franc Swiss gold coin, a Russian 5 rouble, Netherlands 10 guilder, 2 ducat – even a Mexico 2 ducat trade coin and a French 20 franc coin.

Here's the list of the original gold coin portfolio that helped people jump start their rare coin retirement.

World Gold Coin Portfolio with Selected Platinum Issues

Australia	1896	Sovereign	Unc.	$110.00
Austria	1881A	8 Florin/20 Franc	XF	$87.00
Austria		1 Ducat	XF-AU	$43.95
Austria	1915	1 Ducat (restrike)	BU	$42.95
Bahamas	1974	$100	Proof	$130.00
Barbados	1975	$100	Proof	$60.00
Belgium		20 Francs	XF-AU	$70.00
Belize	1981	$100 National Independence	Proof	$125.00
Belize	1981	$50	Proof	$40.00
Belize	1985	$100	Proof	$45.00
Bermuda	1975	$100	Proof	$105.00
Bermuda	1977	$50	Proof	$75.00
Bolivia	1952	7 Gramos	BU	$95.00
Brit. Virgin Islands	1981	$50	Proof	$55.00
Brit. Virgin Islands	1975	$100	Proof	$100.00
Bulgaria	1894	10 Leva	VF	$100.00
Canada		1/15 oz Maple Leaf	BU or PF	$57.50
Canada		1/10 oz Platinum Maple Leaf	BU	$52.65
Canada	1987	Olympic $100	Proof	$99.00
Canada		1/10 oz Platinum Lynx $30	Proof	$109.95

World Gold Coin Portfolio with Selected Platinum Issues

Canada	1989	Indian		$102.00
Canada	1976	Olympic $100	Unc	$94.00
Canada	1997	Maple leaf	1/4 oz	$96.50
Cayman Islands		$25	BU	$83.00
Columbia	1913	5 Pesos	AU	$105.00
Comoros	1976	10,000 Francs	Pf	$125.00
Cook Islands	1975	$100	Proof	$130.00
Cook Islands	1988	Bison	Proof	$45.00
Cuba	1916	2 Peso	BU	$119.00
Egypt	1930	100 Piastres	AU	$100.00
El Salvador	1971	50 Colones	Proof	$100.00
El Salvador	1971	25 Colones	Proof	$75.00
Equatorial Guinea	1970	250 Pesetas	Proof	$100.00
Finland	1882	100 Maarka	BU	$99.00
France	1801	(AN 12A) 20 Francs	VF	$125.00
France	1815	20 Fr Bordeaux Louis XVIII	VF	$115.00
France	1814	20 Francs	XF	$95.00
France	1886	20 Francs (3d Republic)	AU	$78.00
France		20 Francs	XF-AU	$70.00
France	(1899-1914)	20 Franc Rooster	BU	$79.95
France	1856	A 5 Francs	VF	$51.00
Germany		10 Marks	BU	$115.00
Germany		20 mark	XF/AU	$84.50
Gibralter	1997	Classical Heads (set of 4)		$198.00
Great Britain		Sovereign Eliz. II	XF-AU	$84.00
Great Britain		Sovereign Old style	XF-AU	$87.00
Great Britain	1989	Sovereign	Proof	$100.00
Great Britain	1986	½ Sovereign	Proof	$61.00
Guernsey	1981	£1	Proof	$125.00
Guinea	1970	1000 Francs	Proof	$75.00
Guyana	1976	$100	Proof	$50.00
Haiti	1973	200 Gourdes	Proof	$75.00
Haiti	1973	100 Gourdes	Proof	$60.00
Hungary	1885	20 Fr/8 Florin	XF	$82.00

World Gold Coin Portfolio with Selected Platinum Issues

India	1918	Sovereign	BU	$105.00
Iran	AH1322	5000 Dinars	XF	$75.00
Iran	1342	AH ½ Toman	VF-XF	$39.00
Iran	1971	500 Rials (Fr 109)	Pf	$125.00
Italy		20 Lire	XF-AU	$68.00
Jamaica	1975	$100	Proof	$100.00
Japan	1835	2 Shu	XF	$52.00
Liberia	1977	$100	Proof	$125.00
Luxembourg	1953	20 Francs (KM #1M)	BU	$100.00
Malaysia	1976	200 Ringgit	Pf	$100.00
Malta	1974	20 Pounds	Proof	$90.00
Malta	1974	10 Pounds	Proof	$60.00
Mexico		2 Pesos	BU	$24.95
Mexico	1906	5 Pesos	Unc.	$55.00

Australia 1993 $200 Gold
Teletrade

Swiss shooting Thaler Platinum
Teletrade

Russia 3 Roubles Platinum
Teletrade

Australia 1990 $50 Platinum
Heritage (www.HA.Com)

France 5 Franc 1989
Teletrade

David L. Ganz

Barbados 1975 $100 Gold
Heritage (www.HA.Com)

Austria 1927 100 Schilling
Heritage (www.HA.Com)

Great Britain 1917 Gold Sovereign
Heritage (www.HA.Com)

World Gold Coin Portfolio with Selected Platinum Issues

Mexico	1946	2½ Pesos	BU	$42.00
Mexico	1905	10 Pesos	XF-AU	$99.00
Mexico		5 Pesos	BU	$43.00
Mexico		10 Pesos	BU	$82.50
Mexico		2½ pesos	BU	$32.95
Mexico	1985	250 Pesos	BU	$99.00
Netherlands		10 Guilder	XF-AU	$72.50
Netherlands	1988	2 Ducats	Proof	$120.00
Netherlands	1975	1 Ducat	Proof	$60.00
Netherlands Antilles	1979	50 Gulden	BU	$40.00
Panama	1975	100 Balboas	Proof	$90.00
Papua New Guinea	1975	100 Kina	Proof	$110.00
Peru	1965	100 Soles	BU	$65.00
Russia		5 Roubles Nicholas II	XF-AU	$47.95
S. Africa	1964	Proof Set	Proof	$135.00
South Africa	(1961-83)	2 Rands 1/4 oz	BU	$88.00
South Africa	1894	½ Pond	VF	$75.00
South Africa	1982	Krugerrand 1/10 oz	BU	$42.95

World Gold Coin Portfolio with Selected Platinum Issues

Spain	1878	Alfonso XII (Fr 343R)	BU	$85.00
Sudan	1978	25 pounds (Fr 4)	Proof	$135.00
Switzerland		20 Francs	XF-AU	$70.00
Switzerland	10 Francs	XF-AU	$100.00	
Turkey	1969	50 Kurish	MS-64	$75.00
Turks & Caicos	1976	50 Crowns	Proof	$100.00
Turks & Caicos	1981	100 Crowns	Proof	$90.00
Turks & Caicos	1976	25 Crowns	Proof	$75.00
USA	1987	Constitution $5 commemorative	BU or Pf	$99.00
USA	1997	Gold 1/10 oz Eagle	BU	$43.00
USA	1997	Gold 1/4 oz Eagle	BU	$96.00
USA	1988	Olympic $5	BU or Pf	$99.00
USA		$1 Type 1 (1849-1854)	VF	$103.00
USA		$1 Type 3 (1856-1889)	VF	$107.00
USA		$2½ Indian (1908-1929)	VF	$119.00
Venezuela	1905	20 Bolivares (Fr 6)	MS-64	$100.00
Venice	1789	Zecchino (Fr. 1445)	VF-XF	$155.00
Yugoslavia	1982	5000 Dinara	Proof	$100.00
Total				$9,001.75
Average/per coin (1998)				$86.56

Gold's Historical Role with Coinage

Not too long ago, gold was down for the count and some financial analysts discounted its future. Gold's amazing climb stumbled around Aug. 1, 2008 as the precious metal dropped below $800 an ounce for the first time that year, completing a slide that had begun five months earlier on March 17, 2008, when the London daily fix topped out at $1,023.50, silver weighed in at $20.92, and platinum was at exactly $2,000 an ounce.

The London Fix, since 1919, has governed worldwide gold transactions. Current members of the Fix are: The Bank of Nova Scotia - Scotia Mocatta; HSBC (formerly Hong Kong Shanghai Bank Corp.); Deutsche Bank AG London; Societe Generale Corporate & Investment Banking; and Barclays Capital.

The procedure followed by the five member firms is designed to fix a price for settling contracts between members of the London bullion market. The fix takes place twice a day, and is now done by telephone at 10:30 a.m. and 3 p.m. local (London) Greenwich mean time.

Significant golden events since 1960

According to the U.S. Geological Survey, a government agency, there are a number of significant events affecting U.S. gold prices over the half century:

1961 – The London gold pool was established in which U.S. central banks and seven other nations agreed to buy and sell gold to support the $35 per troy ounce price that had been established on Jan. 31, 1934.

1968 – The London gold pool sustained enormous losses and was discontinued. The two-tier gold price was established. One tier was for official monetary transactions, the other for open-market transactions

1971 – President suspends convertibility of dollar into gold, dollar devalued by 7.9%.

1972 – Official U.S. gold price increased to $38 per ounce.

1973 – Official U.S. gold price increased to $42.22, dollar devalued, two-tier gold price terminated, Organization of Petroleum Exporting Countries (OPEC) oil embargo begins.

1974 – U.S. citizens allowed to hold gold bullion and coins for the first time in 40 years.

1975 – U.S. Treasury begins public sales of gold stocks .

1976 – International Monetary Fund (IMF) begins five-year gold sales program. IMF auctions and lower inflation outlook drive gold prices down.

1977 – Hiatus in U.S. Treasury gold sales.

1978 – U.S. Treasury resumes selling gold. Middle Eastern investors increase gold purchases

1979 – Soviet Union invades Afghanistan; political upheaval in Iran, taking of U.S. hostages

1980 – Gold price peaks at an historic daily high of $850 per ounce on Jan. 21. IMF completes 5-year gold sales program.

1982-1988 – Fluctuating world currency exchange rates, increasing concern about U.S. trade and budget deficits, banking problems and Third World debt.

1989-1991 – Conflict in the Persian Gulf and the breaking up of the Soviet Union. There is an erosion of gold's role as a safe haven for investors; generally weak economic growth worldwide .

1992-1996 – Gold price remains relatively stable.

1997-1998 – Central banks of several countries sell large shares of gold holdings to meet common-currency criteria for European Union or to demonetize; bank failures or insolvencies in East and Southeast Asian countries.

2001 – Shanghai gold exchange opens in China.

2009 – Gold tops $1,189 (November), an all-time record, goes above $1,250 in December.

2010 - Gold is near $1,200 on May 1.

First fix took place on Sept. 12, 1919, among the five principal gold bullion traders and refiners of the day: N.M. Rothschild & Sons, Mocatta & Goldsmid, Pixley & Abell, Samuel Montagu & Co. and Sharps Wilkins. The gold price then was £4 18s 9p, (four pounds 18 shillings and ninepence (GBP 4.9375)) per troy ounce or about $24 an ounce. The official price was still $20.67 an ounce.

Today, gold prices are fixed in United States dollars (USD [$]), pound sterling (GBP [£]) and European euros (EUR [€]). Originally, the offices of N.M . Rothschild & Sons in St. Swithin's Lane were used for a table side meeting of five competitors; but since May 5, 2004, it has been done by phone. In April, 2004, Rothschild withdrew from gold trading and Barclays Bank took its place.

At the Rothschild board room, participants could raise a small Union flag on their desk to pause proceedings. With the telephone fixing system, participants can sill register a pause by saying the word "flag." A rotating chair ends the meeting with the phrase, "There are no flags, and we're fixed."

Gold's price history probably should be divided into three parts. First, is the period prior to 1933, when President Franklin Roosevelt effectively nationalized gold and prohibited private gold ownership. Second, is the period from 1934 to Dec.31, 1974, when U.S citizens lost the right to own gold, except for "rare and unusual" gold coins – numismatic items. Third, is the period from Jan. 1, 1975, to the present, when Americans fully participated in the gold market. A fourth period may be in the future when the Chinese are able to fully participate in a developed gold market, opening up 300 million middle-class purchasers to this exciting field.

Gold's price history has been remarkably stable over the past century and a half. The accompanying chart shows this stability from 1837 until 1933, with various spikes characteristic of a free market, but aware nonetheless of a giant overhang of bullion held by the world's central banks. The U.S. stockpile is at Fort Knox and the Federal Reserve Bank vaults on Liberty Street in lower Manhattan, not far from the former World Trade Center site.

The U.S. gold reserve is a tough cookie to measure, in part because it does not value the gold at market, but instead at the "official" price set by Congress at $42.22 in 1973. That changed the value from $38 an ounce and effectively devalued the dollar since that was the unit the most banks used to define net worth.

Most gold is in long term storage – over 258 million ounces – a huge overhang that has led some to suspect price manipulation by the Treasury, which values this at $10.9 billion (about $258.3 billion at current prices). The Treasury denies this, going so far as to say on a government Web site that "We would like to emphasize that the Treasury Department does not seek to manipulate the price of gold or any other metal by intervening in or otherwise interfering with the market."

Gold's recent price trends since 2000

The year 2000 started with $282 an ounce gold, about the same as the prior year ($278). The average for 2001 was $278,70. In 2002, gold's price went to $346.70. The next year closed at $414.80. By 2004, the price was at $438.10, then rapidly rose to $517.20 in 2005, $636.30 in 2006 and $833.20 in 2007.

And it kept climbing, reaching $901 in 2008, $1,090 in 2009 and hitting $1,247.60 on May 13, 2010, before beginning a slow slide.

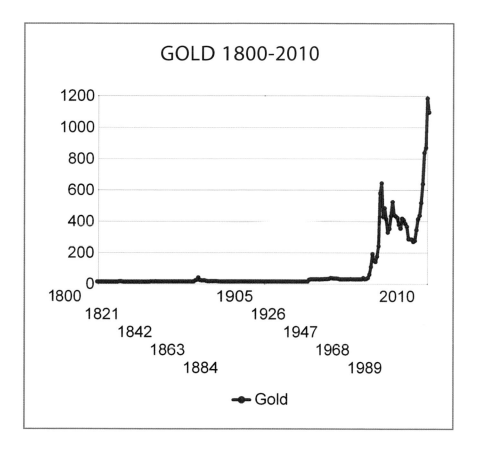

America's history with gold is an uneven one. Gold at the nation's beginning did not have its role of today as an asset of last resort but rather it was a primary asset of wealth. When the United States was founded as a nation, the Constitution was leery of the colonial experience with currency "not worth a Continental."

Indeed, the Constitution was thought to ban the issuance of "money" that was not gold and silver. That didn't mean copper coinage couldn't be issued for change, and indeed, just three years after the Constitution was adopted, the Mint Act of 1792 called for gold, silver and copper coinage. But copper had a

Charlotte & Dahlonega Gold Coin Examples
Heritage (www. HA.com)

limited legal tender value, where gold did not.

Gold and silver metal, bullion, foreign coin or plate could be deposited with the Mint where, for a small service or convenience fee (half of one percent), the Mint would smelt it down and coin it into national money using prescribed weights and sizes. The value of gold and silver per ounce was determined, the volume of metal legislated, and coinage was ready as soon as the Mint director and chief coiner filed their bonds, which took two years.

Each gold coin had its full weight and measure, that is, a gold eagle had just about $10 worth of gold in it. Silver dollars were similarly regulated, as were subsidiary coinage, but the historic problem is that precious metal prices are generally unstable absent a market-maker who guarantees a fixed price.

The result was that American silver coinage was worth more melted than coined. Deposits all but ceased, coinage flowed abroad to settle debts or for smelting, and by the turn of the 19th century, silver dollar coinage was entirely suspended, not to be restarted until the mid-1830s. Lacking a domestic source of gold until deposits were discovered decades later in the Carolinas and Georgia, there wasn't much gold coinage either.

Through the early 1800s there was a real need for coinage, and Congress tried to rectify the problem by regulating the value of foreign coins that circulated domestically. For example, the Act of April 29, 1816, regulates the legal tender value of foreign coins from Britain and Portugal.

Another law signed March 3, 1819, continued in force legal tender values of foreign coins. Two years later, the act of March 3, 1821, regulated 5 franc and crown legal tender values; it was renewed on March 3, 1823.

Congress had a hard time getting it right; the bullion market was constantly changing. As a result, on June 28, 1834, the legal tender value of foreign silver coins of Mexico, Peru, "Chili" and Central America were fixed; the same day, another law reduced weight of foreign gold coins per dollar, thus revaluing the U.S. dollar in the process.

1837 - $21.60	1879 - $20.67	1927 - $20.67	1969 - $35.40
1838 - $20.73	1880 - $20.67	1928 - $20.67	1970 - $37.60
1839 - $20.73	1881 - $20.67	1929 - $20.67	1971 - $43.80
1840 - $20.73	1882 - $20.67	1930 - $20.67	1972 - $65.20
1841 - $20.67	1883 - $20.67	1931 - $20.67	1973 - $114.50
1842 - $20.69	1884 - $20.67	1932 - $20.67	1974 - $195.20
1843 - $20.67	1885 - $20.67	1933 - $32.32	1975 - $150.80
1844 - $20.67	1886 - $20.67	1934 - $35.00	1976 - $145.10
1845 - $20.67	1887 - $20.67	1935 - $35.00	1977 - $179.20
1846 - $20.67	1888 - $20.67	1936 - $35.00	1978 - $244.90
1847 - $20.67	1889 - $20.67	1937 - $35.00	1979 - $578.70
1848 - $20.67	1890 - $20.67	1938 - $35.00	1980 - $641.20
1849 - $20.67	1891 - $20.67	1939 - $35.00	1981 - $430.80
1850 - $20.67	1892 - $20.67	1940 - $34.50	1982 - $484.50
1851 - $20.67	1893 - $20.67	1941 - $35.50	1983 - $415.00
1852 - $20.67	1894 - $20.67	1942 - $35.50	1984 - $331.30
1853 - $20.67	1895 - $20.67	1943 - $36.50	1985 - $354.20
1854 - $20.67	1896 - $20.67	1944 - $36.25	1986 - $435.20
1855 - $20.67	1897 - $20.67	1945 - $37.25	1987 - $522.90
1856 - $20.67	1898 - $20.67	1946 - $38.25	1988 - $441.00
1857 - $20.71	1899 - $20.67	1947 - $43.00	1989 - $433.40
1858 - $20.67	1900 - $20.67	1948 - $42.00	1990 - $423.80
1859 - $20.67	1901 - $20.67	1949 - $40.50	1991 - $379.90
1860 - $20.67	1902 - $20.67	1950 - $40.25	1992 - $356.30
1861 - $20.67	1903 - $20.67	1951 - $40.00	1993 - $419.20
1862 - $27.54	1904 - $20.67	1952 - $38.70	1994 - $409.80
1863 - $31.39	1905 - $20.67	1953 - $35.50	1995 - $385.60
1864 - $46.36	1906 - $20.67	1954 - $35.25	1996 - $367.80
1865 - $29.90	1907 - $20.67	1955 - $35.15	1997 - $288.80
1866 - $27.49	1908 - $20.67	1956 - $35.20	1998 - $288.00
1867 - $27.59	1909 - $20.67	1957 - $35.25	1999 - $287.50
1868 - $27.83	1910 - $20.67	1958 - $35.25	2000 - $272.15
1869 - $24.73	1911 - 1918	1959 - $35.25	2001 - $278.70
1870 - $22.89	- $20.67	1960 - $36.50	2002 - $346.70
1871 - $22.53	1919 - $20.67	1961 - $35.50	2003 - $414.80
1872 - $23.15	1920 - $20.67	1962 - $35.35	2004 - $438.10
1873 - $22.79	1921 - $20.67	1963 - $35.25	2005 - $517.20
1874 - $23.12	1922 - $20.67	1964 - $35.35	2006 - $636.30
1875 - $23.33	1923 - $20.67	1965 - $35.50	2007 - $833.20
1876 - $22.12	1924 - $20.67	1966 - $35.40	2008 - $901.00
1877 - $21.24	1925 - $20.67	1967 - $35.50	2009 - $1,090
1878 - $20.67	1926 - $20.67	1968 - $43.50	2010 - $1,192*
			*as of May 19

In 1837 Congress set the value of gold at $20.67 an ounce, a rate that would hold for nearly a century through the California gold field discoveries, the Civil War, the expansion of America meeting its manifest destiny, and to World War I and beyond. The U.S. double eagle $20 gold piece contained $19.999 worth of gold.

To be sure there were spikes, such as when Jay Gould attempted to corner the gold market (1869), but that overall stability came at a price – the monetary system could not expand easily and the government had difficulty assisting the economy. Once, during the Civil War, the government literally ran out of money and had to print paper substitutes.

This innovation, by Treasury Secretary Salmon P. Chase, saved the Union – only to be declared unconstitutional after the emergency was over by newly appointed Chief Justice of the Supreme Court, Salmon P. Chase; yes, the same one.

Starting around 1867, silver discoveries in Nevada began to impact the marketplace and it became impossible for the government to allow unregulated quantities of metal to be converted into coin, for instead of costing a dollar to mint a silver dollar, the cost with metal was more like 67 cents.

By the time that the Coinage Act of 1873 was passed in April of that year, silver had moved to all-time lows and aside from Trade dollars, which contained the heavier 412.5 grains but were not a legal tender. There was no right to coin silver by depositing metal. The Crime of '73 all but demonetized silver, an act made complete with the passage of the Gold Standard Act for 1900.

America's golden era ceased with the Great Depression of 1929 when the U.S. sneezed and the world economy caught pneumonia. Gold reserves started an outflow, and it simply never stopped. By the time of the 1932 presidential election, the Depression worsened and a political switch to the policies of Franklin Delano Roosevelt lay in the wings.

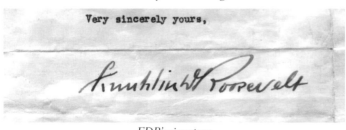

FDR's signature

Author's autograph collection

FDR took office March 4, 1933, and shortly thereafter, the New Deal required millions of dollars worth of gold coinage to be turned in by citizens who held them, acting on a government mandate and under a Presidential Proclamation requiring it.

Only "rare and unusual gold coin" was exempt – enough to allow coin collectors to maintain and keep a collection, assuming that they would be able to do that during the depths of economic despair of 1934. (The exemption had as much to do with the fact that Treasury Secretary William H. Woodin was an experienced coin collector who fully understood the value of coin rarities).

Executive Order 6102 was signed on April 5, 1933, by FDR. It prohibited the "hoarding" of privately held gold coins and bullion in the United States. The order was given under the auspices of the Trading with the Enemy Act of 1917, as recently amended. The government required holders of significant quantities of gold to sell their gold at the prevailing price of $20.67 per ounce.

Shortly after this forced sale, the price of gold from the Treasury for international transactions was raised to $35 an ounce. The U.S. government thereby devalued the dollars (which it had just forced citizens to accept in exchange for their gold) by 41 percent of its former value. The order specifically exempted "customary use in industry, profession or art"– a provision that covered artists, jewelers, dentists, and electricians, among others. The order further permitted any person to own up to $100 in gold coins (equivalent to about $1,800 as of 2010). Section 9 of the order noted the punishment for failure to comply could include a fine of up to $10,000 or up to 10 years in prison. Nevertheless, anecdotal accounts later related that many persons who possessed large amounts of gold simply ignored the order and hid their gold until the order ceased to be in effect. (This is the section that purports to sweep up the 1933 $20 gold pieces).

Gold was frozen in a $35 an ounce realm as the United States slowly pulled out of the Great Depression while simultaneously accumulating a huge supply of the world's gold. Americans could freely collect coins ("rare and unusual") but could not own bullion. As a result, the coins developed a premium market all their own.

Americans lost the ability to own gold privately in 1933. Those limitations, however, as well as those of the Gold Reserve Act of 1934 and various executive orders issued pursuant to the Trading with the Enemy Act of 1917, still allowed ownership of gold abroad (subject to their regulation by the country of residence).

It took a separate executive order in the Kennedy administration to prohibit Americans from owning gold abroad (Executive Order No. 11037, July 20, 1962, by President John F. Kennedy, which prohibits Americans from owning gold outside the continental limits of the United States).

Once the 1933-34 recall was completed, the government re-valued gold to $35 an ounce – effectively devaluing the dollar by about 60 percent. No wonder that the government recalled the old; anyone retaining it got an instant benefit that was meant for the nation as a whole.

From 1933 until Dec.31, 1974, Americans had no ability to own gold other than as numismatic gold coins that sold substantially above the price of bullion. A $20 gold piece, for example, with $33.86 (official price) worth of gold, routinely sold for about $48 to $49 from dealers and the Bank of Nova Scotia, which made a regularly quoted market in the early 1960s.

These were for common-date, typically uncirculated Saints or Liberty heads. The "numismatic premium" was really a penalty for an inability to own gold except in numismatic coin form.

Government officials constantly warned that private gold ownership was only one step away from economic democracy and disaster. They took themselves and their pronouncements seriously, and indeed, rumors could cause gold's price to spike 50 cents or a dollar. That sounds minuscule, but in those same days, if the Dow Jones average rose or fell 10 points, it made the headlines of many newspapers, not just a small article in the financial section.

Starting in the early 1970s, a group of "gold bugs" began to advocate private gold ownership rights and eventually they found the ear of some congressmen and senators who bought into their fairness theory and the claimed illegality of the gold seizures and recalls of the 1930s.

In a truly bizzare episode, they tacked a resolution allowing for private gold ownership onto the foreign aid package that the Nixon Administration wanted. Presidential vetoes were threatened and an alarmist attitude prevailed at the main Treasury building.

Into the middle of this stepped Mint Director Mary T. Brooks. In office since 1970, in 1973 she was promoting bicentennial coinage. I had an interview with her in which I asked her about the possibility of a gold commemorative coin for the bicentennial, and she was quite positive about it. That was real news.

A couple of hours later, I got a call from her key aide, Roy C. Cahoon, interdicting the entire conversation – unless I was willing to drop the gold coin remark. I did and the Republic was safe. But Mrs. Brooks made the same comment weeks later to Russ Rulau, a competitor, then editor of *Numismatic Scrapbook*, and he printed it. The Republic was still safe and, for me, a valuable lesson learned; the government didn't always know what was best.

Author with Mary T. Brooks, director of the Mint, when she made a suggestion for a gold bicentennial coin that nearly caused an international economic incident.

The foreign aid bill with its non-germane gold ownership clause finally made it to a vote in which truly conservative members such as Rep. Phil Crane, R-Ill., and others voted with liberal Democrats. Crane said to me later it was the only foreign aid bill that he voted for in his long congressional career. His rationale was that it was more important to get private gold ownership than argue the vagarities of a single year's foreign aid package.

Flash forward a couple of years when Congress began the debate over whether the U.S. should compete with the Krugerrand. Treasury fought it mightily. Hearings were held in the Senate Banking Committee, and some real heavyweights came out to make out the case of why the U.S. government shouldn't be in the bullion business.

C. Fred Bergsten, a respected international economist and then assistant secretary of the Treasury, testified instead of Secretary W. Michael Blumenthal. He declared, "The [Carter] Administration believes that issuance of gold medallions would be unwise and inappropriate for several reasons," which he enumerated.

First, he said, "the issuance of these medallions would tend to create the erroneous impression that the U.S. government needs to supply the public with an officially issued gold piece as a hedge against inflation."

Second, "the production and sale of an American medallion ... could be interpreted as a U.S. government effort to encourage investment in gold. "

Third, issuance of gold medallions "would be inconsistent with U.S. policy of continuing progress toward demonetizing gold."

He postulated that, horror of horrors, a legal tender version of the medallions might follow – or that the medallions themselves would be monetized.

Dr. Edward M. Bernstein, a respected economist who formerly was a high Treasury Department official, active with the International Monetary Fund, and the Bretton Woods agreements, also spoke out on economic and policy grounds.

An apologist for the official, long-held view that gold ownership should not be allowed privately, and that the metal should be demonetized, Bernstein's positional history carried a lot of Congressional weight. He was professor of economics at the University of North Carolina, 1935-1940; principal economist for the United States Treasury Department, 1940-1946; assistant to the secretary of the United States Treasury Department, 1946; research director of the International Monetary Fund, 1944-1958; President of EBB (Ltd.) Research Economists, 1958-1981; and guest scholar at the Brookings Institution beginning in 1982.

His advice, on the day that gold topped $198 an ounce in London: "it's a terrible mistake to offer Americans this extra inducement to buy gold coins."

His rationale: "It is really not right for the government of the United States to offer an inducement to people to buy gold coins by giving them a nice looking medallion for which they would have to pay 12 percent above the bullion value." Put differently, "it's not a good hedge."

Standing up for the right to own gold and for the medallions was President of the American Numismatic Association Grover C . Criswell Jr. I accompanied him, and wrote his written testimony, in my capacity as ANA legislative counsel.

Grover C. Criswell, Jr.
Central State Numismatic Society

Criswell's summary of five reasons why gold medallions were appropriate (it being obvious that Congress was at least several years away from authorizing gold coins): (1) it helps the balance of payments; (2) it provides clear domestic economic beneficial effects from the sale; (3) it denies $600 million in assistance to South Africa; (4) it returns gold to the people who gave it to the government in the first place – the American people; and (5) it raises more money than the government's auction plans for gold bricks in $80,000 units and above.

As it turned out, Criswell was right. The medallions became collectibles in their own right. Bergsten and Bernstein were right, too. Placing the name and seal of the United States on them gave the medallions an imprimatur around the world. Though many were melted, they are still around today as a popular if short-lived series. Their stats are as follows:

American Arts Gold Medallions

	1/2oz		1 oz	
Date	Design	Mintage	Design	Mintage
1980	Marian Anderson	281,624	Grant Wood	312,709
1981	Willa Cather	97,331	Mark Twain	116,371
1982	Frank Lloyd Wright	348,305	Louis Armstrong	409,098
1983	Alexander Calder	74,571	Robert Frost	390,669
1984	John Steinbeck	32,572	Helen Hayes	33,546

Bernstein contended that "gold is gold. A person who buys a Krugerrand has just the same gold... My objection to the medallion is not that we are selling the gold but that we are putting the symbol of the United States on it which will make it more attractive." As future events would show, gold is not gold – and U.S. legal tender gold coinage consistently sells for more than the South African counterpart or private bars or medals. (But that doesn't mean that they are not collected; just that there is a differentiation in value that, perhaps you can use to your advantage).

From August 1978 until January 2010, gold has gone up, down and sideways (see chart page 111), parking temporarily at over $1,100 an ounce. But those who would have bought bullion issued from 1980 to 1984, didn't do that badly.

The return on investment in gold from 1978 to 2009 is about 3.93 percent compounded annually. It barely outpaced inflation, which averaged 3.3 percent during the same period. The rare coin fund index that Salomon Brothers used to compare measurements – which I extended from 1978-90 to 2010, shows rare coins advanced 8.5 percent during the same period.

Putting this all in some kind of perspective, the last 40 years of private gold ownership has been a bit of a roller coaster ride. But with the ups sand the downs, gold has remained an asset of historic importance and one which is likely to be looked at, collected, and utilized for quite some time to come.

Tax law weighs in

When the government worked on regulations under Section 6045 of the Internal Revenue Code, it issued temporary regulations recognizing the difference between numismatic and non-numismatic products, using 15 percent over spot as the demarcation line. They put it in the Federal Register for all to see.[14]

We return to March 1968 when we saw LBJ set up a two-tiered market for gold based on the official price of $35 an ounce and a free market price that was permitted to float somewhat higher.

The price of gold jumped, moving to heights of $43 an ounce. Almost overnight double eagles, which had traditionally traded at about 48 percent above the spot price of gold, went from $48 a coin to $60 for uncs.

Gold coins were traded and available internationally on a widespread basis, even British sovereigns of the modern era – but if any were made after 1960, they could not be legally imported into the United States without a permit from the Office of Domestic Gold and Silver Operations.

Dr. Leland Howard, an assistant director of the Mint, became head of the ODGSO, and his task in 1968 was to protect the integrity of the Roosevelt seizure order, while simultaneously allowing rare and unusual coin to be imported. Doc Howard may have been the driving force behind the post-war seizure of as many as 10 double eagles bearing the 1933 date.

But even he bowed to the inevitable and recognized that coin collectors should be able to own "rare and unusual" coin – mostly because his boss, the Treasury Secretary, and later the President, wanted it so. And old Doc Howard found that the way to do it was with logic and precision, but not a lot of common sense.

Eventually, an arbitrary line in the sand was drawn with 1960 as the demarcation point. If it was minted before 1960, then, it was "rare and unusual" – even if it was a 1958 sovereign with 8.7 million pieces produced; if it was minted after 1960, it was common, and not importable with a license – even if it was a 1962 sovereign with only 3 million pieces manufactured.

The official approach, at least initially, was never reduced to writing. The rationale was explained orally to Harvey G. Stack, a prominent dealer who later would be President of the Professional Numismatists Guild, Inc. Stack has recounted the government's policy and rationale publicly on a number of occasions, including the welcome address to the business meeting of the American Numismatic Association, 98th Anniversary Convention, Pittsburgh, 1989. He revealed that the Friedberg book, Gold Coins of the World, was used as the Treasury guidepost. Any coin valued at 25 percent or more above its bullion content in the book was deemed "rare and unusual," while anything below that, even if in obvious error, was denied the requisite import license.

As gold faced the real market for the first time following 1968, it was inevitable that economic forces that traditionally had driven the price upward – inflation, war, and economic fears – could also drive its price down.

On April 26, 1969, the Office of Domestic Gold & Silver Operations finally codified what had existed de facto for years. It would permit the importation without a license of gold coins made before 1934. Licenses would be required to import any gold coins made during 1934 or later. Licenses for importation could be issued for coins minted before 1960 if they were recognized to have special value to collectors of rare and unusual coin.

1847 $1 Reverse
Heritage Rare Coins

The specific terms of the regulations signed by Paul A. Volcker, Under Secretary of the Treasury for Monetary Affairs, provided "Gold coin made during or subsequent to 1934 may be imported only pursuant to a specific or general license issued by the Director, Office of Domestic Gold and Silver Operations. Licenses under this paragraph may be issued only for gold coin made prior to 1960, which can be established to the satisfaction of the Director to be of recognized special value to collectors of rare and unusual coin and to have been originally issued for circulation within the country of issue.

1850-O $1 Obverse
Heritage Rare Coins

"Licenses may be issued for gold coin made during or subsequent to 1960 in cases where the particular coin was licensed for importation prior to April 30, 1969. Application for a specific license under this paragraph shall be executed on Form TG-31 and filed in duplicate with the Director."

But even this was not the end of trying to regulate which gold coin could be legally bought and imported into the United States, and which could not. As of May 1968, post-1933 gold coinage from 22 nations or states were permitted to be imported into the United States, including coinage of Afghanistan, Albania, Austria, Croatia, Czechoslovakia,, Egypt, France (100 franc issue, 1953-6), Great Britain (proof of issue of 1937), Greece, India, Italy, Liechtenstein, Mexico, Monaco, Nepal, Rumania, South Africa, Switzerland, Syria, Tunis, Turkey and the Vatican.

In July 1972, the Dominican Republic 30 pesos were added. Some post-1960 issues were also finally allowed.

Putting it all to a coda, a year before gold ownership was once again unconditionally allowed, the ODGSO, in December 1973, pronounced that "all foreign gold coins minted from 1934 through 1959, if genuine and of legal issue, are now considered to be of such recognized special value to collectors of rare and unusual coins as to warrant the issuance of a general license for their importation into the United States under §54.20(e) of the gold regulations for numismatic purposes."

Thus, under the government's own standards, British sovereigns struck in the 1957-59 series of Elizabeth II (Friedberg 275), and earlier issues would be deemed numismatic, as would French 10 and 20 franc issues (Friedberg 336-337). Mintage figures for the British sovereign show that there were about two million pieces manufactured in 1957, eight million in 1958 and 1.3 million in 1959. None of those produced in the 1962-68 period, or the 1974-1981 period, come close to the eight million produced in 1958. (The 1978, with 6.6 million, and the 1963 and 1966 with 7.4 million and 7.0 million respectively, come closest).

So, if the quantitative standards alone are applicable, an argument can be made for those pieces likewise having numismatic value, despite a high degree of their trading value being set by bullion worth. The morass seems almost endless, and would be nothing but an historic footnote except for the position the IRS took in 1984 in proposing a tax regulation that set a 15 percent premium above face value to be declared "numismatic" and below nothing but bullion.

And so it was that in the early days of 1970, Under Secretary of the Treasury Paul Volcker (later chairman of the Federal Reserve) announced Jan. 16 that the new gold agreement signed with South Africa provided "no assured 'floor price' for gold speculators," and with that the metal dropped to its lowest price in London free trading in 16 years – below the official floor ($34.90).

In a letter to Rep. Henry Reuss, D-Wis., chair of an international economic subcommittee and later Chair of the House Banking Committee, Volcker called the agreement with South Africa "consistent with a two-tiered system" of pricing gold.

Rep. Henry Reuss, D-Wis., chairman of the House Banking Committee, with the author, 1973, in Washington.

A couple of years later, in an interview with me while serving as *Numismatic News* Washington Correspondent, Reuss would say that this marked the real beginning of the drive for private gold ownership, which did not take place until Dec. 31, 1974.

Gold's importance to the overall numismatic market wasn't overlooked in the 1970s. Indeed, I often wrote of the parallel that seemed obvious between the way that the price of gold bullion moved and the manner in which the coin market responded.

The events of January 1970 were at once liberating as well as thought provoking. In a totally free market, gold could rise or fall and without an official price, the metal price could go below an official buy price of the government.

Ironically, within 18 months, inflation would be ravaging the nation and on Aug. 15, 1971, President Nixon would suspend the dollar's convertibility into gold, slamming down the gold exchange window and setting the stage for the dramatic rise of gold – and the numismatic market – for decades to come.

Once again the dollar was devalued, raising the official price of gold to $38 an ounce. (Still later, it would go to its present official price of $42.22 an ounce). But ironically, with or without an official price, the run on the metal proved the historic truism that gold was, and is, king of precious metals.

In 1973, gold regulations were eased slightly to allow more gold coins minted between 1933 and 1961 to be admitted to the country as "rare" coins. However, a drive in Congress to reverse the action of four decades before failed when the House failed by a single vote to call for immediate ownership.

By early 1974, the President had gained the legal authority from Congress to allow private gold ownership at any time he felt it is in the best interests of the international economic situation of the United States. We all thought it would be Nixon, the Cold War warrior, who would release gold, but his resignation left that to Gerald R. Ford.

Gold's price rose in the 1979-80 commodity surge to $800 an ounce, but then relented. Gold coin prices for common typical uncirculated pieces closely mirrored the bullion price, with a modest numismatic surcharge. Charting the coins over an extended period of time shows that they still make a valid investment as well as inflation hedge – better in fact than bullion.

In retrospect, the fight to regaining old ownership – and the governmental battle to prevent it – seems silly. Today, people buy gold, invest in it and hold gold coins without giving the metal a second thought. The international monetary system did not fall apart with private gold ownership, and neither did the American economy. What was ultimately shown is that those who held onto rare coins – rare gold coins– were richly rewarded.

The 2009 cycle, without question, has been one of the most exciting, and one which portends a bright future. (The same holds true for other precious metals such as silver and platinum). Here's what the 2009 picture is of the 1998 coin portfolio:

World Gold Coin Portfolio with Selected Platinum Issues				1998 Portfolio	Estimated Value 12-09	Gain
Australia	1896	Sovereign	Unc.	$110	$408.00	270.91%
Austria	1881A	8 Florin/20 Franc	XF	$87	$242.50	178.16%
Austria		1 Ducat	XF-AU	$43.95	$205.00	365.91%
Austria	1915	1 Ducat (restrike)	BU	$42.95	$205.00	376.74%
Bahamas	1974	100	Proof	$130	$235.00	80.77%
Barbados	1975	100	Proof	$60	$149.43	148.33%
Belgium		20 Francs	XF-AU	$70	$242.50	245.71%
Belize	1981	$100 national Independence	Proof	$125	$149.43	19.20%
Belize	1981	50	Proof	$40	$36.09	-10.00%
Belize	1985	100	Proof	$445	$149.43	-66.52%
Bermuda	1975	100	Proof	$105	$304.56	189.52%
Bermuda	1977	50	Proof	$75	$175.49	133.33%
Bolivia	1952	7 Gramos	BU	$95	$337.05	254.74%
Brit. Virgin Islands	1981	50	Proof	$55	$64.39	16.36%
Brit. Virgin Islands	1975	100	Proof	$100	$302.00	202.00%
Bulgaria	1894	10 Leva	VF	$100	$139.70	39.00%
Canada		1/15 oz Maple Leaf	BU or Pf	$57.50	$375.56	546.55%
Canada		1/10 oz Platinum Maple Leaf	BU	$52.65	$229.00	332.08%
Canada	1987	Olympic $100	Proof	$99	$456.88	360.61%
Canada		1/10 oz Platinum Lynx $30	Proof	$109.95	$229.00	108.18%
Canada	1989	Indian		$102	$374.33	266.67%
Canada	1976	Olympic $100	Unc	$94	$475.00	405.32%
Canada	1997	Maple leaf 1/4 oz		$96.5	$374.33	285.57%
Cayman Islands	$25		BU	$83	$150.63	80.72%
Columbia	1913	5 Pesos	AU	$105	$349.33	232.38%
Comoros	1976	10,000 Francs	Pf	$125	$132.96	5.60%
Cook Islands	1975	100	Proof	$130	$415.96	219.23%
Cook Islands	1988	Bison	Proof	$45	$59.89	33.09%
Cuba	1916	2 Peso	BU	$119	$350.00	194.12%
Egypt	1930	100 Piastres	AU	$100	$358.01	258.00%
El Salvador	1971	50 Colones	Proof	$100	$255.59	155.00%
El Salvador	1971	25 Colones	Proof.	$75	$127.27	69.33%
Equatorial Guinea	1970	250 Pesetas	Proof	$100	$152.43	52.00%
Finland	1882	10 Maarka	BU	$99	$242.50	144.44%
France	1801	(AN 12A) 20 Francs	VF	$125	$242.50	93.60%
France	1815	20 Fr Bordeaux Louis XVIII	VF	$115	$242.50	110.43%
France	1814	20 Francs	XF	$95	$242.50	154.74%

World Gold Coin Portfolio with Selected Platinum Issues				1998 Portfolio	Estimated Value 12-09	Gain
France	1886	20 Francs (3d Republic)	AU	$78	$242.50	210.26%
France		20 Francs	XF–AU	$70	$242.50	245.71%
France	(1899-1914)	20 Franc Rooster	BU	$79.95	$242.50	202.50%
France	1856	A 5 Francs	VF	$51	$69.89	37.25%
Germany		10 Marks	BU	$115	$139.78	20.87%
Germany		20 Marks	XF/AU	$84.5	$279.55	228.24%
Gibralter	1997	Classical heads (4)		$198	$374.33	88.89%
Great Britain		Sovereign	XF–AU	$84	$316.75	276.19%
Great Britain		Sovereign	XF–AU	$87	$316.75	263.22%
Great Britain	1989	Sovereign	Proof	$100	$316.75	216.00%
Great Britain	1986	½ Sovereign	Proof	$61	$176.24	188.52%
Guernsey	1981	£1	Proof	$125	$316.75	152.80%
Guinea	1970	1000 Francs	Proof	$75	$173.24	130.67%
Guyana	1976	100	Proof	$50	$138.20	176.00%
Haiti	1973	200 Gourdes	Proof	$75	$126.08	68.00%
Haiti	1973	100 Gourdes	Proof	$60	$62.74	3.33%
Hungary	1885	20 Fr/8 Florin	XF	$82	$242.50	195.12%
India	1918	Sovereign	BU	$105	$349.00	232.38%
Iran	AH1322	5000 Dinars	XF	$75	$62.29	-17.33%
Iran	1342	AH ½ Toman	VF-XF	$39	$176.24	351.28%
Iran	1971	500 Rials (Fr 109)	Proof	125	$281.95	124.80%
Italy		20 Lire	XF–AU	$68	$242.50	255.88%
Jamaica	1975	100	Proof	$100	$339.15	239.00%
Japan	1835	2 Shu	XF	$52	$77.99	48.08%
Liberia	1977	100	Proof	$125	$473.61	278.40%
Luxembourg	1953	20 Francs (KM #1M)	BU	$100	$299.47	199.00%
Malaysia	1976	200 Ringgit	Proof	$100	$316.24	216.00%
Malta	1974	20 Pounds	Proof	$90	$529.16	487.78%
Malta	1974	10 Pounds	Proof	$60	$250.95	316.67%
Mexico		2 Pesos	BU	24.95	$65.20	160.00%
Mexico	1906	5 Pesos	Unc.	$55	$147.00	167.27%
Mexico	1946	2½ Pesos	BU	$42	$79.50	89.29%
Mexico	1905	10 Pesos	XF–AU	$99	$487.60	391.92%
Mexico		5 Pesos	BU	$43	$147.00	241.86%
Mexico		10 Pesos	BU	$82.5	$487.60	486.75%
Mexico		2½ pesos	BU	$32.95	$79.50	139.39%
Mexico	1985	250 Pesos	BU	$99	$316.75	219.19%
Netherlands		10 Guilder	XF–AU	$73	$336.00%	360.27%
Netherlands	1988	2 Ducats	Proof	$120	$407.00	239.17%
Netherlands	1975	1 Ducat	Proof	$60	$205.00	241.67%
Netherlands Antilles	1979	50 Gulden	BU	$40	$145.39	262.50%

World Gold Coin Portfolio with Selected Platinum Issues				1998 Portfolio	Estimated Value 12-09	Gain
Panama	1975	100 Balboas	Proof	$90	$353.52	292.22%
Papua New Guinea	1975	100 Kina	Proof	$110	$188.36	70.91%
Peru	1965	10 Soles	BU	$65	$202.95	210.77%
Russia		5 Roubles Nicholas II	XF-AU	$47.95	$242.50	404.17%
S. Africa	1964	Proof Set	Proof	$135	$528.71	291.11%
South Africa	(1961-83)	2 Rands 1/4 oz	BU	$88	$374.33	325.00%
South Africa	1894	½ Pond	VF	$75	$316.75	321.33%
South Africa	1982	Krugerrand 1/10 oz	BU	$42.95	$149.73	246.51%
Spain	1878	Alfonso XII (Fr 343R)	BU	$$85	$139.70	63.53%
Sudan	1978	25 pounds (Fr 4)	Pf	$135	$364.15	169.63%
Switzerland		20 Francs	XF-AU	$70	$242.50	245.71%
Switzerland		10 Francs	XF-AU	$100	$139.78	39.00%
Turkey	1969	50 Kurish	MS64	$75	$216.66	188.00%
Turks & Caicos	1976	50 Crowns	Proof	$100	$149.73	49.00%
Turks & Caicos	1981	100 Crowns	Proof	$90	$433.63	381.11%
Turks & Caicos	1976	25 Crowns	Proof	$75	$295.00	293.33%
USA	1987	Constitution $5 commemorative	BU or Proof	$99	$362.17	265.66%
USA	1997	Gold 1/10 oz Eagle	BU	$43	$149.73	246.51%
USA	1997	Gold 1/4 oz Eagle	BU	$96	$315.00	228.13%
USA	1988	Olympic $5	BU or Pf	$99	$300.00	203.03%
USA	(1849-1854)	$1 Type 1	VF	$103	$210.00	103.88%
USA	(1856-1889)	$1 Type 3	VF	$107	$310.00	189.72%
USA	(1908-1929)	$2½ Indian VF	VF	$119	$175.00	47.06%
Venezuela	1905	20 Bolivares (Fr 6)	MS64	$100	$242.50	142.00%
Venice	1789	Zecchino (Fr. 1445)	VF-XF	$155	$332.26	114.19%
Yugoslavia	1982	5000 Dinara	Pf	$100	$346.63	246.00%
Totals				**$9,001.75**	**$26,342.15**	
Average				**$85.73**	**$250.88**	193.94%

Gold has been promising and had an excellent outlook in the 21st century. There's some suggestion that the sharp rise in 2009 is a "bubble" and that those who invest are setting themselves up for a giant fall. But the use of gold in products that need expensive (but accurate) conductivity and the need for a non-tarnishing malleable metal in outer space and elsewhere, suggest that even before considering jewelry, gold has a bright future.

Some of the contemporary issues that concern some collectors and investors is whether precious metals such as gold should be (or can be) legally incorporated into their retirement planning in Individual Retirement accounts. There are also those who wonder whether or not the government is planning – or if circumstances might not just push Uncle Sam into a "seizure" mode to take control of the economy.

Gold and gold coins in IRAs

Some of the following discussion is technical. Forgive me. The lawyer in me says that it has to be technical, at least in part, to fully understand what is going on. But I've spent years explaining the complex and making it digestible, comprehensible, and hopefully interesting to readers of Numismatic News and other periodicals.

Coins in individual retirement accounts (IRAs) are a "used-to-be"that existed before the Tax Reform & Fiscal Responsibility act of 1981 (TEFRA), with only a few narrow exceptions. Most bullion products are also prohibited, except in highly regulated circumstances, as are stamps, Scotch whiskey, and anything else deemed a collectible.

Two recent developments challenge conventional thinking about this blanket statement, and in each instance, the final resolution may have to wait until either the Internal Revenue Service (IRS) or Congress sorts it all out. The taxpayer, and the collector, are the loser in the meanwhile, but there are some things that you can do if you want Uncle Sam to be your partner in purchasing precious metal or gold coinage.

At issue in 2010, and for a couple of years earlier, is the role that certified coins (i.e., graded, encapsulated) American eagles have or may have in IRAs and, secondarily, whether the now relatively new, popular Buffalo nickel gold bullion coin can have a role, together with any 99.9 percent gold coin made by the Mint under authority of either Congress or the Secretary of the Treasury.

Governing all this is the Internal Revenue Code of 1986, as amended, and in particular section 408(m) of Title 26 of the U.S. Code, the body of law in which the taxing authorities laws are codified. (There is also the Code of Federal Regulations, but that only complicates the discussion).

Here's what the law says:

"(m) Investment in collectibles treated as distributions. –

(1) In general. –The acquisition by an individual retirement account or by an individually-directed account under a plan described in section 401(a) of any collectible shall be treated (for purposes of this section and section 402 as a distribution from such account in an amount equal to the cost to such account of such collectible.

(2) Collectible defined. – For purposes of this subsection, the term "collectible" means--

(A) any work of art,

(B) any rug or antique,

(C) any metal or gem,

(D) any stamp or coin,

(E) any alcoholic beverage, or

(F) any other tangible personal property specified by the Secretary for purposes of this subsection.

(3) Exception for certain coins and bullion. – For purposes of this subsection, the term "collectible" shall not include –

(A) any coin which is--"(I) a gold coin described in paragraph (7), (8), (9), or (10) of section 5112(a) of title 31, United States Code,

(II) a silver coin described in section 5112(e) of title 31, United States Code,

(iii) a platinum coin described in section 5112(k) of title 31, United States Code, or

(iv) a coin issued under the laws of any State, or

(B) any gold, silver, platinum, or palladium bullion of a fineness equal to or exceeding the minimum fineness that a contract market (as described in section 7 of the Commodity Exchange Act, 7 U.S.C. 7 requires for metals which may be delivered in satisfaction of a regulated futures contract, if such bullion is in the physical possession of a trustee described under subsection (a) of this section."

What's at stake

Since 1981, and the passage of section 408(m) of the Internal Revenue Code, rare coin investments in individual retirement accounts (IRAs) have been largely prohibited by legislatively declaring that such an investment acts as a taxable distribution, causing the holder all kinds of financial penalties.

It does not prevent it, outright, but taxes it so heavily that no one with a legitimate aim of preserving capital or making a gain would follow such a course of action. But as long as a trustee for a private pension is satisfied that rare coins are a "prudent investment," not only has their use been appropriate, it has never been expressly disapproved.

Other individuals have done likewise, just not with their individual retirement account assets since 1981.

It was three decades ago that Americans lost an important investment option,the right to put rare coins and some other collectibles into self-directed individual retirement accounts (IRAs) and Keogh accounts (the 401-K plans that are so popular among the self-employed, and some businesses).

Those who were involved in the coin market at the time remember the consequence: a precipitous decline in coin prices as a once fertile ground for placement of assets dried up as a potential purchasing source.

For a number of years since, a coalition of interested parties led by the Industry Council for Tangible Assets (ICTA) has led the battle to overturn the 1981 legislation, which makes it useful to examine what brought about the prohibition, and why the right should be restored.

Named for Congressman Eugene Keogh of New York, the Keogh account was intended to provide small businesses with the equivalent of a pension, but

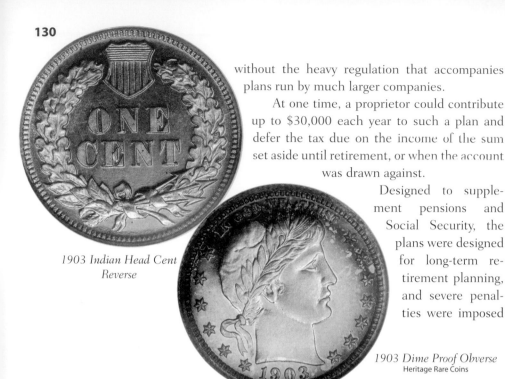

1903 Indian Head Cent Reverse

without the heavy regulation that accompanies plans run by much larger companies.

At one time, a proprietor could contribute up to $30,000 each year to such a plan and defer the tax due on the income of the sum set aside until retirement, or when the account was drawn against.

Designed to supplement pensions and Social Security, the plans were designed for long-term retirement planning, and severe penalties were imposed

1903 Dime Proof Obverse
Heritage Rare Coins

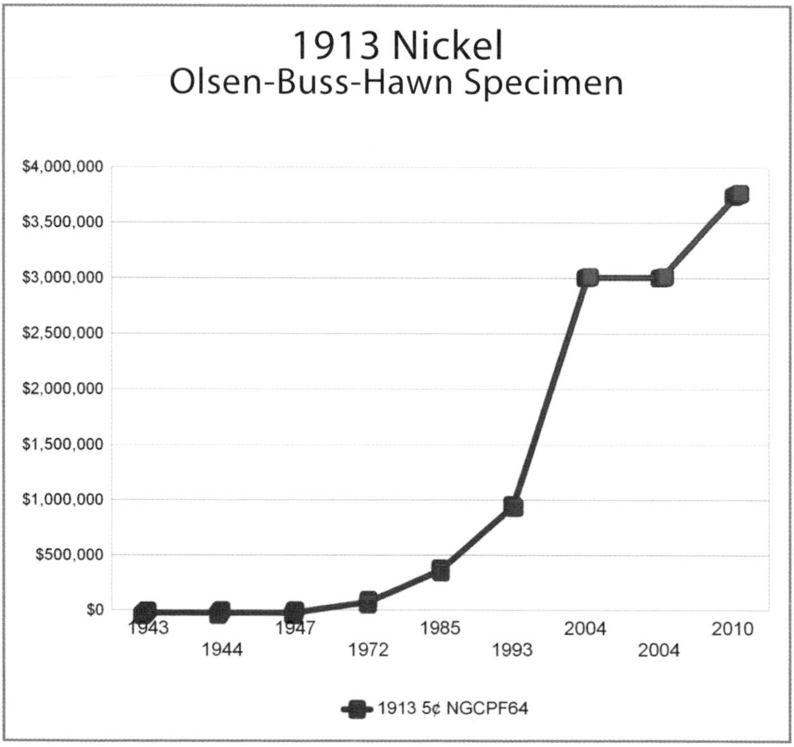

1913 Nickel
Olsen-Buss-Hawn Specimen

[Chart showing value of 1913 5¢ NGCPF64 from 1943 to 2010, rising from near $0 to approximately $3,750,000. X-axis labels: 1943, 1944, 1947, 1972, 1985, 1993, 2004, 2004, 2010. Y-axis: $0 to $4,000,000.]

■ 1913 5¢ NGCPF64

1903 Silver Dollar Proof Reverse
Heritage Rare Coins

to make certain that the retirement plans were used as intended.

Still later, those who were not self-employed or working for small companies that lacked pension plans were allowed to set up their own plans known universally under the IRA acronym, and at one time set aside up to $2,000 a year (also as deferred income). The limits today are as follows (see IRS publication 590 for more details): 2010 Combined Traditional and Roth IRA Contribution Limits

If you are under 50 years of age at the end of 2010 the maximum contribution that you can make to a traditional or Roth IRA is the smaller of $5,000 or the amount of your taxable compensation for 2010. This limit can be split between a traditional and a Roth IRA but the combined limit is $5,000. The maximum contribution to a Roth IRA and the maximum deductible contribution to a traditional IRA may be reduced depending upon your modified adjusted gross income (modified AGI).

If you are 50 years of age or older before 2011 the maximum contribution that can be made to a traditional or Roth IRA is the smaller of $6,000 or the amount of your taxable compensation for 2010. This limit can be split between a traditional and a Roth IRA but the combined limit is $6,000. The maximum contribution to a Roth IRA and the maximum deductible contribution to a traditional IRA may be reduced depending upon your modified AGI.

Deferred compensation means that it isn't taxed now, but rather is taxed when it is withdrawn, typically as part of an actuarially sound plan after a person reaches retirement age. The tax is paid on the sum withdrawn based on then-current tax rates.

Penalties & Prohibitions

Those who draw upon the resources before reaching age 59½ are subject to premature withdrawal penalties that include an immediate surtax on the sum withdrawn, the indignity of having to also pay income tax on the sum removed, and a prohibition against making further contributions for a period of five years.

Virtually all of the plans that were set up were self-directed, meaning that the owner had the right to designate how the funds were invested. The choice could be a simple bankbook (which back then was paying 5 percent simple interest), the equities market, corporate bonds, real estate mortgages, real estate, collectibles or in fact virtually any asset not otherwise illegal to own.

Wall Street's dirty little secret is that billions of dollars went into the equities market with the self-directed plan as a source. Buy-ins were cheap. The government was in essence a partner for the marginal tax rate and there was no capital gains tax (because it is collected only based on distributions).

Now here's a novel result: the government sets up a system that allows unfettered investment virtually without regulation or taxation, and the equities market grows from a Dow Jones Industrial Average of 1,000 in 1972 to more than 11,000 today. There have been highs, lows, and bumps along the way.

TEFRA in 1981 was intended as genuine tax reform by the Reagan Administration and substantially reduced the taxes that most Americans paid. It also placed on a list of prohibited acquisition assets for self-directed plans

Reasons cited for the prohibition were that the assets weren't productive, and simply did not help the economy. The underlying rationale: the assets were risky, and people also shouldn't be able to put a retirement asset in their homes, on their walls, or even be able to enjoy them before they were taxed on the consequences –" the ultimate Puritan work ethic."

Now, let me be bold and ask you to imagine who would have been the proponent of such a move to prohibit placing collectibles such as oriental rugs, rare coins, and Scotch whiskey into a retirement plan. Probably not rug manufacturers or antique dealers. Most likely the distilled spirits industry didn't propose it, either. Hmmm.

Here's a tough one. Who had an interest in preventing diversification?

Penny stocks that were highly volatile were permissible inclusions in a retirement account even if it was highly likely that a pensioner would lose his shirt and underwear before he saw a profit.

Junk bonds that promised high returns but had little collateral behind them, and which frequently could (and did) go into default were eligible, too. And they were hyped to the max by securities industry salesmen.

Intelligent people can draw their own conclusions from facts and arguments, and who sponsored the proposal probably doesn't matter anyway. They left no fingerprints, just a lot of circumstantial evidence.

Practical effect of the ban that took place was an immediate market disruption — just as if the government had said that you could no longer buy and sell real estate in your own name, and had to only do it corporately.

Prices plummeted, because a major buyer (those with IRA and Keogh assets) was removed from the marketplace, without warning, and without replacement plans on the drawing board.

(It's worthwhile noting that non-self-directed plans can and do still include rare coins in their portfolios, but that requires an independent trustee to make the decision, to determine that it is prudent to do so, and to assume full liability if it is not. Some, but not many, are willing to make that choice).

ICTA

About the only fortuitous result of this is that a National Association of Coin & Precious Metals Dealers was founded to help fight future assaults on the hobby, and later, an Industry Council for Tangible Assets was born to have a permanent Washington presence.

Burt Blumert, who practically invented the coin dealer's teletype in the 1950s, was a prime mover in the National Association. The NAC+PMD organization folded into ICTA a few years later and since then, the Washington lobbying organization has saved the hobby's proverbial cookies on more than one occasion, including the attack by the Internal Revenue Service on broker reporting that at one time threatened the sale of even a simple Roosevelt dime.

By 1986, America – the government and the Mint – had gotten into the business of selling gold and silver to the public. It occurred to the best and the brightest that the U.S. Mint's product line had a serious problem in the investment community that sold the bullion coins.

If the vendor made a sale and sold 500 ounces of silver as a bar, it could be kept in an IRA or Keogh account. But if the item purchased was 500 silver Eagle coins, the inclusion into the IRA or Keogh account would trigger all of the negative provisions of section 408(m) of the Internal Revenue Code.

These included considering the purchase a distribution –" making it taxable, with penalties – and prohibiting future additions for a five year period of time.

Sensing that there was good profit to be made, and that there was not much difference between 500 ounces of brick silver and 500 silver Eagles, there was intense pressure to change the law relative to coins in IRAs.

Add the Eagles

And so on Oct. 11, 1986, another Tax Reform Act was passed, replete with an obscure provision that allowed Eagles to be placed in self-directed plans. The race was on to sell gold and silver Eagles, whose sales soared to record heights. In 1986, the Mint sold 5.3 million ounces of silver through its one ounce Eagle programs. The IRA addition came late in the fourth quarter of 1986. By 1987, sales soared to 11.4 million ounces.

In 1996, a platinum Eagle was authorized, but for obscure legal reasons, a tax bill had to be prepared to allow its inclusion in self-directed retirement plans. That happened and as Goldline Web site remarks, "The United States government allows both proof and bullion American Eagles to be utilized in Individual Retirement Accounts (IRAs). Whether you prefer gold, silver, platinum, or a combination, these official U.S. coins can be added to your retirement savings by opening a new IRA account or transferring funds through an IRA rollover.

By the early 1990s, ICTA began to form a coalition designed to achieve equity and fairness in the treatment of the rare coin industry and appeared to have finally beaten back the non-productive asset argument. Small wonder. What stock is ever productive? What stock purchase ever created a job, except in the same way that the sale of a rare coin creates one? But that battle continues even into the new decade.

Yet in 2010, even as legislation has again been introduced to allow these self-directed plans to include rare coins, there remains a specter of continued prohibition. There are those who will argue that rare coins have no business in a retirement account, that purchasing silver has proven to be a bad investment, that gold buying is speculative, and that rare coins can't be accurately valued and are prone to abuse.

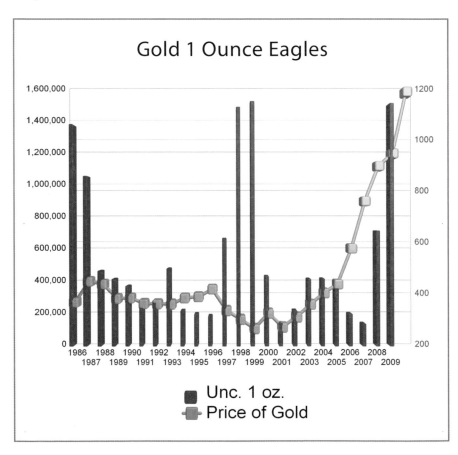

The same can be said about stocks and bonds. ake a real blue chip, like IBM. I bought some shares in the 1980s when the stock was trading at about $89 a share. It promptly dropped to $67 a share (where I bought still more).

That sort of reminded me about the time that I decided to add American silver Eagles into my retirement account, both as a hedge against inflation, as a strong affirmative statement that coins can be an investment tool, and to practice what I preach.

IBM went down, still more, to $43 a share. The silver Eagles that I bought declined less, but still I lost over $1 an ounce on several thousand ounces before IBM began a very profitable march toward $200 a share. (The 2010 Statistical Abstract ssays that 40 percent of the population has retirement assets in IRAs. Fortunately for me, I sold out my interest in IBM before its subsequent share decline). If I had held the silver, it would have increased about six-fold.

Congress look-see

Some of the questions that Congress has asked is what type of revenue is involved in the rare coin field, what was the total dollar volume of coins held in individual retirement accounts when it was permitted (between 1974-81). Also asked was what constitutes a reasonable estimate of the ratio between coins and bullion and other assets that were in IRAs and pension accounts during the same timeframe.

Answers are elusive, but there are some guideposts that can be employed. According to the Mutual Fund Fact Book and the Investment Company In-stitute of Washington, of $1.169 trillion in Individual Retirement Accounts in 1995, 6 percent was kept in savings institutions (compared with 28 percent in 1985, and 54 percent in 1981).

In 2005, a decade later, the amount is changed several-fold. First, total as-sets in IRAs (according to the 2005 statistical abstract of the United States, exceed $3,007 billion. Of this, most ($1,117 billion) is in securities and $1,306 billion is in mutual funds. Banks and thrifts have $268 billion worth or about 8.9 percent of the total.

As savings banks held fewer assets, commercial bank holdings have also declined, but perhaps less because some commercial institutions permit self-directed plans to make riskier investments such as brokerage transactions, mort-gages, and similar items.

Today, about 9 percent of the IRAs are in commercial banks compared with 12 percent in 1995 and 22.2 percent in 1981. The equities market has tapped the interest of IRA holders, rising from a 1981 low of 9.9 percent to a 1995 high of about 35 to 37 percent for stocks alone and 43 percent for mutual funds.

Life insurance and credit unions took up 11 percent in 1995 (compared with 13.4 percent in 1981 and 10.4 percent today), meaning that the remainder constitutes self-directed plans which can be in coins under very narrow circumstances.

In 1995, the Statistical Abstract of the United States (1997 edition) estimated that 36 percent of people's IRA assets are in self-directed plans, compared with no estimate at all in 1981, 14 percent in 1985 and 22 percent in 1990. About 40 million households representing a little less than half the population has an IRA, the 2006 Statistical Abstract says.

The 401-k plans (which had $105 billion in assets in 1985, $300-billion in 1990, an estimated $675 billion in 1995 and $923 trillion in 2003 (latest year available) by contrast has only about 6 percent in assets other than equity, money market, balanced accounts, bond funds or company stock.

While no one quite knows what volume of business the coin industry does, in the banner year of 1980, one of the largest coin and bullion houses apparently had about $800-million in sales. Another major house had $400 million in overall sales.

Probably, the 10 largest firms had about $2 billion in sales, with the next 100 largest firms having another $1 billion in sales. That means, likely as not, that the numismatic industry in 1980 was a $3.5 billion target.

Of that gross, my best guess is that no more than a third or about $1-billion of 1980 sales was driven by the IRA benefits for bullion and gold; some of that is still hidden in accounts (as it may lawfully be, so long as it was put in before August, 1981).

So as Congress legislates what can and can't be done, there probably are "trapped" assets in IRAs of about $3billion that constitute rare coins and bullion, a powerful sum considering that a buyer with even $1 million in fresh cash can substantially move an auction sale.

This in its own turn becomes important because the purchasers in 1981, if they were then 35, turn 64 in 2010, and are almost at a time when the law requires that they start to dispose of assets, a second disruption to normal market forces that could well be more dangerous than the original prohibition.

Of course, coins with 5 percent or less of the tangible assets that were included in IRAs are small potatoes in all this. But the same logic affects the other investors and their areas of preference.

What's allowed

As it currently stands, only those coins found in paragraphs 7 through 10 of title 31, section 5112 of the U.S. Code are allowed in IRAs – they can be proof, uncirculated, and probably stored in envelopes or encapsulated holders (though some argue that this is another issue to be decided).

That excludes paragraph 11 ("A $50 gold piece– weighing one ounce of gold that is 99.99 percent pure" and subparagraph (q) "$50 gold bullion and proof coins – bearing the original design by James Earl Fraser which appears on the 5-cent coin commonly referred to as the "Buffalo nickel – or the 1913 type 1."

It leaves in and allowable (7) a $50 gold piece weighing 33.931 grams and containing 1 troy ounce of gold (22k), (8) a $25 half ounce coin (22k), a $10 quarter ounce (22K) and a $5 tenth of an ounce, also 22k. The specs are written into the law.

(The silver and platinum eagles are allowed, too, but are not an issue since there is no alternative investment).

You can also put one ounce bullion bars into your IRA account, or 100 ouncers, because they can be used to settle Commodity Futures Trading Commission contracts. The CFTC has the authority to regulate transactions for delivery of silver bullion, gold bullion, and bulk silver and gold coins pursuant to standard margin or leverage account contracts.

The Commodity Futures Trading Commission and the mercantile exchanges are not concerned with legislating small, minor purchases of one ounce, 10 ounces, bars, nor numismatic items, because their statutory concern is directed toward preventing "excessive speculation" causing price fluctuations in the marketplace, which small units are incapable of causing.

What is being regulated is futures trading, nothing less than the buying and selling of standardized contracts for the future delivery of a specific grade and amount of a commodity.

There's no rational basis to exclude the new bullion coins; Congress simply forgot the law of unintended consequences and likely forgot to make the change. (I leave the issue of certified eagles in IRAs for another day's discussion, and including again coins in IRAs for a discussion worthy of the issue). If Congress wanted to correct the measure, it would be easy to do so:

Government gold seizure 21st century style

Here's the scenario: a multi-billion mortgage bail-out package on the table, Wall Street investment bank Lehman Brothers in bankruptcy, brokerage giant Merrill Lynch sold, and the appearance of economic chaos on at least three continents – North America, Europe and Asia, and in late 2009, even Dubai – gold has moved to the forefront and with it issues that parallel 1933-34.

The question fairly rises as to whether or not the government is moving to consolidate its economic power by an outright gold seizure or whether it is prepared to allow the free gold market to speak about the dollar bill and a gaggle of other foreign currencies. Some wonder if it is willing to let the dollar's purchasing power slip away entirely.

Cause of the initial crisis: bad bank loans. RealtyTrac® (realtytrac.com), a leading online marketplace for foreclosure properties, released its second quarter 2008 U.S. Foreclosure Market Report, which shows foreclosure filings were reported on 739,714 U.S. properties during the second quarter, The report also showed that one in every 171 U.S. households received a foreclosure filing during the quarter. A year later in February, 2010, Realty Trac reports that one in every 418 U.S. housing units received a foreclosure filing

The change from $750 on Sept. 12 to $869 on Sept. 19 was at a rate of 15.8 percent in just a week. Meanwhile, Lehman Brothers stock, which was $67 in 2007, was trading at 19 cents a share. Five thousand shares, which a year earlier had a value of $335,000, could be purchased for a mere $1,000.

Prior to 1933, a search for "gold seizure" in the *New York Times* historical data base, yields six news stories, all of which refer to wars in South Africa and elsewhere. The story is different by early 1934 when President Franklin D. Roosevelt used executive orders –without Congressional approval – to claim the nation's gold stock, including its coinage. (There were some exceptions).

The Jan. 13, 1934, issue of the *New York Times* had a series of articles whose headlines and sub-heads tell the central points of the dispute. "Roosevelt Claims Power to Capture Reserve Bank Gold," the first headline began. The sub-point: "Believes He Has Ample Authority, but Does Not Disclose His Intentions."

How was this accomplished? With the connivance of the attorney general. Again the *Times* headlines: "Cummings Gives Ruling But Definite Word on the Attorney General's Conclusions Is Withheld."

There is more to the headlines: "No Central Bank Plan," followed by "Roosevelt Declares That Such Reports of Aims Are Only Very Bad Guesses" and goes on to make the summary point: "President Claims He Can Seize Gold".

Over the next few weeks, there is more drama, more headlines: "Gold Bill Constitutional, Cummings Tells Senate; Early Passage Expected" is one thought. But there are those who claim that the seizure contemplated is unconstitutional – which headlines address, too.

There was opposition. Sen. Carter Glass of Virginia was opposed, as the headlines of the day disclose. Says the *Times*: "Held for 'Public Service' Glass Is Not Convinced While Reserve Board Is Inclined to Give Up Profit Only. House Group Scores Point Beats Rival Committee to Floor with Bill – Stabilization Reports Persist. Reports Gold Bill Is Constitutional"

Carter Glass, Woodrow Wilson's Secretary of the Treasury, and also FDR's choice (he declined) had been U.S. Senator (Democrat) from Virginia since 1920 when he did battle with FDR over gold seizure. Again, the Times summarizes in its headlines the problems of the day: "Glass Denounces Aims of Gold Bill; Silver Men Rally."

Glass's principal objection was taking gold from the Federal Reserve. He charged that Britain and Germany did not cripple their central banks when they went off the gold standard. That would be changed in the final executive order and the eventual custodian, which was the Fed.

Citizens once had the right to deposit silver or gold bullion with the Mint and receive, in return, a full measure of precious metal coinage, less the cost of coining. (The specifics are found in the original Mint Act of April 2, 1792, sections 14-15.) The government and the population could thus control currency supplies.

The right to deposit these metals was called "free coinage," though this was hardly so since there was a modest charge by the Mint for the service. Free coinage of silver ended with passage of the Coinage Act of 1873; general circulation gold coinage itself was halted in 1933, when FDR acted on his announcement discussed above, and created the first modern government regulatory function: controlling those numismatic coins that were exempted from an otherwise nation-wide recall of gold coins.

Passage of the Trading with the Enemy Act of 1917 authorized the President to regulate, investigate, and prohibit "under such Rules and regulations as he may prescribe ... any transactions in foreign exchange, export or earmarkings of gold or silver coin or bullion or currency ... by any person within the United States ..."

Prof. Henry Mark Holzer, in a remarkable 1973 article in the *Brooklyn Law Review* entitled "How Americans lost the right to own gold—and became criminals in the process" wrote of this. "The war emergency and the President's duty to fight the war provided Congress with a convenient rationale for the Act. The fact is, however, that the Constitution nowhere empowers Congress to prohibit dealing in gold, much less authorizes Congress to delegate that power to a coordinate branch of government."

First came Presidential Proclamation No.2038 (48 Stat. 1689 (1933), whose prefatory language sets up the explanation of national calamity.

"Whereas there have been heavy and unwarranted withdrawals of gold and currency from our banking institutions for the purpose of hoarding; and

"Whereas continuous and increasingly extensive speculative activity abroad in foreign exchange has resulted in severe drains on the Nation's stocks of gold; and

"Whereas these conditions have created a national emergency; * * * [and a banking holiday would be in the national interest]...

"Now Therefore I, Franklin D. Roosevelt, President of the United States of America, in view of such national emergency and by virtue of the authority vested in me by said Act and in order to prevent the export, hoarding, or earmarking of gold or silver coin or bullion or currency, do hereby proclaim, order, direct and declare that from Monday, the sixth day of March, to Thursday, the ninth day of March, Nineteen Hundred and Thirty Three, both dates inclusive, there shall be maintained and observed by all banking institutions and all branches thereof located in the United States of America, including the territories and insular possessions, a bank holiday, and that during said period all banking transactions shall be suspended."

The order was then specific about coins and other items: "During such holiday, excepting as hereinafter provided, no such banking institution or branch shall pay out, export, earmark, or permit the withdrawal or transfer in any manner or by any device whatsoever, of any gold or silver coin or bullion or currency or take any other action which might facilitate the hoarding thereof; nor shall any such banking institution or branch pay out deposits, make loans or discounts, deal in foreign exchange, transfer credits from the United States to any place abroad, or transact any other banking business whatsoever."

A generation after World War I and a few months after the initial shot across-the-bow, FDR issued Executive Order 6260 of Aug. 28, 1933 which recalled all gold coins, but exempted "rare and unusual gold coins." What was rare, or unusual, constituted a regulatory function of the Treasury Department in succeeding years. Millions of coins were melted (see chart below), creating rarities and investment possibilities in the process – if only they could be collected.

With the 1933 gold recall, all but rare and unusual coins were required by law to be turned in to the government in exchange for paper currency. Executive Order 6260 provided in pertinent part that "no return ... [is required of](b) gold coins having a recognized special value to collectors of rare and unusual coin ..."

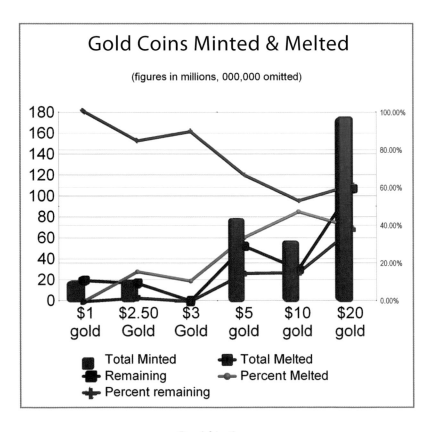

There were other limitations. Because more than $1.5 billion in coins were melted, calculated at their face value, millions of coins were forever destroyed.

Collectors knew, of course, that by virtue of their status as a collector, they were able to continue to hold gold coins, even quarter Eagles (though no more than four of each date and mintmark) while other citizens were forced to surrender their coins. Each of these pieces had been produced at a time when gold was valued at $20.67, and a $20 gold piece contained $19.99 worth of gold.

Simultaneous with the recall came a devaluation of the dollar, which meant that the price of gold was raised from $20.67 and ounce to $35.00. Since each $20 gold piece now contained $33.86 worth of gold, a significant advantage was attained by those collectors who retained their coins over those who patriotically turned them in as directed. (Actually, 1934 Proc. No. 2072, Jan. 31, 1934, 48 Stat. 1730 revalued the dollar to $35 an ounce (15-5/21 grains of .900 fine gold).

There are a host of laws that govern today's national banking and economic emergencies. Among them: title 12 of the U.S. Code (banking), section 4407(national emergencies), which notes as a cross-reference: "The provisions of this Chapter may not be construed to limit the authority of the President under the Trading With the Enemy Act (50 App. U.S.C.A. § 1 et seq.) or the International Emergency Economic Powers Act (50 U.S.C.A. § 1701 et seq.)."

The law lives on today as 50 App. USCA §5 (subsection (b)(1)) which still says that "During the time of war, the President may, through any agency that he may designate, and under such Rules and regulations as he may prescribe, by means of instructions, licenses, or otherwise--

(A) investigate, regulate, or prohibit, any transactions in foreign exchange, transfers of credit or payments between, by, through, or to any banking institution, and the importing, exporting, hoarding, melting, or earmarking of gold or silver coin or bullion, currency or securities..."

If this sounds like something forgotten 90 years ago, be aware that the legislative history tells another tale: it was most recently amended by Congress in 1977, 1988 and 1994. As the headlines play out, and begin to sound eerily repetitive with the 1930s, it is worthy of remembering that Americans were able to own gold abroad until the Kennedy administration prohibited it – also by executive order– in the early 1960s.

By Dec. 31, 1974, Americans regained the right to own gold as Congress repudiated the declaration of national emergency – but none of that precludes a presidential finding of an emergency that is obvious from reading the newspapers – even if it can be reversed by another executive order or congressional action. Put differently, it could happen again and it could happen to you.

For thousands of years, gold has had the allure to drive the world economy and to provide a hedge against inflation. In the 21st century, its storied past continues, and the coins made of it allow for affordable coin investing.

SELECTED AFFORDABLE RARITIES

Note: All of the coins mentioned (except where there are cut-offs) have favorable consideration in the rare coin retirement portfolio.

A. Modern Commemoratives

In planning for your rare coin retirement, the three most common areas to consider are modern commemorative coinage (1982-the present), statehood quarters (the extended series of 11 years that includes all 50 states, Washington, D.C., and five trust territories), mint errors, and the new modern circulating commemorative coins and newly designed coins..

Some of this is going to be hard and some of it is even going to be counterintuitive, but for these new issues, you need to acquire the object or coin involved in uncirculated condition, rather than a proof. Mint spokesmen will give the opposite impressions and suggest that proofs have a popularity that runs three to one – true enough – but that leaves the uncirculated coins a rarity all their own.

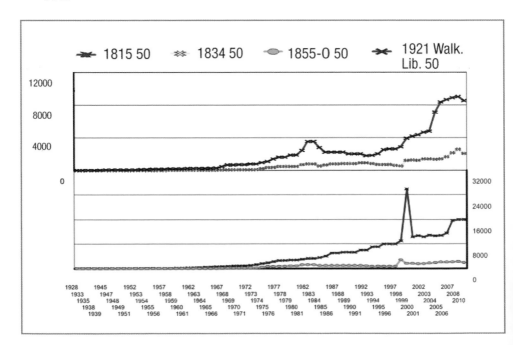

Half Dollars
Heritage Rare Coins

David L. Ganz

From my desk, the single most undervalued area of American numismatics is uncirculated modern commemoratives. First, look at the evidence which is in chart form. I began keeping this chart when I served on the Citizens Commemorative Coin Advisory Committee during the Clinton Administration.

Long after leaving the committee – 14 years ago – I still update the records faithfully because of the useful information that it provides. Note that in analyzing all modern commemorative issues, the combined number of coins minted is a little over 60 million pieces of which 47.4 million (or 77 percent) are proof. A mere 12.6 million are struck as uncirculated on average or about 24.8 percent of the pieces coined.

Let's look at this two ways, an original chart done for convenience by denomination and year (easy to find that way):

Half Dollars

Date\Type	Value	Minted	Proof	% Proof	Unc	% Unc	Authorized in Millions	Percent Sold
1982 Washington	$0.50	7,104,502	4,894,044	68.89%	2,210,458	31.11%	10.000	71.05%
1986 Statue of Liberty	$0.50	7,853,635	6,925,627	88.18%	928,008	11.82%	10.000	78.54%
1989 Congress	$0.50	897,401	762,198	84.93%	135,203	15.07%	4.000	22.44%
1991 Mount Rushmore	$0.50	926,011	753,257	81.34%	172,754	18.66%	2.500	37.04%
1992 Columbus	$0.50	525,973	390,255	74.20%	135,718	25.80%	6.000	8.77%
1992 Olympic	$0.50	678,484	517,318	76.25%	161,166	23.75%	6.000	11.31%
1993 Madison	$0.50	775,287	584,350	75.37%	190,937	24.63%	1.000	77.53%
1994 World Cup	$0.50	776,851	609,354	78.20%	168,208	21.80%	5.000	15.54%
1994 WWII	$0.50	512,759	313,801	61.20%	198,958	38.80%	2.000	25.64%
1995 Olympics Basketball	$0.50	340,656	169,655	49.80%	171,001	50.20%	2.000	17.03%
1995 Olympics Baseball	$0.50	282,692	118,087	41.77%	164,605	58.23%	2.000	14.13%
1995 Civil War	$0.50	434,789	322,245	74.12%	112,544	25.88%	2.000	21.74%
1996 Olympics Soccer	$0.50	175,248	122,412	69.85%	52,836	30.15%	2.000	8.76%
1996 Olympic Swimming	$0.50	163,848	114,315	69.77%	49,533	30.23%	3.000	5.46%
2001 Capitol Visitor Center	$0.50	177,119	77,962	44.02%	99,157	55.98%	0.750	23.62%
2003 First Flight Centennial	$0.50	169,295	111,569	65.90%	57,726	34.10%	0.750	22.57%
2008 Bald Eagle	$0.50	277,779	180,280	64.90%	97,499	35.10%	0.750	37.04%

Silver $1

Date\Type	Value	Minted	Proof	% Proof	Unc	% Unc	Authorized in Millions	Percent Sold
1983 Oly	$1	2,219,596	1,577,025	71.05%	642,571	28.95%	50.000	4.44%
1984 OLY	$1	2,252,514	1,801,210	79.96%	451,304	20.04%	50.000	4.51%
1986STAT LIB	$1	7,138,273	6,414,638	89.86%	723,635	10.14%	10.000	71.38%
1987 CONST	$1	3,198,745	2,747,116	85.88%	451,629	14.12%	10.000	31.99%
1988 OLY	$1	1,550,734	1,359,366	87.66%	191,368	12.34%	10.000	15.51%
1989 LONG	$1	931,650	767,897	82.42%	163,753	17.58%	3.000	31.06%
1990 IKE	$1	1,386,130	1,144,461	82.57%	241,669	17.43%	4.000	34.65%
1991 KOREA	$1	831,537	618,488	74.38%	213,049	25.62%	1.000	83.15%
1991 MT RUSHM	$1	871,558	738,419	84.72%	133,139	15.28%	2.500	34.86%
1991 USO	$1	446,233	321,275	72.00%	124,958	28.00%	1.000	44.62%
1992 COLUMBUS	$1	492,252	385,290	78.27%	106,962	21.73%	4.000	12.31%
1992 Olympic	$1	688,842	503,239	73.06%	185,603	26.94%	4.000	17.22%
1992 White House	$1	498,753	375,154	75.22%	123,599	24.78%	0.500	99.75%
1993 Madison	$1	627,995	532,747	84.83%	95,248	15.17%	0.900	69.78%
1994 Capitol Bic	$1	304,421	243,597	80.02%	60,824	19.98%	0.500	60.88%
1994 POW	$1	267,800	213,900	79.87%	53,900	20.13%	0.500	53.56%
1994 Vietnam	$1	275,800	219,300	79.51%	56,500	20.49%	0.500	55.16%
1994 Women in Military	$1	259,100	207,200	79.97%	51,900	20.03%	0.500	51.82%
1994 World Cup	$1	656,567	577,090	87.73%	81,524	12.27%	5.000	13.13%
1994 World War II	$1	445,667	339,358	76.15%	106,309	23.85%	1.000	44.57%
1994 Jefferson	$1	599,844	332,890	55.50%	266,954	44.50%	0.600	99.97%
1995 Civ War Battle	$1	101,112	55,246	54.64%	45,866	45.36%	1.000	10.11%
1995 Olympics Track and Field	$1	161,731	136,935	84.67%	24,796	15.33%	0.750	21.56%
1995 Olympics Cycling	$1	138,457	118,795	85.80%	19,662	14.20%	0.750	18.46%
1995 Olympics Paralympics	$1	166,986	138,337	82.84%	28,649	17.16%	0.750	22.26%
1995 Olympics Gymnastics	$1	225,173	182,676	81.13%	42,497	18.87%	0.750	30.02%
1995 Special Olympics World Games	$1	441,065	351,764	79.75%	89,301	20.25%	1.000	44.11%
1996 Olympics Rowing	$1	168,148	151,890	90.33%	16,258	9.67%	1.000	16.81%
1996 Olympics Tennis	$1	107,999	92,016	85.20%	15,983	14.80%	1.000	10.80%
1996 Olympics High Jump	$1	140,199	124,502	88.80%	15,697	11.20%	1.000	14.02%
1996 Olympics Paralympics Wheelchair	$1	98,777	84,280	85.32%	14,497	14.68%	0.500	19.76%
1996 Smithsonian 150th Anniv.	$1	160,382	129,152	80.53%	31,230	19.47%	0.650	24.67%
1996 National Community Service	$1	125,043	101,543	81.21%	23,500	18.79%	0.500	25.01%
1997 Jackie Robinson	$1	140,502	110,495	78.64%	30,007	21.36%	0.200	70.25%
1997 National Law Enf. Memorial	$1	139,003	110,428	79.44%	28,575	20.56%	0.500	27.80%

Silver $1

Date\Type	Value	Minted	Proof	% Proof	Unc	% Unc	Authorized in Millions	Percent Sold
1998 Black Patriots	$1	112,280	75,070	66.86%	37,210	33.14%	0.500	22.46%
1998 Black Patriots	$1	112,280	75,070	66.86%	37,210	33.14%	0.500	22.46%
1998 Robert F. Kennedy	$1	205,442	99,020	48.20%	106,422	51.80%	0.500	41.09%
1999 DolleyMadison	$1	181,195	158,247	87.34%	22,948	12.66%	0.500	36.24%
1999 Yellowstone	$1	152,260	128,646	84.49%	23,614	15.51%	0.500	30.45%
2000 Leif Erikson	$1	86,762	58,612	67.55%	28,150	32.45%	0.500	17.35%
2000 Library of COngress	$1	249,671	196,900	78.86%	52,771	21.14%	0.500	49.93%
2001 American Buffalo/Indian	$1	500,000	272,869	54.57%	227,131	45.43%	0.500	100.00%
2001 Capitol Visitor Center	$1	179,173	143,793	80.25%	35,380	19.75%	0.500	35.83%
2002 West Point Military Bicen	$1	363,852	267,184	73.43%	96,668	26.57%	0.500	72.77%
2002 Salt Lake City Olympics	$1	202,986	163,773	80.68%	39,213	19.32%	0.400	50.75%
2003 First Flight Centennial	$1	246,847	193,086	78.22%	53,761	21.78%	0.500	49.37%
2004 Edison	$1	253,518	194,189	76.60%	59,329	23.40%	0.500	50.70%
2004 Lewis & Clark	$1	314,342	234,541	74.61%	79,801	25.39%	0.400	78.59%
2005 Ch Justice Marshall	$1	180,407	133,368	73.93%	47,039	26.07%	0.400	45.10%
2005 Marines 230th anniv.	$1	500,000	370,000	74.00%	130,000	26.00%	0.600	83.33%
2006 Ben Franklin 300 youth	$1	130,000	85,000	65.38%	45,000	34.62%	0.400	32.50%
2006 Ben Franklin old	$1	130,000	85,000	65.38%	45,000	34.62%	0.400	32.50%
2006 San Francisco Mint	$1	227,970	160,870	70.57%	67,100	29.43%	0.500	45.59%
2007 Jamestown 400th	$1	289,880	213,065	73.50%	76,815	26.50%	0.500	57.98%
2007 Little Rock	$1	127,698	89,742	70.28%	37,956	29.72%	0.500	25.54%
2008 Bald Eagle	$1	340,799	249077	73.09%	91722	26.91%	0.5	68.16%
2009 Louis Braille bicentennial	$1	179,454	131726	73.40%	47728	26.60%	0.4	44.86%
2009 Abraham Lincoln Bicentennial	$1	450,000	325000	72.22%	125000	27.78%	0.45	100.00%

Half Eagle ($5)

Date\Type	Value	Minted	Proof	% Proof	Unc	% Unc	Authorized in Millions	Percent Sold
1986 Statue of Liberty	$5	499,261	404,013	80.92%	95,248	19.08%	0.500	99.85%
1987 Congress	$5	865,884	651,659	75.26%	214,225	24.74%	1.000	86.59%
1988 Olympics	$5	413,055	281,465	68.14%	131,590	31.86%	1.000	41.31%
1989 Congress	$5	211,589	164,690	77.83%	46,899	22.17%	1.000	21.16%
1991 Mt. Rushmore	$5	143,950	111,991	77.80%	31,959	22.20%	0.500	28.79%

Date\Type	Value	Minted	Proof	% Proof	Unc	% Unc	Authorized in Millions	Percent Sold
1992 Columbus	$5	104,065	79,734	76.62%	24,331	23.38%	0.500	20.81%
1992 Olympics	$5	104,214	76,499	73.41%	27,715	26.59%	0.500	20.84%
1993 Madison	$5	101,928	78,654	77.17%	23,274	22.83%	0.300	33.98%
1994 World Cup	$5	112,066	89,614	79.97%	22,447	20.03%	5.000	2.24%
1994 WWII	$5	90,434	66,837	73.91%	23,597	26.09%	0.300	30.14%
1995 Civil War Battle	$5	67,981	55,246	81.27%	12,735	18.73%	0.300	22.66%
1995 Olympics Runner	$5	72,117	57,442	79.65%	14,675	20.35%	0.175	41.21%
1995 Olympics Stadium	$5	53,703	43,124	80.30%	10,579	19.70%	0.175	30.69%
1996 Olympics Flag Bearers	$5	42,060	32,886	78.19%	9,174	21.81%	0.300	14.02%
1996 Olympics Cauldron/ Flame	$5	47,765	38,555	80.72%	9,210	19.28%	0.300	15.92%
1996 Smithsonian 150th Anniv	$5	30,840	21,772	70.60%	9,068	29.40%	0.100	30.84%
1997 Franklin D. Roosevelt	$5	41,368	29,474	71.25%	11,894	28.75%	0.100	41.37%
1997 Jackie Robinson	$5	29,748	24,546	82.51%	5,202	17.49%	0.100	29.75%
1999 George Washington	$5	55,038	35,656	64.78%	19,382	35.22%	0.100	55.04%
2001 Capitol Visitor's Center	$5	65,669	27,652	42.11%	38,017	57.89%	0.100	65.67%
2002 Salt Lake City Olympics	$5	42,523	32,351	76.08%	10,172	23.92%	0.080	53.15%
2006 San Francisco	$5	51,200	35,841	70.00%	15,359	30.00%	0.080	64.00%
2007 Jamestown	$5	60,805	43,609	71.72%	17,196	28.28%	0.080	76.01%
2008 Bald Eagle	$5	48,152	34021	70.65%	14131	29.35%	0.1	48.15%
Eagle ($10)								
1984 $10 Olympic Gold	$10	573,364	497,478	86.76%	75,886	13.24%	1.000	57.34%
2000 Library of Congress	$10	33,850	27,167	80.26%	6,683	19.74%	0.200	16.93%
2003 First Flight	$10	31,975	21,846	68.32%	10,129	31.68%	0.100	31.98%
Combined Totals		60,042,337	47,442,118	77.14%	12,602,972	255.04%	.249	39.06%

Now you can conveniently look up each modern commemorative and find, for example, how low the 1996 Olympic coinage silver dollars are. But again for convenience, let's sort the chart listing, lowest to highest, those coins in the order of total mintage. This groups by series because one postulate is that people collect by design type and don't always care whether or not they have uncirculated or proof, but do care about the design.

This chart shows that combined, the Jackie Robinson $5 gold piece is the lowest; uncs and proofs combined are less than 30,000 pieces.

Commemoratives Mintages Low to High

Date\Type	Value	Combined Minted	Proof	% Proof	Unc	% Unc
1997 Jackie Robinson 50th Anniv	$5	29,748	24,546	82.51%	5,202	17.49%
1996 Smithsonian 150th Anniv	$5	30,840	21,772	70.60%	9,068	29.40%
2003 First Flight	$10	31,975	21,846	68.32%	10,129	31.68%
2000 Library of Congress	$10	33,850	27,167	80.26%	6,683	19.74%
1997 Franklin D. Roosevelt	$5	41,368	29,474	71.25%	11,894	28.75%
1996 Olympics Flag Bearers	$5	42,060	32,886	78.19%	9,174	21.81%
2002 Salt Lake City Olympics	$5	42,523	32,351	76.08%	10,172	23.92%
1996 Olympics Cauldron/Flame	$5	47,765	38,555	80.72%	9,210	19.28%
2008 Bald Eagle	$5	48,152	34021	70.65%	14131	29.35%
2006 San Francisco	$5	51,200	35,841	70.00%	15,359	30.00%
1995 Olympics Stadium	$5	53,703	43,124	80.30%	10,579	19.70%
1999 George Washington	$5	55,038	35,656	64.78%	19,382	35.22%
2007 Jamestown	$5	60,805	43,609	71.72%	17,196	28.28%
2001 Capitol Visitor's Center	$5	65,669	27,652	42.11%	38,017	57.89%
1995 Civil War Battle	$5	67,981	55,246	81.27%	12,735	18.73%
1995 Olympics Runner	$5	72,117	57,442	79.65%	14,675	20.35%
2000 Leif Erikson	$1	86,762	58,612	67.55%	28,150	32.45%
1994 WWII	$5	90,434	66,837	73.91%	23,597	26.09%
1996 Olympics Paralympics Wheelchair	$1	98,777	84,280	85.32%	14,497	14.68%
1995 Civ War Battle	$1	101,112	55,246	54.64%	45,866	45.36%
1993 Madison	$5	101,928	78,654	77.17%	23,274	22.83%
1992 Columbus	$5	104,065	79,734	76.62%	24,331	23.38%
1992 Olympics	$5	104,214	76,499	73.41%	27,715	26.59%
1996 Olympics Tennis	$1	107,999	92,016	85.20%	15,983	14.80%
1994 World Cup	$5	112,066	89,614	79.97%	22,447	20.03%
1998 Black Patriots	$1	112,280	75,070	66.86%	37,210	33.14%

1932 Eagle Obverse
Heritage Rare Coins

1868 2-Cent Obverse
Heritage Rare Coins

1868 Quarter
Heritage Rare Coins

*1868 Shield Nickel
Obverse*
Heritage Rare Coins

*1868 Half Dime
Obverse*
Heritage Rare Coins

1868 Half Dollar
Reverse
Heritage Rare Coins

1868 Dollar
Heritage Rare Coins

1876 20-Cent
Reverse

1868 Half Obverse
Heritage Rare Coins

1868 3-Cent Obverse
Heritage Rare Coins

Commemoratives Mintages Low to High

Date/Type	Value	Combined Minted	Proof	% Proof	Unc	% Unc
1998 Black Patriots	$1	112,280	75,070	66.86%	37,210	33.14%
1996 National Community Service	$1	125,043	101,543	81.21%	23,500	18.79%
2007 Little Rock	$1	127,698	89,742	70.28%	37,956	29.72%
2006 Ben Franklin Diplomat	$1	130,000	85,000	65.38%	45,000	34.62%
2006 Ben Franklin Youth	$1	130,000	85,000	65.38%	45,000	34.62%
1995 Olympics Cycling	$1	138,457	118,795	85.80%	19,662	14.20%
1997 National Law Enf. Memorial	$1	139,003	110,428	79.44%	28,575	20.56%
1996 Olympics High Jump	$1	140,199	124,502	88.80%	15,697	11.20%
1997 Jackie Robinson	$1	140,502	110,495	78.64%	30,007	21.36%
1991 Mt. Rushmore	$5	143,950	111,991	77.80%	31,959	22.20%
1999 Yellowstone	$1	152,260	128,646	84.49%	23,614	15.51%
1996 Smithsonian 150th Anniv.	$1	160,382	129,152	80.53%	31,230	19.47%
1995 Olympics Track and Field	$1	161,731	136,935	84.67%	24,796	15.33%
1996 Olympic Swimming	$0.50	163,848	114,315	69.77%	49,533	30.23%
1995 Olympics Paralympics	$1	166,986	138,337	82.84%	28,649	17.16%
1996 Olympics Rowing	$1	168,148	151,890	90.33%	16,258	9.67%
2003 First Flight Centennial	$0.50	169,295	111,569	65.90%	57,726	34.10%
1996 Olympics Soccer	$0.50	175,248	122,412	69.85%	52,836	30.15%
2001 Capitol Visitor Center	$0.50	177,119	77,962	44.02%	99,157	55.98%
2001 Capitol Visitor Center	$1	179,173	143,793	80.25%	35,380	19.75%
2009 Louis Braille bicentennial	$1	179,454	131726	73.40%	47728	26.60%

Commemoratives Mintages Low to High

Date/Type	Value	Combined Minted	Proof	% Proof	Unc	% Unc
2005 Chief Justice Marshall	$1	180,407	133,368	73.93%	47,039	26.07%
1999 DolleyMadison	$1	181,195	158,247	87.34%	22,948	12.66%
2002 Salt Lake City Olympics	$1	202,986	163,773	80.68%	39,213	19.32%
1998 Robert F. Kennedy	$1	205,442	99,020	48.20%	106,422	51.80%
1989 Congress	$5	211,589	164,690	77.83%	46,899	22.17%
1995 Olympics Gymnastics	$1	225,173	182,676	81.13%	42,497	18.87%
2006 San Francisco Mint	$1	227,970	160,870	70.57%	67,100	29.43%
2003 First Flight Centennial	$1	246,847	193,086	78.22%	53,761	21.78%
2000 Library of Congress	$1	249,671	196,900	78.86%	52,771	21.14%
2004 Edison	$1	253,518	194,189	76.60%	59,329	23.40%
1994 Women in Military	$1	259,100	207,200	79.97%	51,900	20.03%
1994 POW	$1	267,800	213,900	79.87%	53,900	20.13%
1994 Vietnam	$1	275,800	219,300	79.51%	56,500	20.49%
2008 Bald Eagle	$0.50	277,779	180,280	64.90%	97,499	35.10%
1995 Olympics Baseball	$0.50	282,692	118,087	41.77%	164,605	58.23%
2007 Jamestown 400th	$1	289,880	213,065	73.50%	76,815	26.50%
1994 Capitol Bic	$1	304,421	243,597	80.02%	60,824	19.98%
2004 Lewis & Clark	$1	314,342	234,541	74.61%	79,801	25.39%
1995 Olympics Basketball	$0.50	340,656	169,655	49.80%	171,001	50.20%
2008 Bald Eagle	$1	340,799	249077	73.09%	91722	26.91%
2002 West Point Military Bicen	$1	363,852	267,184	73.43%	96,668	26.57%
1988 Olympic	$5	413,055	281,465	68.14%	131,590	31.86%
1995 Civil War	$0.50	434,789	322,245	74.12%	112,544	25.88%
1995 Special Olympics World Games	$1	441,065	351,764	79.75%	89,301	20.25%
1994 World War II	$1	445,667	339,358	76.15%	106,309	23.85%
1991 USO	$1	446,233	321,275	72.00%	124,958	28.00%
2009 Abraham Lincoln Bicentennial	$1	450,000	325000	72.22%	125000	27.78%
1992 Columbus	$1	492,252	385,290	78.27%	106,962	21.73%
1992 White House	$1	498,753	375,154	75.22%	123,599	24.78%
1986 Statue of Liberty	$5	499,261	404,013	80.92%	95,248	19.08%
2001 American Buffalo/Indian	$1	500,000	272,869	54.57%	227,131	45.43%
2005 Marines 230th anniv.	$1	500,000	370,000	74.00%	130,000	26.00%
1994 WWII	$0.50	512,759	313,801	61.20%	198,958	38.80%
1992 Columbus	$0.50	525,973	390,255	74.20%	135,718	25.80%
1984 Olympic Gold	$10	573,364	497,478	86.76%	75,886	13.24%

1881 Trade Dollar
Obverse
Heritage Rare Coins

1913 Liberty 5-Cent
Reverse
Stack's Rare Coins

1881 Proof 50-Cent
Reverse
Heritage Rare Coins

1904 Half Dollar
Heritage Rare Coins

1868 Proof
Heritage Rare Coins

Commemoratives Mintages Low to High

Date/Type	Value	Combined Minted	Proof	% Proof	Unc	% Unc
1994 Jefferson	$1	599,844	332,890	55.50%	266,954	44.50%
1993 Madison	$1	627,995	532,747	84.83%	95,248	15.17%
1994 World Cup	$1	656,567	577,090	87.73%	81,524	12.27%
1992 Olympic	$0.50	678,484	517,318	76.25%	161,166	23.75%
1992 Olympic	$1	688,842	503,239	73.06%	185,603	26.94%
1993 Madison	$0.50	775,287	584,350	75.37%	190,937	24.63%
1994 World Cup	$0.50	776,851	609,354	78.20%	168,208	21.80%
1991 Korea	$1	831,537	618,488	74.38%	213,049	25.62%
1987 Constitution	$5	865,884	651,659	75.26%	214,225	24.74%
1991 Mount Rushmore	$1	871,558	738,419	84.72%	133,139	15.28%
1989 Congress	$0.50	897,401	762,198	84.93%	135,203	15.07%
1991 Mount Rushmore	$0.50	926,011	753,257	81.34%	172,754	18.66%
1989 Congress	$1	931,650	767,897	82.42%	163,753	17.58%
1990 Eisenhower	$1	1,386,130	1,144,461	82.57%	241,669	17.43%
1988 Olympic	$1	1,550,734	1,359,366	87.66%	191,368	12.34%
1983 Olympic	$1	2,219,596	1,577,025	71.05%	642,571	28.95%

Commemoratives Mintages Low to High

Date\Type	Value	Combined Minted	Proof	% Proof	Unc	% Unc
1984 Olympic	$1	2,252,514	1,801,210	79.96%	451,304	20.04%
1987 Constitution	$1	3,198,745	2,747,116	85.88%	451,629	14.12%
1982 Washington	$0.50	7,104,502	4,894,044	68.89%	2,210,458	31.11%
1986 Statue of Liberty	$1	7,138,273	6,414,638	89.86%	723,635	10.14%
1986 Statue of Liberty	$0.50	7,853,635	6,925,627	88.18%	928,008	11.82%

The highest (and thus most popular), but by the same token least likely to increase in value is the Statue of Liberty 50-cent piece with 7.8 million pieces struck. That pleases me for an entirely different reason.

About 25 years ago, I was engaged by the Statue of Liberty Centennial Foundation to work on this very coin program when it was conceptually consisting of a silver dollar and a $5 or $10 gold coin.

Remember at this time the only prior experience was with the U.S. Mint's Olympic gold $10 coin from 1984. I thought the $350 price point was way high and that there was nothing of a "souvenir" price point for the visitor to the Games, no less the visitor to the world of coins and coin collecting.

I made a bet with the Foundation's executive director along with a recommendation. I said that a switch to $5 gold would increase sales and surcharges, and that addition of a copper-nickel clad 50-cent piece would yield both a surcharge reward and simultaneously broaden the appeal of the coin program.

Looking at it in 2010, it seemed obvious; then it was daring. I won the bet. There were 6.9 million proof half dollars (7.8 million total) with $3 a coin surcharges that brought in more than $22 million. The dollar coin brought in another $70 million (7.1 million at $10 each) and finally the piece de la resistance: a $5 gold coin that literally sold out: 499,221 pieces with a half million authorized by law to be issued, for $17 million in surcharges, yielding over $100 million to pay for the restoration project it was to fund. I won the bet but am still waiting for Executive Director Steve Brigandi to arrange dinner with chair Lee Iacocca.

1881 Trade Dollar Obverse
Heritage Rare Coins

But to get to the best value in buying low mintage, you need another chart sort, one that allows proofs and uncs to be compared equally. This is time consuming, and without the use of spreadsheets would be almost impossible to do quickly or efficiently, or to undertake some what if scenarios. Anyway, here is the result: of more than 200 coins, "P" for proof, "U" for uncirculated, of the 30 lowest mintages, the first 20 are all uncirculated; there are some proofs in numbers 20-30.

1884 Silver Dollar Obverse
Heritage Rare Coins

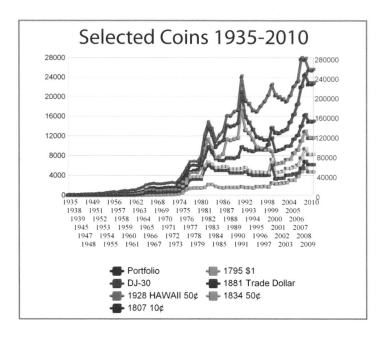

Selected Coins 1935-2010

Legend:
- Portfolio
- DJ-30
- 1928 HAWAII 50¢
- 1807 10¢
- 1795 $1
- 1881 Trade Dollar
- 1834 50¢

Commemoratives Uncirculated Mintages Low to High

Date/Type	Scarcer Strike Quality	Denom.	Total Mintage	Unc.	%Unc.
1997 Jackie Robinson 50th Anniv	U	$5	29,748	5,202	17.49%
2000 Library of Congress	U	$10	33,850	6,683	19.74%
1996 Smithsonian 150th Anniv	U	$5	30,840	9,068	29.40%
1996 Olympics Flag Bearers	U	$5	42,060	9,174	21.81%
1996 Olympics Cauldron/Flame	U	$5	47,765	9,210	19.28%
2003 First Flight	U	$10	31,975	10,129	31.68%
2002 Salt Lake City Olympics	U	$5	42,523	10,172	23.92%
1995 Olympics Stadium	U	$5	53,703	10,579	19.70%
1997 Franklin D. Roosevelt	U	$5	41,368	11,894	28.75%
1995 Civil War Battle	U	$5	67,981	12,735	18.73%
2008 Bald Eagle	U	$5	48,152	14131	29.35%
1996 Olympics Paralympics Wheelchair	U	$1	98,777	14,497	14.68%
1995 Olympics Runner	U	$5	72,117	14,675	20.35%
2006 San Francisco	U	$5	51,200	15,359	30.00%
1996 Olympics High Jump	U	$1	140,199	15,697	11.20%
1996 Olympics Tennis	U	$1	107,999	15,983	14.80%
1996 Olympics Rowing	U	$1	168,148	16,258	9.67%
2007 Jamestown	U	$5	60,805	17,196	28.28%
1999 George Washington	U	$5	55,038	19,382	35.22%
1995 Olympics Cycling	U	$1	138,457	19,662	14.20%
1996 Smithsonian 150th Anniv	P	$5	30,840	21,772	70.60%

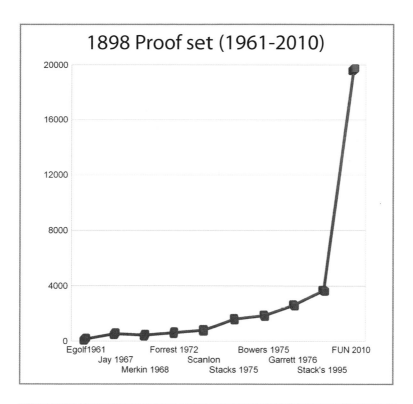

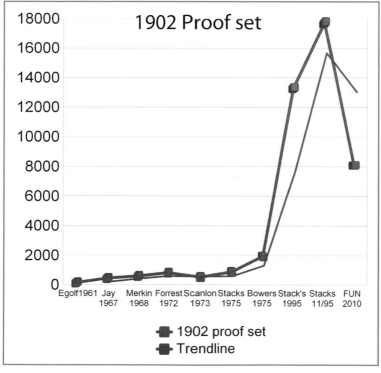

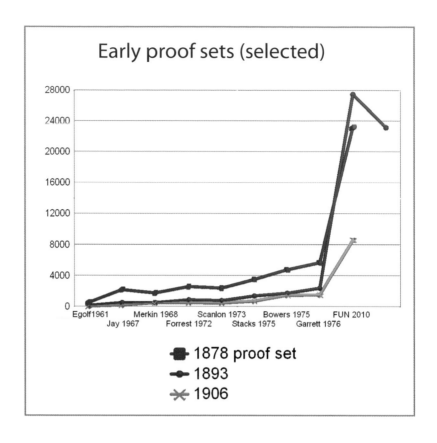

Early proof sets (selected)

28000
24000
20000
16000
12000
8000
4000
0

Egolf 1961   Merkin 1968   Scanlon 1973   Bowers 1975   FUN 2010
   Jay 1967   Forrest 1972   Stacks 1975   Garrett 1976

— 1878 proof set
— 1893
— 1906

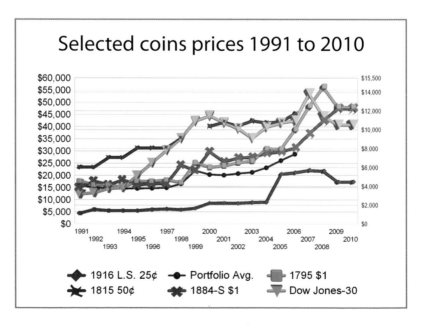

Selected coins prices 1991 to 2010

$60,000 $15,500
$55,000 $14,000
$50,000
$45,000 $12,000
$40,000 $10,000
$35,000
$30,000 $8,000
$25,000 $6,000
$20,000
$15,000 $4,000
$10,000 $2,000
$5,000
$0 $0

1991 1994 1997 2000 2003 2006 2009
   1992 1995 1998 2001 2004 2007 2010
      1993 1996 1999 2002 2005 2008

— 1916 L.S. 25¢   — Portfolio Avg.   — 1795 $1
— 1815 50¢   — 1884-S $1   — Dow Jones-30

Commemoratives Uncirculated Mintages Low to High

Date/Type	Scarcer Strike Quality	Denom.	Total Mintage	Unc.	% Unc.
2003 First Flight	P	$10	31,975	21,846	68.32%
1994 World Cup	U	$5	112,066	22,447	20.03%
1999 DolleyMadison	U	$1	181,195	22,948	12.66%
1993 Madison	U	$5	101,928	23,274	22.83%
1996 National Community Service	U	$1	125,043	23,500	18.79%
1994 WWII	U	$5	90,434	23,597	26.09%
1999 Yellowstone	U	$1	152,260	23,614	15.51%
1992 Columbus	U	$5	104,065	24,331	23.38%
1997 Jackie Robinson 50th Anniv	P	$5	29,748	24,546	82.51%
1995 Olympics Track and Field	U	$1	161,731	24,796	15.33%
2000 Library of Congress	P	$10	33,850	27,167	80.26%
2001 Capitol Visitor's Center	P	$5	65,669	27,652	42.11%
1992 Olympic	U	$5	104,214	27,715	26.59%
2000 Leif Erikson	U	$1	86,762	28,150	32.45%
1997 National Law Enf. Memorial	U	$1	139,003	28,575	20.56%
1995 Olympics Paralympics	U	$1	166,986	28,649	17.16%
1997 Franklin D. Roosevelt	P	$5	41,368	29,474	71.25%
1997 Jackie Robinson	U	$1	140,502	30,007	21.36%
1996 Smithsonian 150th Anniv.	U	$1	160,382	31,230	19.47%
1991 Mount Rushmore	U	$5	143,950	31,959	22.20%
2002 Salt Lake City Olympics	P	$5	42,523	32,351	76.08%
1996 Olympics Flag Bearers	P	$5	42,060	32,886	78.19%
2008 Bald Eagle	P	$5	48,152	34021	70.65%
2001 Capitol Visitor Center	U	$1	179,173	35,380	19.75%
1999 George Washington	P	$5	55,038	35,656	64.78%
2006 San Francisco	P	$5	51,200	35,841	70.00%
1998 Black Patriots	U	$1	112,280	37,210	33.14%
1998 Black Patriots	U	$1	112,280	37,210	33.14%
2007 Little Rock	U	$1	127,698	37,956	29.72%
2001 Capitol Visitor's Center	U	$5	65,669	38,017	57.89%
1996 Olympics Cauldron/flame	P	$5	47,765	38,555	80.72%
2002 Salt Lake City Olympics	U	$1	202,986	39,213	19.32%
1995 Olympics Gymnastics	U	$1	225,173	42,497	18.87%
1995 Olympics Stadium	P	$5	53,703	43,124	80.30%
2007 Jamestown	P	$5	60,805	43,609	71.72%
2006 Ben Franklin 300 youth	U	$1	130,000	45,000	34.62%
2006 Ben Franklin old	U	$1	130,000	45,000	34.62%
1995 Civ War Battle	U	$1	101,112	45,866	45.36%

Commemoratives Uncirculated Mintages Low to High

Date/Type	Scarcer Strike Quality	Denom.	Total Mintage	Unc.	% Unc.
1989 Congress Bicentennial	U	$5	211,589	46,899	22.17%
2005 Ch ief Justice Marshall	U	$1	180,407	47,039	26.07%
2009 Louis Braille Bicentennial	U	$1	179,454	47,728	26.60%
1996 Olympic Swimming	U	$0.50	163,848	49,533	30.23%
1994 Women in Military	U	$1	259,100	51,900	20.03%
2000 Library of Congress	U	$1	249,671	52,771	21.14%
1996 Olympics Soccer	U	$0.50	175,248	52,836	30.15%
2003 First Flight Centennial	U	$1	246,847	53,761	21.78%
1994 POW	U	$1	267,800	53,900	20.13%
1995 Civ War Battle	P	$1	101,112	55,246	54.64%
1995 Civil War Battle	P	$5	67,981	55,246	81.27%
1994 Vietnam	U	$1	275,800	56,500	20.49%
1995 Olympics Runner	P	$5	72,117	57,442	79.65%
2003 First Flight Centennial	U	$0.50	169,295	57,726	34.10%
2000 Leif Erikson	P	$1	86,762	58,612	67.55%
2004 Edison	U	$1	253,518	59,329	23.40%
1994 Capitol Bicentennial	U	$1	304,421	60,824	19.98%
1994 WWII	P	$5	90,434	66,837	73.91%
2006 San Francisco Mint	U	$1	227,970	67,100	29.43%
1998 Black Patriots	P	$1	112,280	75,070	66.86%
1998 Black Patriots	P	$1	112,280	75,070	66.86%
1984 Olympic Gold	U	$10	573,364	75,886	13.24%
1992 Olympic	P	$5	104,214	76,499	73.41%
2007 Jamestown 400th	U	$1	289,880	76,815	26.50%
2001 Capitol Visitor Center	P	$0.50	177,119	77,962	44.02%
1993 Madison	P	$5	101,928	78,654	77.17%
1992 Columbus	P	$5	104,065	79,734	76.62%
2004 Lewis & Clark	U	$1	314,342	79,801	25.39%
1994 World Cup	U	$1	656,567	81,524	12.42%
1996 Olympics Paralympics Wheelchair	P	$1	98,777	84,280	85.32%
2006 Ben Franklin old	P	$1	130,000	85,000	65.38%
2006 Ben Franklin 300 youth	P	$1	130,000	85,000	65.38%
1995 Special Olympics World Games	U	$1	441,065	89,301	20.25%
1994 World Cup	P	$5	112,066	89,614	79.97%
2007 Little Rock	P	$1	127,698	89,742	70.28%

Commemoratives Uncirculated Mintages Low to High

Date/Type	Scarcer Strike Quality	Denom.	Total Mintage	Unc.	% Unc.
2008 Bald Eagle	U	$1	340,799	91722	26.91%
1996 Olympics Tennis	P	$1	107,999	92,016	85.20%
1993 Madison	U	$1	627,995	95,248	15.17%
1986 Statue of Liberty	U	$5	499,261	95,248	19.08%
2002 West Point Military Bicen	U	$1	363,852	96,668	26.57%
2008 Bald Eagle	U	$0.50	277,779	97,499	35.10%
1998 Robert F. Kennedy	P	$1	205,442	99,020	48.20%
2001 Capitol Visitor Center	U	$0.50	177,119	99,157	55.98%
1996 National Community Service	P	$1	125,043	101,543	81.21%
1994 World War II	U	$1	445,667	106,309	23.85%
1998 Robert F. Kennedy	U	$1	205,442	106,422	51.80%
1992 Columbus	U	$1	492,252	106,962	21.73%
1997 National Law Enf. Memorial	P	$1	139,003	110,428	79.44%
1997 Jackie Robinson	P	$1	140,502	110,495	78.64%
2003 First Flight Centennial	P	$0.50	169,295	111,569	65.90%
1991 Mount Rushmore	P	$5	143,950	111,991	77.80%
1995 Civil War	U	$0.50	434,789	112,544	25.88%
1996 Olympic Swimming	P	$0.50	163,848	114,315	69.77%
1995 Olympics Baseball	P	$0.50	282,692	118,087	41.77%
1995 Olympics Cycling	P	$1	138,457	118,795	85.80%
1996 Olympics Soccer	P	$0.50	175,248	122,412	69.85%
1992 White House	U	$1	498,753	123,599	24.78%
1996 Olympics High Jump	P	$1	140,199	124,502	88.80%
1991 USO $1	U	$1	446,233	124,958	28.00%
2009 Abraham Lincoln Bicentennial	U	$1	450,000	125000	27.78%
1999 Yellowstone	P	$1	152,260	128,646	84.49%
1996 Smithsonian 150th Anniv.	P	$1	160,382	129,152	80.53%
2005 Marines 230th Anniv.	U	$1	500,000	130,000	26.00%
1988 Olympics	U	$5	413,055	131,590	31.86%
2009 Louis Braille Bicentennial	P	$1	179,454	131726	73.40%
1991 Mount Rushmore	U	$1	871,558	133,139	15.28%
2005 Chief Justice Marshall	P	$1	180,407	133,368	73.93%
1989 Congress Bicentennial	U	$0.50	897,401	135,203	15.07%
1992 Columbus	U	$0.50	525,973	135,718	25.80%
1995 Olympics Track and Field	P	$1	161,731	136,935	84.67%

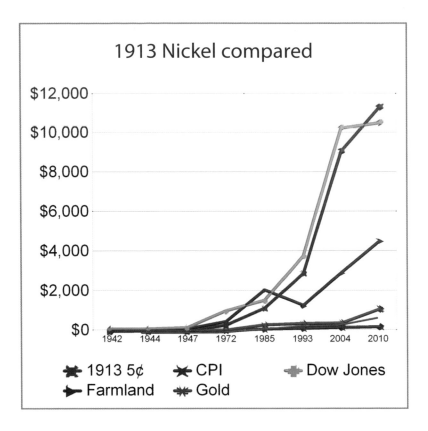

Commemoratives Uncirculated Mintages Low to High

Date/Type	Scarcer Strike Quality	Denom.	Total Mintage	Unc.	% Unc.
1995 Olympics Paralympics	P	$1	166,986	138,337	82.84%
2001 Capitol Visitor Center	P	$1	179,173	143,793	80.25%
1996 Olympics Rowing	P	$1	168,148	151,890	90.33%
1999 DolleyMadison	P	$1	181,195	158,247	87.34%
2006 San Francisco Mint	P	$1	227,970	160,870	70.57%
1992 Olympic	U	$0.50	678,484	161,166	23.75%
1989 Congress Bicentennial	U	$1	931,650	163,753	17.58%
2002 Salt Lake City Olympics	P	$1	202,986	163,773	80.68%
1995 Olympics Baseball	U	$0.50	282,692	164,605	58.23%
1989 Congress Bicentennial	P	$5	211,589	164,690	77.83%
1994 World Cup	U	$0.50	776,851	168,208	21.65%
1995 Olympics Basketball	P	$0.50	340,656	169,655	49.80%
1995 Olympics Basketball	U	$0.50	340,656	171,001	50.20%
1991Mount Rushmore	U	$0.50	926,011	172,754	18.66%

Commemoratives Uncirculated Mintages Low to High

Date/Type	Scarcer Strike Quality	Denom.	Total Mintage	Unc.	% Unc.
2008 Bald Eagle	P	$0.50	277,779	180,280	64.90%
1995 Olympics Gymnastics	P	$1	225,173	182,676	81.13%
1992 Olympics	U	$1	688,842	185,603	26.94%
1993 Madison	U	$0.50	775,287	190,937	24.63%
1988 Olympics	U	$1	1,550,734	191,368	12.34%
2003 First Flight Centennial	P	$1	246,847	193,086	78.22%
2004 Edison	P	$1	253,518	194,189	76.60%
2000 Library of Congress	P	$1	249,671	196,900	78.86%
1994 WWII	U	$0.50	512,759	198,958	38.80%
1994 Women in Military	P	$1	259,100	207,200	79.97%
1991 Korea	U	$1	831,537	213,049	25.62%
2007 Jamestown 400th	P	$1	289,880	213,065	73.50%
1994 POW	P	$1	267,800	213,900	79.87%
1987 Constitution	U	$5	865,884	214,225	24.74%
1994 Vietnam	P	$1	275,800	219,300	79.51%
2001 American Buffalo/Indian	U	$1	500,000	227,131	45.43%
2004 Lewis & Clark	P	$1	314,342	234,541	74.61%
1990 Eisenhower	U	$1	1,386,130	241,669	17.43%
1994 Capitol Bicentennial	P	$1	304,421	243,597	80.02%
2008 Bald Eagle	P	$1	340,799	249077	73.09%
1994 Jefferson	U	$1	599,844	266,954	44.50%
2002 West Point Military Bicen	P	$1	363,852	267,184	73.43%
2001 American Buffalo/Indian	P	$1	500,000	272,869	54.57%
1988 Olympic	P	$5	413,055	281,465	68.14%
1994 WWII	P	$0.50	512,759	313,801	61.20%
1991 USO	P	$1	446,233	321,275	72.00%
1995 Civil War	P	$0.50	434,789	322,245	74.12%
2009 Abraham Lincoln Bicentennial	P	$1	450,000	325000	72.22%
1994 Jefferson	P	$1	599,844	332,890	55.50%
1994 World War II	P	$1	445,667	339,358	76.15%
1995 Special Olympics World Games	P	$1	441,065	351,764	79.75%
2005 Marines 230th Anniv.	P	$1	500,000	370,000	74.00%
1992 White House	P	$1	498,753	375,154	75.22%
1992 Columbus	P	$1	492,252	385,290	78.27%
1992 Columbus	P	$0.50	525,973	390,255	74.20%
1986 Statue of Liberty	P	$5	499,261	404,013	80.92%
1984 Olympic	U	$1	2,252,514	451,304	20.04%
1987 Constitution	U	$1	3,198,745	451,629	14.12%
1984 Olympic Gold	P	$10	573,364	497,478	86.76%
1992 Olympic	P	$1	688,842	503,239	73.06%

Commemoratives Uncirculated Mintages Low to High

Date/Type	Scarcer Strike Quality	Denom.	Total Mintage	Unc.	% Unc.
1992 Olympics	P	$0.50	678,484	517,318	76.25%
1993 Madison	P	$1	627,995	532,747	84.83%
1994 World Cup	P	$1	656,567	577,090	87.73%
1993 Madison	P	$0.50	775,287	584,350	75.37%
1994 World Cup	P	$0.50	776,851	609,354	78.20%
1991 Korea	P	$1	831,537	618,488	74.38%
1983 Olympics	U	$1	2,219,596	642,571	28.95%
1987 Constitution	P	$5	865,884	651,659	75.26%
1986 Statue of Liberty	U	$1	7,138,273	723,635	10.14%
1991 Mount Rushmore	P	$1	871,558	738,419	84.72%
1991 Mount Rushmore	P	$0.50	926,011	753,257	81.34%
1989 Congress Bicentennial	P	$0.50	897,401	762,198	84.93%
1989 Congress Bicentennial	P	$1	931,650	767,897	82.42%
1986 Statue of Liberty	U	$0.50	7,853,635	928,008	11.82%
1990 Eisenhower	P	$1	1,386,130	1,144,461	82.57%
1988 Olympics	P	$1	1,550,734	1,359,366	87.66%
1983 Olympics	P	$1	2,219,596	1,577,025	71.05%
1984 Olympics	P	$1	2,252,514	1,801,210	79.96%
1982 Washington	U	$0.50	7,104,502	2,210,458	31.11%
1987 Constitution	P	$1	3,198,745	2,747,116	85.88%
1982 Washington	P	$0.50	7,104,502	4,894,044	68.89%
1986 Statue of Liberty	P	$1	7,138,273	6,414,638	89.86%
1986 Statue of Liberty	P	$0.50	7,853,635	6,925,627	88.18%

So, using the data that has already been sorted once, we find that the Jackie Robinson coin (uncirculated) is the scarcest, and that the proof version is scarce too in 30th place. All 30 of these coins have a total mintage of under 490,000 pieces combined. The Jackie Robinson uncirculated has a total mintage of 5,202 pieces. The gold-platinum Library of Congress coin is low mintage as well at under 6,700 pieces.

Even the highest mintage of these 30 coins in the chosen group has a mere 24,546 coins produced. Let's consider some equivalents. A 1937 proof set has a mere 5,542 pieces of each design, but there are similar designs. How about the Grant gold commemorative dollar (4,256 pieces) or the Panama Pacific $2.50 (6.749 pieces)? With mintages this low, at the high end, the future is bright.

Lowest Mintage Commemoratives by Type

Date/Type	Scarcer Strike Quality	Denomination	Total (U+P)	Mintage this coin
1997 Jackie Robinson 50th Anniv	U	$5	29,748	5,202
2000 Library of Congress Gold/Platinum	U	$10	33,850	6,683
1996 Smithsonian 150th Anniv	U	$5	30,840	9,068
1996 Olympics Flag Bearers	U	$5	42,060	9,174
1996 Olympics Cauldron/Flame	U	$5	47,765	9,210
2003 First Flight	U	$10	31,975	10,129
2002 Salt Lake City Olympics	U	$5	42,523	10,172
1995 Olympics Stadium	U	$5	53,703	10,579
1997 Franklin D. Roosevelt	U	$5	41,368	11,894
1995 Civil War Battle	U	$5	67,981	12,735
2008 Bald Eagle	U	$5	48,152	14131
1996 Olympics Paralympics Wheelchair	U	$1	98,777	14,497
1995 Olympics Runner	U	$5	72,117	14,675
2006 San Francisco	U	$5	51,200	15,359
1996 Olympics High Jump	U	$1	140,199	15,697
1996 Olympics Tennis	U	$1	107,999	15,983
1996 Olympics Rowing	U	$1	168,148	16,258
2007 Jamestown	U	$5	60,805	17,196
1999 George Washington	U	$5	55,038	19,382
1995 Olympics Cycling	U	$1	138,457	19,662
1996 Smithsonian 150th Anniv	P	$5	30,840	21,772
2003 First Flight	P	$10	31,975	21,846
1994 World Cup	U	$5	112,066	22,447
1999 DolleyMadison	U	$1	181,195	22,948
1993 Madison	U	$5	101,928	23,274
1996 National Community Service	U	$1	125,043	23,500
1994 WWII	U	$5	90,434	23,597
1999 Yellowstone	U	$1	152,260	23,614
1992 Columbus	U	$5	104,065	24,331
1997 Jackie Robinson 50th Anniv	P	$5	29,748	24,546
Total			2,322,259	489,561

For a long time, I collected American gold pieces in well circulated condition that had a mintage of under 30,000 pieces. I reasoned that they were scarce and that they were essentially irreplaceable. You could expand the 30 coins listed by a few to add a few more coins that are worthwhile to add to your investment portfolio. Now these are scarce coins.

Scarcer Coins to Add to Portfolio

Date & Design	U or P	Denomination	Total U+P	Mintage this coin	% of whole
1995 Olympics Track and Field	U	$1	161,731	24,796	15.33%
2000 Library of Congress	P	$10	33,850	27,167	80.26%
2001 Capitol Visitor's Center	P	$5	65,669	27,652	42.11%
1992 Olympic	U	$5	104,214	27,715	26.59%
2000 Leif Erikson	U	$1	86,762	28,150	32.45%
1997 National Law Enf. Memorial	U	$1	139,003	28,575	20.56%
1995 Olympics Paralympics	U	$1	166,986	28,649	17.16%
1997 Franklin D. Roosevelt	P	$5	41,368	29,474	71.25%
1997 Jackie Robinson	U	$1	140,502	30,007	21.36%

1860 $1 Gold
107 Teletrade.com

David L. Ganz

B. Early proof sets (1858-1915) and early modern proof sets (1936-1955)

Another area that I like are modern proof sets from 1936 to the present. In another quarter century, the 1936 set will actually be a hundred years old!

I also like old time proof sets (1858-1916), though for purposes of a portfolio that plans your rare coin retirement, it might be top-heavy to include them as a set when individual pieces might do better. They are ideal because they are low mintage, generally desirable, necessary for completeness, singularly attractive, and usually good value for the money.

In the course of the past half century, early proof sets have been sold many times at auction, usually coin by coin. Rarely have there been significant sales of old time proof sets.

Fortunately for researchers and compilers, a major sales event took place in January 2010 at the FUN convention auction conducted by Heritage Auctions in Orlando. It offered a complete run from 1856 to 1952 from the Boca collection. And while the sets lacked pedigrees, there is a certain sameness that allows comparisons with proofs from earlier eras.

Proof sets manufactured by the U.S. Mint from 1858-1916, when coin collecting was in its infancy, offer one of the surest ways to value the coin market over a long period of time and a solid collection that at once affords the ability to reap substantial financial rewards. The modern proof set era, 1936-1955 is surely another.

Virtually all of the proof sets are assembled sets, contrasted with the sealed, encapsulated sets that are produced by the Mint today. There are exceptions, such as the John Jay Pittman collection (explored elsewhere in this book) whose original proof sets were acquired inexpensively by modern standards and brought fabulous prices when kept together, more when separated.

That separation is ironic, because a century and a half ago, the Mint marketed individual coins, as well as sets, while coin collecting was in its infancy.

Individual proof coins of that era (1858-1955) are commonly available, and not infrequently, auctions will offer assembled subsidiary and minor coinage, together with the silver dollar, as a proof set. But major offerings of many old time proof sets are a modern rarity.

Coin collecting began in earnest in the United States in the late 1850s. One step that significantly helped foster the hobby was the 1858 recommendation of Mint melter and refiner James Booth to sell specimen coins produced by the Philadelphia Mint at a small premium. He called them "proofs."

Mint Director James Ross Snowmen decided to sell minor and subsidiary specimen coinage to collectors as a set. The earliest of the sets consisted of seven coins – cent, silver three cent piece, half dime, dime, quarter, half dollar and dollar – bearing a face value of $1.94.

Selling price of the set was $5.02, and of the $3.08 in surcharge, just 8 cents went toward the cost of producing the proof coins themselves. The remaining sum was utilized for the cost of the box or casket used to hold them, plus a small profit for the Mint.

Originally, gold coins were omitted from the sets, but they were added later. Their cost was a mere 25 cents above face value. They could be ordered individually or as a set. The overall cost of a gold proof set consisting of a $1, quarter eagle, $3, half eagle, eagle and double eagle was $43 (of which $41.50 consisted of face value).

But based on the wages and prices, even fewer could afford that. Hence, low mintages.

Records of early Mint production proof coins is spotty. By 1888, the procedure had been regularized sufficiently for Mint Superintendent Daniel Fox to post regulations stating that "Silver sets are not separated. Proof sets are furnished of the current year only. The Mint has no Coins or Sets of back dates for sale."

By that same year, Mason & Company of Boston was already offering proof coins for sale at modest price gains. For example, the 1865 2-cent piece was selling at 40 cents, the same price as the 1870 tuppence. The 1877 3-cent nickel had a $2 price tag, but all of the other 3-cent nickels from 1879 to 1888 had a 25-cent price tag.

For kicks, I decided to see which offers the better rate of return, the 1804 dollar (assuming it was sold in 1890 for $765 (and resold in 2009 at $2,300,000, as the Childs specimen was), which gives an average compounded rate of return of 6.96 percent; or the 1865 set at $4 which, is similar to one described in "Numisma" 1895 selling for $11,426. That set up a compounded rate of return of 7.87 percent.[15]

Proof coinage has been part of our nation's numismatic history, almost from the founding of the Mint. The 1792 disme pattern coin, with some claim to come from Martha Washington's silver plate, may well have been the Mint's first specimen coin

All proof coinage is struck on specially prepared planchets from a highly polished die of regular coinage design. The die is employed on a coining press , striking the coin with far greater pressure than is usual for a circulation strike.

The effect of this is for the metal to flow to the edges, creating a sharper rim than normal, and for the design to have a slightly greater depth giving it greater definition than on a conventionally issued circulation strike.

Prior to 1817, the number of American proof or specimen coins produced was few. The screw presses utilized in the Mint made proof production difficult; the fire of 1816 resulted in a need for new equipment, which was capable of proof coinage production.

By the 1850s, proof coins were being produced regularly. The 1856 flying eagle cent pattern was produced exclusively as a proof, though worn specimens that found their way into circulation are well-known today. All are actually impaired proofs.

Early sets were offered by the Mint to customers who frequently ordered by mail. For some customers, such as T. Harrison Garrett, the Mint sent extended explanations. In 1880, Garrison transmitted two drafts totaling $51 to the Mint of the United States at Philadelphia. On Feb.10, 1880, Superintendent A. Loudon Snowdon wrote that the Mint was sending by Adams Express a gold proof set of 1880 (cost $43) and two silver sets (cost $4 each, totaling $8).

At that time, as now, regulations of the Mint provided that the price would be approved by the Director. The proof set of silver and minor coins cost $3, and a "minor coins proof set" was available at 12 cents.

1868 Half Dollar
Obverse
Heritage Rare Coins

The 1880 silver set (actually minor coins and silver) that Garrett purchased was sold by Bowers & Ruddy in October 1980 during the dispersal of the fabulous collection that later reposed at Johns Hopkins University.

Bidding on the lot opened at $7,000 and immediately jumped with an oral bid to $15,000. It was finally hammered down in a matter of nine other bids at the $24,000 mark, a record that stood until October 1992 when the Floyd Starr set, also an original from the Mint, brought $26,100.

Using the same formula, Garrett's $3 purchase in 1880, selling a century later for $24,000, returned about 9.4 percent.

Many so-called "original" sets are typically repackaged other than the way that they were received from the Mint; their originality is usually determined based on a uniformity of color and toning. Trade dollars were always available as an extra piece.

Over the years, sets were broken up by collectors and dealers anxious for a particular coin date or denomination; other pieces have been added. Some coins are struck better than others; some have hairlines (resultant from bad cleaning of the dies, or cleaning of the coins after striking). Thus, it is difficult to objectively compare sets that are not specifically pedigreed.

Despite this, it is instructive and useful to look at various significant sales of old time proof sets to ascertain how the market overall has viewed them. The sets can be compared by date, and significantly, the average price per lot is a useful measure.

There are not that many auctions over the last half century that have significant numbers of early proof sets to even allow some basic comparison. In my research, I found them to include the Howard Egolf collection sold by

Stack's in October 1961 as a good starting point. An excellent follow-up is the Charles Jay collection, which Stack's landmarked in October 1967.

Next on my list is the Lester Merkin sale of March 1968; the S.S. Forest sale in October 1972; the George Scanlon sale a year later, October 1973; an unnamed sale by Stack's in May 1975; a Bowers & Ruddy sale of the Kensington collection in December 1975; the first Garrett collection sale (by Stack's in March, 1976), the Teich family sale in January 1990; the Floyd Starr collection sold by Stack's in October 1992, the Stack's sale of October 1995, and now the 2010 FUN "Boca collection."

In 1961, the Howard Egolf sale was virtually complete in its issues from 1859-1915. (It was missing the 1858, the 1912 and the 1914 set). The average price per lot was $434 (the median price was $320 per set). Representative prices included $250 for the 1892, 1894, 1897, 1900, 1901, 1904, and 1911 sets

When the Charles Jay complete collection of early proof sets (1858-1915) was sold by Stack's in October 1967, there had already been a significant change in the price line. The average set sold for $1,205 (median price was $920). Nearly all of the sets had doubled in price in the intervening six years.

By October 1972, the S.S. Forrest collection was sold by Stack's and, like Jay's, was complete from 1858 to 1915. George Scanlon's collection, also complete, was sold the following October 1973. Prices declined in the Scanlon sale when compared to Forrest, but compared to 1967 or 1961, it was a whopping gain.

Other sales were significant in 1975 and 1976. Bowers & Ruddy's Kensington collection, in 1975, was especially important since the sets were first auctioned individually, and then re-sold as a single lot for more than $100,000. (The individual pieces and lots were re-offered at a 5 percent premium above the highest winning bid.)

The number of collectors who could have relatively complete offerings of older proof sets are actually quite few. Only 380 proof quarters and proof half dollars were manufactured in 1914, for example. Thus, many otherwise complete collections are lacking dates like that. Egolf, for example, didn't have a complete 1914 set.

Floyd Starr's fabulous collection came to the auction block in 1992. It was truly a proof set collection from an old time collector, who had actually died almost 20 years earlier and had acquired these gems in a bygone era.

His proofs alone garnered $1.5 million, the most to its day ever achieved for a complete run, but included an 1884 set, complete with the rare Trade dollar, which made a $177,600 price for the record books.

Many of Starr's sets were original pieces that had strong pedigrees, and the prices realized reflected fully their value. So, too, in the 60th anniversary sale conducted by Stack's, and in the *Numisma* '95 offering, several of the coins and sets offered had pedigrees all their own.

Trying to set a parameter for availability of these coins is difficult because Mint records are spotty. Breen estimates that many coins are far below announced mintage levels because of subsequent meltings by the Mint. The 1859 set, for example, shows strikes of 800 coins, but Stack's and Breen, estimate that fewer than 100 sets exist today.

At the October 1995 sale, the example was a pedigreed set that was offered at the 1976 ANA convention, where it realized $4,250. The 1995 price for the identical set of seven coins was $15,890, a three-fold gain in the intervening years.

Another pedigreed set was that of 1866, lacking the 3-cent silver piece in October, 1995, just as it was when it was sold in the C. Ramsey Bartlett auction of February 1966. In 1966, it realized $2,700; in 1995, the price fetched was $11,426.50. In 2010, a similar set realized $37,375

Not every set always goes up continually. The 1883 proof set including the Trade dollar (a proof only issue) traced its origins to the Century collection, which Superior sold in February 1992 for $52,800. The 1995 resale price was a respectable $30,222.50.

Another pedigreed piece was the 1885 proof set (lacking the elusive Trade dollar, of course) which brought $825 at the Stack's sale conducted in December, 1964. In 1995, the resale price of the set jumped to $3,074.50, a respectable increment that averages a rate of return at 9 percent annually; the compound rate would be 4.3 percent annually.

The final pedigreed set of the 1995 offering was the six-coin 1901, cent to dollar, which traced its last sale back to the 1976 ANA convention. Back then, the price of the set was $1,900; in 1995, the resale price at auction crossed the block at $17,600, a hefty gain indeed and a compound return of 12.4 percent annually.

Old time proof sets do offer a unique view of the marketplace and the rare opportunity to compare prices of yesterday with those of today. In the case of these early sets, that comparison has not only been favorable, it's been one that has meant that the buyers, and sellers, have made a substantial profit in the process.

The 2010 pricing shows that some can be included in your rare coin retirement portfolio (the larger one) depending on your tolerance for over-weight risk.

Proof Set Values Since 1961

Date	Egolf	Jay	Forrest	Scanlon	Floyd Starr	Heritage
	Oct. 67	Oct. 76	Oct. 73	May 75	Oct. 95	2010FUN
1856						$69,000
1857						$43,125
1858		$5,320	$7,500	$8,500	$101,000	$37,375
1859	$775	$1,950	$2,750	$3,000	$35,450	$18,400
1860	$470	$1,295	$2,100	$2,100	$36,500	$25,300
1861	$480	$1,118	$1,900	$2,100	$33,800	$27,600
1862	$430	$935	$1,600	$1,600	$46,000	$17,250
1863	$430	$1,190	$1,800	$1,600	$39,600	$17,250
1864	$600	$1,935	$4,000	$2,900	$101,350	$18,400
1865	$550	$1,530	$2,800	$2,600	$35,050	$17,250
1866	$825	$2,716	$3,200	$3,800	$23,850	$37,375
1867	$550	$1,317	$2,100	$2,400	$23,850	$17,250
1868	$550	$1,317	$1,800	$2,300	$25,875	$9,488
1869	$550	$1,562	$1,900	$2,300	$35,700	$19,550
1870	$450	$1,572	$1,700	$1,200	$33,700	$16,675
1871	$600	$1,405	$1,800	$1,750	$24,350	$18,400
1872	$500	$1,500	$1,900	$2,000	$23,925	$18,400
1873	$1,400	$3,425	$4,500	$3,400	$32,875	$37,375
1874	$525	$1,457	$2,400	$1,800	$33,025	$12,650
1875	$475	$1,230	$2,000	$2,100	$5,725	$11,500
1876	$360	$1,062	$1,900	$1,800	$28,325	$19,550
1877	$1,500	$4,022	$5,750	$4,000	$39,750	$25,300
1878	$675	$2,300	$2,700	$2,500	$38,300	$23,000
1879	$350	$970	$1,500	$1,000	$23,650	$13,225
1880	$280	$1,015	$1,500	$1,520	$26,100	$18,400
1881	$285	$920	$1,300	$1,000	$30,800	$13,800
1882	$300	$854	$16,500	$1,450	$29,600	$15,065
1883	$350	$1,102	$1,700	$1,550	$44,625	$25,300
1884	$270	$438	$950	$825	$177,600	$11,500
1885	$440	$773	$1,050	$1,150	$22,750	$9,775
1886	$370	$752	$1,150	$850	$15,925	$9,775
1887	$340	$775	$1,100	$950	$16,250	$10,925
1888	$260	$657	$1,100	$950	$11,125	$16,100
1889	$320	$482	$900	$850	$23,450	$9,488
1890	$310	$593	$900	$800	$17,550	$138,000
1891	$275	$400	$950	$750	$11,340	$13,800
1892	$250	$447	$900	$625	$11,065	$12,133
1893	$280	$635	$1,000	$900	$12,875	$23,000

Date	Egolf	Jay	Forrest	Scanlon	Floyd Starr	Heritage
	Oct. 67	Oct. 76	Oct. 73	May 75	Oct. 95	2010FUN
1894	$250	$920	$1,400	$1,150	$14,060	$17,250
1895	$1,500	$5,280	$6,000	$6,250	$40,400	$86,250
1896	$300	$660	$900	$1,000	$29,400	$10,925
1897	$250	$562	$900	$900	$17,150	$14,950
1898	$260	$650	$725	$900	$21,090	$19,550
1899	$245	$553	$950	$900	$15,900	$11,500
1900	$250	$582	$800	$875	$16,725	$8,338
1901	$250	$557	$850	$1,050	$13,950	$14,950
1902	$230	$530	$900	$600	$10,125	$8,085
1903	$290	$592	$800	$650	$10,240	$10,350
1904	$250	$620	$900	$550	$8,725	$9,200
1905	$200	$422	$650	$625	$8,355	$27,600
1906	$200	$340	$650	$600	$10,800	$8,625
1907	$210	$352	$650	$800	$9,645	$12,075
1908	$230	$435	$600	$775	$7,555	$7,475
1909	$200	$450	$650	$900	$12,360	$21,850
1910	$270	$360	$700	$650	$8,330	$7,475
1911	$250	$440	$750	$500	$7,725	$8,625
1912		$520	$750	$600	$6,950	$5,750
1913	$400	$1,240	$1,900	$950	$8,000	$14,950
1914		$1,305	$1,900	$1,350	$9,575	$12,368
1915	$925	$1,560	$2,000	$1,400	$6,500	$9,775
Total	$24,335	$69,901	$116,925	$94,895	$1,566,265	$1,245,663
Average	$435	$1,205	$2,016	$1,636	$27,005	$19,544
Median	$340	$920	$1,450	$1,100	$23,100	$12,104
	$1,961	$1,967	$1,972	$1,973	$1,992	$2,010
Dow	$670	$879	$740	$850	$3,301	$10,248

Stack's May 1975 and Kensington 12/75 combined (12/75 bold italic)
Stack's Oct. & Nov. 1995 sales combined, Numisma '95 bold and italic

To include in your rare coin portfolio of affordable rare coins to invest in right now, there is a potential problem of overweight; that is, the sets are expensive as a set or even as component parts. Yet in the Boca collection sold at FUN in January, 20120, of 600 sets from 1856 to 1915, some 48 had a price realized under $20,000; 32 under $15,000 and 16 under $10,000. Given cost averaging and the number of coins in a set, most of the sets in the under $15,000 price range ought to be acceptable risks for retirement planning, or current investment.

For the most part, this involves coins that are appropriate. To augment it, you might consider one or more gold coins, say a proof quarter eagle or half eagle that will not break the bank and will complement the collection. Having a nice velvet display box made to hold it completes the illusion.

C. American Eagles-gold, silver, platinum

An opportunity can also be found in modern American Eagles, both the proof coins and the uncirculated counterparts (though for these, high grade condition is important). In taking this route, the investment is plainly in gold – there is a premium to be paid for numismatic content. But, the mintage statistics of gold, silver and platinum eagles is something to also consider.

From 1980 to the present, the price of gold has several different periods, but a trading range of $300-$450 an ounce was once a dominant feature. It then came off a 1980 high of $800 an ounce. The last several years has made us used to a four-figure price above $1,000 an ounce.

With this as background, a reader of my "Under the Glass" column in *Numismatic News* inquired recently whether I thought it better to acquire gold as bullion, Krugerrands, U.S. Eagles or U.S. numismatic gold coinage. The real question is what performs better: numismatic coinage or gold bullion?

I undertook an analysis – not scientific, but rather random– using several different coins designed to mimic a numismatic coin with more bullion content than numismatic worth. That meant condition ran from about uncirculated to MS-63, but most were plain old MS-60.

The coins included an 1850-O gold dollar, an 1880-CC $5, a 1932 $10 in MS-60, an 1880-S in MS-63, an 1890 quarter eagle in MS-60, a 1925-D $2.50 in MS-60 and three double eagle $20 gold pieces, an 1889 in MS-60, a 1909-D in AU-50 and a 1916-S in MS-60.

Look at the accompanying graph, which shows bullion's average price from 1980-2010. It's consistently the lowest line on the chart. Then compare trend lines of the double Eagles. There is no comparison. The small numismatic premium yields greater rewards.

While the floor is the bullion, the numismatic differential gives a greater rate of return that is immediately visible on the graph. There are certainly other ups and downs and bumps on the coin prices, even the about uncirculated 1909-D double Eagle doesn't follow the bullion price, but instead charts its own course.

What the numbers make clear is that those who thought gold's role in the monetary system or even governing collectibles was dead and buried need to re-think their position. A new era for gold may have begun.

My advice on collecting silver proof Eagles for growth possibilities is to cut off acquisition at coins with lower than 500,000 pieces (1996 on the chart); the three best relative values are: 1992, 1996 and 1998.

Silver Eagle Proofs

Date	Mintage	Date	Mintage
1986	1,446,778	1999	549,769
1987	997,732	2000	600,000
1988	557,370	2001	746,398
1989	617,694	2002	647,342
1990	695,510	2003	747,831
1991	511,925	2004	801,602
1992	498,654	2005	701,606
1993	405,913	2006	1,043,602
1994	372,168	2007	827,106
1995	438,511	2008	546,765
1996	500,000	2009	0
1997	435,368	Total	15,139,644
1998	450,000		

Silver Eagle Proofs by Mintage Low to High

Date	Mintage	Date	Mintage	Date	Mintage
1994	372,168	2008	546,765	2001	746,398
1993	405,913	1999	549,769	2003	747,831
1997	435,368	1988	557,370	2004	801,602
1995	438,511	2000	600,000	2007	827,106
1998	450,000	1989	617,694	1987	997,732
1992	498,654	2002	647,342	2006	1,043,602
1996	500,000	1990	695,510	1986	1,446,778
1991	511,925	2005	701,606		

Relative rarity, but not actual or even perceived scarcity, is possible with uncirculated silver eagles. See the accompanying chart showing annual mintage figures:

Uncirculated Silver Eagles Mintages

Date	Mintage	Date	Mintage
1987	11,442,335	1999	7,408,640
1988	5,004,646	2000	9,239,132
1989	5,203,327	2001	9,001,711
1990	5,203,327	2002	10,539,026
1991	7,191,066	2003	8,495,008
1992	5,540,068	2004	8,882,754
1993	6,763,762	2005	8,891,025
1994	4,227,319	2006	10,676,522
1995	4,672,051	2007	9,028,036
1996	3,603,386	2008	20,583,000
1997	4,295,004	2009	0
1998	4,847,549	Total	176,131,699

Again for convenience, here's a sorted version for rarity (or lower mintage, first, anyway): the mintage runs as high as 20.5 million and as low as 3.6 million.

Uncirculated Silver Eagles Ranked by Mintage

Date	Mintage	Date	Mintage
1996	3,603,386	1999	7,408,640
1994	4,227,319	2003	8,495,008
1997	4,295,004	2004	8,882,754
1995	4,672,051	2005	8,891,025
1998	4,847,549	2001	9,001,711
1988	5,004,646	2007	9,028,036
1989	5,203,327	2000	9,239,132
1990	5,203,327	2002	10,539,026
1992	5,540,068	2006	10,676,522
1993	6,763,762	1987	11,442,335
1991	7,191,066	2008	20,583,000

Gold eagles in proofs have much lower mintages, but not yet an impressive price history. That could come. Start with the traditional mintage table, after which we'll sort them by weight to see where the real low mintages are:

That means that there are 11 one ounce pieces within those guidelines, 12 half ounce pieces, eight quarter ounce pieces and three 10th of an ounce coins.

Proof Gold Eagle Coin Mintage

Date	1OZ	½ OZ	1/4OZ	1/10 OZ
1986	446,290	N/A	N/A	N/A
1987	147,498	143,398	N/A	N/A
1988	87,133	76,528	98,028	143,881
1989	54,570	44,798	54,170	84,647
1990	62,401	51,636	62,674	99,349
1991	50,411	53,125	50,839	70,334
1992	44,826	40,976	46,269	64,874
1993	34,369	43,819	46,464	58,649
1994	46,674	44,584	48,172	62,849
1995	46,368	45,388	47,526	62,667
1996	36,153	35,058	38,219	57,047
1997	32,999	26,344	29,805	34,977
1998	25,886	25,374	29,503	39,395
1999	31,427	30,427	34,417	48,428
2000	33,007	32,028	36,036	49,971
2001	24,555	23,240	25,613	37,530
2002	27,499	26,646	29,242	40,864
2003	28,344	28,270	30,292	40,027
2004	28,215	27,330	28,839	35,131
2005	35,246	34,311	37,207	49,265
2006	47,096	34,322	36,127	47,277
2007	51,810	44,025	46,189	58,553
2008	30,237	22,602	18,877	28,116

The rule of thumb that I would use on proof eagles is 35,000 or fewer mintage:

Proof Gold Eagles Ranked by Mintage

Date	1OZ	Date	½ OZ	Date	1/4OZ	Date	1/10 OZ
2001	24,555	1986	N/A	1986	N/A	1986	N/A
1998	25,886	2008	22,602	1987	N/A	1987	N/A
2002	27,499	2001	23,240	2008	18,877	2008	28,116
2004	28,215	1998	25,374	2001	25,613	1997	34,977
2003	28,344	1997	26,344	2004	28,839	2004	35,131
2008	30,237	2002	26,646	2002	29,242	2001	37,530
1999	31,427	2004	27,330	1998	29,503	1998	39,395
1997	32,999	2003	28,270	1997	29,805	2003	40,027
2000	33,007	1999	30,427	2003	30,292	2002	40,864
1993	34,369	2000	32,028	1999	34,417	2006	47,277
2005	35,246	2005	34,311	2000	36,036	1999	48,428
1996	36,153	2006	34,322	2006	36,127	2005	49,265
1992	44,826	1996	35,058	2005	37,207	2000	49,971
1995	46,368	1992	40,976	1996	38,219	1996	57,047
1994	46,674	1993	43,819	2007	46,189	2007	58,553
2006	47,096	2007	44,025	1992	46,269	1993	58,649
1991	50,411	1994	44,584	1993	46,464	1995	62,667
2007	51,810	1989	44,798	1995	47,526	1994	62,849
1989	54,570	1995	45,388	1994	48,172	1992	64,874
1990	62,401	1990	51,636	1991	50,839	1991	70,334
1988	87,133	1991	53,125	1989	54,170	1989	84,647
1987	147,498	1988	76,528	1990	62,674	1990	99,349
1986	446,290	1987	143,398	1988	98,028	1988	143,881

D. American Arts Gold Medallions

Don't fall over with this next suggestion: the American Arts Gold Medallions, made during the interregnum between prohibited gold ownership and American made gold coins. I had something to do with their legislative creation.

It turns out that my friend, Grover Cleveland Criswell Jr., as president of the American Numismatic Association, gave credibility to the American Arts Gold Medallion program at a time when others were critical of the possibility of any government gold sales. They warned that it could constitute the end of civilization as we know it if gold were issued in a round half ounce or one ounce format.

In 1978, Criswell was president of the American Numismatic Association. I had just been named the organization's first legislative counsel – signifying a new initiative toward dealing with Washington and the various issues that affected organized numismatics.

ANA had previously had an on again, off again, relationship in Washington. For years, there had been the "official" Washington presence at Ellis Edlow's law offices. That had culminated in the battle for America's bicentennial coinage in 1973, the same year that the Hobby Protection Act had passed.

There was considerable involvement of the ANA, Chet Krause, Cliff Mishler, and others in both of these legislative initiatives, but forever looming in the background was the feeling that there was something illegal, or improper, about ANA's involvement in "lobbying" Congress on numismatic matters.

Criswell felt differently, and was persuaded that it made sense to appoint a legislative counsel to deal with Washington issues, and assist in the lobbying effort as well as in offering testimony to various Congressional committees that dealt with coinage matters in a substantive way.

Houston, Texas, in August 1978 was hot, humid, uncomfortable, and the site of ANA's 87th anniversary convention. In the midst of this, Sen. William Proxmire, D-Wis., chairman of the Senate Banking Committee, decided to hold hearings on a bill that would authorize Treasury sales of U.S. gold and the Gold Medallion Act of 1978.

This proposal was nothing less than revolutionary. A scant five years earlier, Sen. Mark Hatfield, R-Ore., a numismatist and one-time ANA member, had proposed a gold commemorative coin for the bicentennial celebration. At the time, private gold ownership was still illegal. Direct response from the Nixon White House, and the Treasury Department was that the President would actually veto the legislation rather than allow a gold coin to be struck; the fear was that international markets would interpret this as demonetizing gold.

Flash forward five years. Sen. Jesse Helms, R-N.C., proposed one ounce and half ounce gold medallions and demanded a hearing, which Proxmire agreed to. I worked on draft remarks for Criswell's testimony. Private gold ownership had become legal on or after Dec. 31, 1974, but the Treasury had never liked the law change and did its level best to inhibit it at every turn.

In the course of more than 30 years as a lawyer, I have worked with many clients who have given speeches that I have written, and many who have testi-

Colorama
Ira & Larry Goldberg

Copy of 86
Stack's Rare Coins

1868 Dime Obverse & Reverse
Heritage Rare Coins

fied before Congressional committees, or other groups. None was so masterful as Criswell, who not only spoke from the written notes as if it were extemporaneous, but came across as very knowledgeable against stiff competition.

The other witnesses were principally U.S. Senators, Assistant Secretary of the Treasury Fred Bergsten and Edward Bernstein, formerly a high government official, who with Bergsten strongly opposed a government medallion or coin.

Stella Hackel, then the Mint director, was at the ANA convention. Dr. Alan Goldman, assistant director for technology, appeared with the official view: that it was impractical to strike medallions. Goldman noted the Mint had never undertaken a program to sell 2.24 million medals before and thought that equipment to produce it might cost $100,000 in otherwise unappropriated funds.

Further modifications of the physical plant would cost $250,000, he said, mailing to the Mint list another $500,000, and by the time he was done, he stated that the Mint would ask for "appropriations of approximately $5 million".

Bergsten, testifying on behalf of Treasury Secretary W. Michael Blumenthal, called "issuance of gold medallions ... unwise and inappropriate." He cited budgetary costs, claimed the issue of the medallions would "raise questions about the Government's determination to fight inflation," that it would "offer official encouragement to U.S. Citizens to invest in a highly speculative commodity", and "call into question the sincerity and credibility of the policy of eliminating the monetary role of gold".

Bernstein, formerly a Treasury economist, objected saying "my position is very simple. Gold is gold. ... My objection to the medallion is not that we are selling them gold, but that we are putting the symbol of the United States on it which will make it more attractive."

Criswell put it all into perspective in extemporaneous remarks responding to both: "I believe that if the United States issued one-half ounce and one ounce gold medallions ... in a year's time such coins might become a standard gold coin for trade throughout the world. I would rather see the words 'Freedom' and 'Liberty and Justice for All' on those coins than the South African seal or the hammer and sickle of Russia."

These remarks were prescient, particularly with the American eagle that eventually emerged following the production run of the American Arts Gold medallions – forming the best and most famous brand in the world.

The end result was the American Arts Gold Medallion Act. The design themes and mintages of the half ounce and one ounce (round) medallions that were the object of such derision:

American Arts Gold Medallions

Date	1/2oz Design	½ oz Mintage	1 oz Design	1 oz Mintage
1980	Marian Anderson	281,624	Grant Wood	312,709
1981	Willa Cather	97,331	Mark Twain	116,371
1982	Frank Lloyd Wright	348,305	Louis Armstrong	409,098
1983	Alexander Calder	74,571	Robert Frost	390,669
1984	John Steinbeck	32,572	Helen Hayes	33,546

Here are the medallions in a single table using mintage as a point of separating.

Date	Design	Mintage	Type
1984	John Steinbeck	32,572	½ oz
1984	Helen Hayes	33,546	1 oz
1983	Alexander Calder	74,571	½ oz
1981	Willa Cather	97,331	½ oz
1981	Mark Twain	116,371	1 oz
1980	Marian Anderson	281,624	½ oz
1980	Grant Wood	312,709	1 oz
1982	Frank Lloyd Wright	348,305	½ oz
1983	Robert Frost	390,669	1 oz
1982	Louis Armstrong	409,098	1 oz
Total		**2,096,796**	

1866 Dollar Obverse
Heritage Rare Coins

1868 Cent Obverse & Reverse
Heritage Rare Coins

By the way, it turns out that the Mint sold about two million medallions of which 1.26 million ounces made a one ounce coin and the remaining 800,000 odd coins were selling about 400,000 troy ounces.

E. State quarters

Begun as America's 50 State Commemorative Quarter circulating coin program, and finished as a 56 coin design program that included the District of Columbia and five exotic, foreign dominions that are U.S. Trust Territories, or, equivalent, the state quarter program offers one of the most exciting collecting opportunities in a generation.

Not only can you acquire a virtual coin collection from pure pocket change – errors, too – but the opportunity to own special silver examples, proofs, uncirculated pieces from pocket change, and to build a storehouse of value abounds.

Every 10 weeks from 1999 to 2009, the United States Mints at Philadelphia and Denver intend to produce a series of new commemorative quarter designs that circulate to this day throughout the United States, and probably the world. All 50 American states are honored as are Washington, D.C., Puerto Rico, Guam, American Samoa, American Virgin Islands and Mariana Islands. The 56 different coin design program is the largest and most ambitious commemorative coin program in history.

Delaware came first, both as a state to ratify the federal Constitution, and as a commemorative coin in this program. The design recommended by its governor: a depiction honoring Caesar Rodney's historic 80 mile ride from Dover to Philadelphia, where he cast the decisive vote in favor of American independence from Great Britain in 1776.

David Ganz with a U.S. Mint employee at the striking of the first Delaware State Quarter, Dec. 9, 1998.

That coin was first struck Dec. 7, 1998, in a first strike ceremony at the Philadelphia Mint. The hydraulic presses doubly struck uncirculated specimens that were slightly more expressive in design than circulation strikes, but not quite proofs. I was at the first strike and was privileged to fire up one of the presses and participate.

The resulting coinage is a long way from what was originally contemplated, and even proposed, by the Citizens Commemorative Coin Advisory Committee, which began a drumbeat in 1993 that reached a crescendo at a Congressional coin hearing in the summer of 1995.

What eventually emerged from a modest proposal to promote "our national ideals ... and our esteem as a nation" grew into a proposal that was described "the most tangible way to touch the lives of every American."

Every good idea that becomes reality has a hundred fathers. In my view,

Rep. Michael Castle, R-Del., is the legislative father. It was his proposal that directed the Mint to strike 50 different coin designs – one for each state over the next 10 years – that was introduced July 11, 1996. The occasion marked the one-year anniversary of hearings held before the subcommittee on Domestic and International Monetary Policy of the House Banking & Financial Services Committee, which Castle then chaired. It has charge of all coinage matters.

At that hearing on July 12, 1995, Castle had picked up on the remarks of a panelist who participated, Harvey G. Stack, to suggest a commemorative program honoring the first 13 colonies, just as Canada had commemorated each of its 12 provinces.

Several panelists present that day, including Beth Deisher, Dr. Alan Stahl of the American Numismatic Society, Philip Diehl, and me – both as a member of the CCCAC and as President of the American Numismatic Association – also picked up on that theme to suggest a commemorative program for America's states.

I could brag about the role that I had in bringing about this collectible, but instead I'll let Philip Diehl, former director of the Mint, give you the short version:

"The idea of a circulating commemorative has been around the hobby for decades, but frankly, good ideas are a dime a dozen. Far more rare is the ability to move an idea to reality, especially in the rough and tumble environment of Washington, D.C. From my vantage point, the lion's share of the credit for making the 50 States program a reality goes to David Ganz, for his persistence as an advocate, and Congressman Michael Castle for championing the proposal through Congress. David gradually persuaded me of the merits of the proposal, and we at the Mint, in turn, convinced Treasury and the Hill that it was doable. There are other claimants, to be sure, but the hobby owes a debt of gratitude to Congressman Castle and Mr. Ganz."

–Philip N. Diehl,
Director of the United States Mint, Washington, D.C.,
(Dec. 11, 1998).
Reprinted by permission of Numismatic News (Krause Publications, Iola, Wis.)

Let's assume that you've decided to make an investment in America's state quarters. The next question is how? There are almost as many ways that you can collect them as there are coin designs.

First you have to decide whether you want to collect a set of them, or if you'd prefer individual acquisition.

If, for example, you decide you want to acquire a set of uncirculated MS-70 state quarters, one of each date and mintmark – the best of the best, 56 "P" mintmarks, " 56 "D" mintmarks (no "S" because they are proof) – you're in for a disappointment.

The Professional Coin Grading Service (PCGS) and Numismatic Guaranty Corp. (NGC) has certified only a handful of MS-70 coins of all dates and mint-marks combined for all statehood quarters minted 1999-2009. (Just five MS-70 uncirculated coins of a total of 109,000 Mint State coins certified.

Over 18,000 proof-70s have been certified and slabbed or encapsulated for one service; over 212,000 proof-70 for the other, which also did 411,000 in proof-69).

Proof coins are more forgiving when it comes to perfection – and there are a six-figure worth of certified coins, where the uncirculated model, with hundreds of millions of coins to choose from, has few.

But the next thing to consider is how you might want to hold your collection (see chapter 6); generally, an album is the way to go, but you have to decide whether you want merely one of each design or one of each mintmark (there are albums that cater to that).

Here are some general thoughts on how you can collect and invest in statehood quarter coins:

- The complete set by date (56 coins), mintmark (168 coins), metal composition (additional 56 coins) method of strike (proofs, an additional 56 coins)
- Roll Sets
- By design (56 coins)
- By designer (sculptor, engraver)
- By theme
- By type
- By timeframe (i.e., 2004-2005, or some other arrangement).
- By circulated coin issues (i.e., Philadelphia and Denver, a 112-coin set) or of a single Mint
- By proof coin ("S" mint only) (56 coin type set)
- By condition (say MS-68 or proof 68, 69 or 70)
- Alphabetically by state (Alabama, Alaska, Arizona, Arkansas, etc.)
- By design, such as those showing state maps: Pennsylvania, Georgia, South Carolina, Ohio, Indiana, Louisiana, Illinois, Michigan, Texas, Minnesota, etc.
- By those depicting natural phenomena, such as the Connecticut charter oak tree, New Hampshire's late Old Man of the Mountain, Vermont maple trees, etc.
- By those depicting animals, such as Delaware's horse bearing Caesar Rodney, South Carolina's Carolina wren, Louisiana's pelican, Wisconsin's cow, the California eagle, Kansas bison, Nevada's wild mustangs, North Dakota's bison, etc.
- By historical figure, such as Delaware's Caesar Rodney, New Jersey's Washington crossing the Delaware, the Massachusetts Minute Man, Ohio's Neil Armstrong, Illinois' Lincoln, Alabama's Helen Keller, California's John Muir, etc.

- By error. There are an amazing number of double and triple struck state quarter coins and a collection of them, although expensive to acquire, is fascinating to look at side by side.
- With other coins struck in honor of one or more of the 56 states and territories. The U.S. Mint, at the behest of Congress, struck commemorative coins honoring the statehood of a number of states, ending with Iowa in 1946. These include: Alabama, Arkansas, California, Connecticut, Delaware, Illinois, Iowa, Maine, Maryland, Missouri, Oregon, Rhode Island, Texas, Vermont, and Virginia.
- By a combination of these methods.

There's no correct way to collect or invest in coins, and no incorrect way, except by definition. If you say you are collecting every design, then if you have "all" 40 designs, you are several short. You simply have to find out what works for you.

When I started collecting coins nearly a half century ago, I began because I found a 1906 Indian Head cent in pocket change and was fascinated by it. So when the statehood quarters came along, I decided to collect from pocket change – but not in the traditional way of one of every date and mintmark. I figured that one date and design was sufficient, so that a 56-coin collection would be complete. I also decided to make an investment in them, and chose error coins which have the added benefit of having a neat look to them.

To assist in the process, I bought a Commercial album that had one slot for each state – then 50 in all, now it would be 56 – and began to fill them up. After awhile, I wanted to do more and got a Littleton album that allowed me to put in both Philadelphia and Denver, and to have room for proof "S" San Francisco as well as silver proof coins. It's all about what you want to do and what you can afford.

While you can collect state quarters out of circulation, you can also collect them as certified coins of a certain grade. A set of the best of the best available would cost over $15,000, or an average of between $140 to $180 a coin.

You can also invest in the proof versions of state quarters, where it is advisable to look only at the high-end condition (Proof-68 or better).

Quite unlike the process of examining circulated coins for minor defects, proof coinage is made differently, looks very different, and in at least one respect is much easier to grade. Proof coins are struck on specially selected planchets that were previously cleaned in a cream of tartar solution that leaves them with a mirror-like sheen. They are produced on a hydraulic press that can strike several coins a minute at a maximum, contrasted with hundreds of coins a minute on a regular production press. Regular coins are struck just once, while proof coins are struck twice (or more) to bring up the design while simultaneously maintaining a mirror-like finish in the fields. Sometimes the design elements are struck in a mirror-like manner; other times they have a "matte" finish because of a production technique that has no effect on condition.

In the 21st century, virtually all proof coins, off the press and into the packet, will have a grade of at least Proof-65, and some will go higher quite easily. At an earlier time, even in the modern era of the 20th century, Mint production, storage, and coin interaction many times lowered the grade into the Proof-62 or Proof-63 range. It is always useful to remember that when it comes to the grades Proof-68, Proof-69 and Proof-70, there really aren't a lot of coins that merit these descriptions. Hence, even though the Mint might offer a proof set at $32.50 complete with the original 50 state coins, a single 50 state coin 18 months out of production in Proof-68 Condition typically had a $30 price tag, which means a five-fold return on the investment if all coins in the set were of the same grade and condition.

A word about buying "raw" proof coins that you intend to submit for subsequent slabbing. Traditionally, collectors have emphasized the condition of the obverse over the condition of the reverse. Thus, if a coin was MS-65 on the obverse and not quite as nice on the reverse, it probably would get a higher designation of MS-65. On the other hand, historically, if the reverse was MS-65 and the obverse was MS-63 or MS-64, it would never achieve an MS-65 grade.

The verdict is not in on this yet, but it is apparent because of the heavy focus on the 56 states and territories portion of the program, that collectors will give far more emphasis to the reverse side of the series than to the obverse. The little "scratch" or the little "ding" or contact mark on the reverse will more likely have a greater substantive effect on condition than before.

State quarters are widely available, but some are downright scarce – especially in superior condition. Here are some rough stats to keep in mind:

- NGC has had 109,000 Mint State submissions.
- There are 28,700 MS-67 state quarters that NGC has certified.
- PCGS has certified 397,000 state quarters as PF-69.
- NGC has certified 212,965 state quarters as PF-70.
- NGC has certified 412,000 state quarters as PF-69.

The key to modern coinage investment is knowledge. That means knowing mintages, how many have been encapsulated (slabbed) and what condition is available. Up-to-date information on NGC's slabbing practices is on the Numismatic Guaranty Web site and the Professional Coin Grading Service (PCGS) Web site.

Looking at state quarters from the standpoint of unlocking future value requires patience, fortitude and knowledge of the facts. The hardest thing to acquire is basic knowledge (the mintage production figures of each date and mintmark.) Here's the data, sorted, so that low mintage coins are listed first, highest last. The 2009 designs for Washington, D.C., and the remainder of the commonwealth or territorial series is where these coins found a good home that lasts today – if low mintage is a sole criteria:

State Quarters with Mintages under 100 million

Mintmark	State	Ter #	Date	Mintage	Mintmark	State	Ter #	Date	Mintage
P	MARIANA	56	2009	35,200,000	P	Am SAMOA	54	2009	42,600,000
D	MARIANA	56	2009	37,600,000	P	GU	53	2009	45,000,000
D	Am SAMOA	54	2009	39,600,000	P	PR	52	2009	53,200,000
D	VI	55	2009	41,000,000	P	DC	51	2009	83,600,000
P	VI	55	2009	41,000,000	D	PR	52	2009	86,000,000
D	GU	53	2009	42,600,000	D	DC	51	2009	88,800,000

State Quarters with Mintages over 100 million

Mintmark	State	Ter #	Date	Mintage	Mintmark	State	Ter #	Date	Mintage
D	OK	46	2008	194,600,000	D	IA	29	2004	251,800,000
P	IA	29	2004	213,800,000	D	UT	45	2007	253,200,000
P	TN	17	2002	217,200,000	P	HI	50	2008	254,000,000
P	ME	23	2003	217,400,000	D	AK	49	2008	254,000,000
P	OK	46	2008	222,000,000	P	UT	45	2007	255,000,000
P	MO	24	2003	225,000,000	D	MT	41	2007	256,240,000
P	AL	22	2003	225,000,000	P	MT	41	2007	257,000,000
D	MI	26	2004	225,800,000	P	CA	31	2005	257,200,000
P	IL	21	2003	225,800,000	D	TX	28	2004	263,000,000
P	WI	30	2004	226,400,000	D	CA	31	2005	263,200,000
D	WI	30	2004	226,800,000	P	KS	34	2005	263,400,000
P	AR	25	2003	228,000,000	D	HI	50	2008	263,600,000
D	MO	24	2003	228,200,000	D	AZ	48	2008	265,000,000
D	AR	25	2003	229,800,000	P	WA	42	2007	265,200,000
D	ME	23	2003	231,400,000	D	SD	40	2006	265,800,000
D	AL	22	2003	232,400,000	D	NE	37	2006	273,000,000
P	MI	26	2004	233,800,000	P	CO	38	2006	274,800,000
D	IL	21	2003	237,400,000	P	NV	36	2006	277,000,000
P	MN	32	2005	239,600,000	P	TX	28	2004	278,800,000
P	FL	27	2004	240,200,000	D	WA	42	2007	280,000,000
D	FL	27	2004	241,600,000	D	OH	15	2002	286,468,000
P	WY	44	2007	243,600,000	D	ID	43	2007	286,800,000
P	NM	47	2008	244,200,000	D	MS	20	2002	289,600,000
D	NM	47	2008	244,400,000	P	MS	20	2002	290,000,000
P	AZ	48	2008	244,600,000	D	CO	38	2006	294,200,000
P	SD	40	2006	245,000,000	P	ID	43	2007	294,600,000
D	MN	32	2005	248,400,000	D	NJ	3	1999	299,028,000
P	AK	49	2008	251,800,000	D	KS	34	2005	300,000,000

Mintmark	State	Ter #	Date	Mintage	Mintmark	State	Ter #	Date	Mintage
P	AND	39	2006	305,800,000	P	RI	13	2001	423,000,000
D	NV	36	2006	312,800,000	P	VT	14	2001	423,400,000
P	OR	33	2005	316,200,000	D	NC	12	2001	427,876,000
P	NE	37	2006	318,000,000	D	RI	13	2001	447,100,000
D	WY	44	2007	320,800,000	P	GA	4	1999	451,188,000
D	IN	19	2002	327,200,000	D	VT	14	2001	459,404,000
P	PA	2	1999	349,000,000	D	GA	4	1999	488,744,000
P	KY	16	2001	353,000,000	D	NH	9	2000	495,976,000
D	WV	35	2005	356,200,000	D	MA	6	2000	535,184,000
D	PA	2	1999	358,332,000	D	MD	7	2000	556,532,000
D	AND	39	2006	359,000,000	D	SC	8	2000	566,208,000
P	OH	15	2002	361,600,000	D	NY	11	2001	619,640,000
P	LA	18	2002	362,000,000	P	NC	12	2001	627,600,000
P	IN	19	2002	362,600,000	P	MA	6	2000	628,600,000
P	NJ	3	1999	363,200,000	D	VA	10	2000	651,616,000
P	WV	35	2005	365,400,000	P	NY	11	2001	655,400,000
D	KY	16	2001	370,564,000	D	CT	5	1999	657,880,000
P	DE	1	1999	373,400,000	P	NH	9	2000	673,040,000
D	DE	1	1999	401,424,000	P	MD	7	2000	678,200,000
D	LA	18	2002	402,204,000	P	CT	5	1999	688,744,000
D	OR	33	2005	404,000,000	P	SC	8	2000	742,576,000
D	TN	17	2002	414,832,000	P	VA	10	2000	943,000,000

It's hard to look at state quarters and the territorial counterparts and not want to draw comparisons. Indeed, you can't help but compare Washington quarters of the 1950s – with relatively low mintages (say 14 million for the 1953-S) and then look at the Mariana Islands coinage with a 35 million mintage for circulation in 2009.

Here's why.

The 1953 estimated U.S. population was 160 million people. Today, its estimated at 315 million, or 96 percent higher. The ratio of 14 million to 160 million people contrasts to equivalent of 27.5 million mintage to be in equal demand.

But try 1955 (18 million quarters struck) and you have that near perfect match up (35.4 million). In MS-67, the 1955 quarter is a $360 coin in *Numis-Media*'s first 2010 issue (Modern #60).

State quarters themselves, if certified (slabbed) in superior condition, can be a nice purchase. A complete set (50 states, Washington, D.C., and the five former colonial territories) using "highest price" at auction, can run over $20,000! Check out the citations on the accompanying chart which shows why Teletrade is so widely popular and successful for these coins.

In the chart that follows, each state was given one coin date (including mint-mark) and total (non-proof) uncirculated coinage with the price at auction realized for the collector to truly appreciate what transpired. A complete set of these 56 coins and nothing more is over $15,000.

State Quarters Auction Prices Listed by State

State	Date	Auction	Grade	Price	State	Date	Auction	Grade	Price
AL	2003-P	11-28-06TT	MS-68	$90	NM	2008-P	9-25-08TT	MS-67	$75
AK	2003-D	11-18-06TT	MS-68	$120	NY	2001-P	11-19-06TT	MS-69	$1,050
AZ	2008-d	11-16-08TT	MS69	$600	NC	2001-D	11-26-06TT	MS-68	$320
AR	2003-D	11-8-06TT	MS-68	$120	AND	2006-D	10-23-06TT	MS-69	$65
CA	2005-D	11-3-06TT	MS-69	$300	OH	2002-P	5-31-03H	MS-69	$494
CO	2006-D	10-3-06TT	MS-69	$45	OK	2008P/D	10-05-08TT	MS-69	$360
CT	1999-P	10-11-06TT	MS-68	$120	OR	2005-D	2-26-06TT	MS-69	$130
DE	1999-D	10-23-06TT	MS-67	$260	PA	1999-D	11-19-06TT	MS-67	$340
FL	2004-P	05-09-05TT	MS-69	$320	RI	2001-D	12-11-06TT	MS-68	$525
GA	1999-P	10-9-06TT	MS-67	$280	SC	2000-P	10-23-06TT	MS-67	$70
HI	2008-P	11-30-08TT	MS-69	$275	SD	2006-P	11-29-06TT	MS-69	$70
ID	2007-D	02-08-08TT	MS-69	$50	TN	2002-D	11-02-05TT	MS-68	$140
IL	2003-D	121806TT	MS-68	$475	TX	2004-P	10-11-06TT	MS-68	$50
IN	2002-P	053103Her	MS-69	$690	UT	2007-P	7-30-08TT	MS-69	$80
IA	2004-D	10-18-06TT	MS-69	$130	VT	2001-D	11-19-06TT	MS-68	$70
KS	2005-P	8-28-06TT	ANACS65	$70	VA	2000-P	10-25-0-6TT	MS-68	$110
KY	2001-D	5-15-05TT	MS-68	$210	WA	2007D	2-17-08TT	MS-67	$28
LA	2002-P	12-09-03H	MS-69	$346	WV	2005-D	12-13-06TT	MS-69	$1,600
ME	2003-P	11-12-06TT	MS 68	$525	WI	2004-D (error)	07-06H	MS-66	$2,530
MD	2000-D	11-19-06TT	MS-68	$260	WY	2007-D	072708TT	MS-65	$85
MA	2000-D	5-15-05TT	MS-68	$140	DC	2009-D	7-20-09TT	MS-67	$60
MI	2004-D	10-11-05TT	MS-69	$625	PR	2009-D	7-20-09TT	MS--67	$60
MN	2005-D	9-13-06TT	MS-69	$200	Guam	2009-P&D	4-22-10TT	MS-67(2)	$50
MS-	2002-D	12-3-06TT	MS-68	$33	AM Samoa	2009-P	1-27-10TT	MS-67	$45
MO	2003-D	10-11-06TT	MS-68	$360	V ISLANDS	2009-P	2-10-10TT	MS-68	$210
MT	2007-P	5-07TT	MS-67	$55	Mariana	2009-P	3-31-10	MS-67	$33
NE	2006-D	9-24-06TT	MS-69	$60					
NV	2006-D	10-23-06TT	MS-69	$100	TT=Teletrade			Total	$16,144
NH	2000-P	10-11-06TT	MS-68	$210	H=Heritage			Average	$288
NJ	1999-D	10-11-06TT	MS-67	$425					

The key to studying this chart is to see how it goes from $28 a coin to over $2,500.

State Quarters Lowest to Highest Price

State	Date	Auction Date	Grade	Price	State	Date	Auction Date	Grade	Price
WA	2007-D	2-17-08TT	MS-67	$28.00	IA	2004-D	10-18-06TT	MS-69	$130.00
MS	2002 D	12-3-06TT	MS-68	$33.00	TN	2002-D	11-02-05TT	MS-68	$140.00
Guam	2007		MS-60	$36.00	MA	2000-D	5-15-05TT	MS-68	$140.00
Mariana		NONE	NONE POSTED	$45.00	MN	2005-D	9-13-06TT	MS-69	$200.00
AM Samoa	2009-P	1-27-2010TT	MS- 67	$45.00	NH	2000-P	10-11-06TT	MS-68	$210.00
CO	2006-D	10-3-06TT	MS-69	$45.00	KY	2001-D	5-15-05TT	MS-68	$210.00
TX	2004-P	10-11-06TT	MS-68	$50.00	DE	1999-D	10-23-06TT	MS-67	$260.00
ID	2007-D	2-08-08TT	MS-69	$50.00	MD	2000-D	11-19-06TT	MS-68	$260.00
MT	2007-P	5-07TT	MS-67	$55.00	HI	2008-P	11-30-08TT	MS-69	$275.00
DC	2009-D	7-20-09TT	MS-67	$60.00	GA	1999-P	10-9-06TT	MS-67	$280.00
NE	2006-D	9-24-06TT	MS-69	$60.00	CA	2005-D	11-3-06TT	MS--69	$300.00
V ISLANDS	2009-P	11-28-09TT	MS-68	$60.00	NC	2001-D	11-26-06TT	MS-68	$320.00
PR	2009-D	7-20-09TT	MS-67	$60.00	FL	2004-P	05-09-05TT	MS-69	$320.00
AND	2006-D	10-23-06TT	MS-69	$65.00	PA	1999-D	11-19-06TT	MS-67	$340.00
SD	2006-P	11-29-06TT	MS-69	$70.00	LA	2002-P	12-09-03H	MS-69	$346.00
VT	2001-D	11-19-06TT	MS-68	$70.00	OK	2008-P/D	100508TT	MS-69	$360.00
SC	2000-P	10-23-06TT	MS-67	$70.00	MO	2003-D	10-11-06TT	MS-68	$360.00
KS	2005-P	8-28-06TT	ANACS65	$70.00	NJ	1999-D	101106TT	MS-67	$425.00
NM	2008-P	92508TT	MS-67	$75.00	IL	2003-D	121806TT	MS-68	$475.00
UT	2007-P	73008TT	MS-69	$80.00	OH	2002-P	053103H	MS-69	$494.00
WY	2007-D	072708TT	MS-65	$85.00	RI	2001-D	12-11-06TT	MS-68	$525.00
AL	2003-P	11-28-06TT	MS--68	$90.00	ME	2003-P	11-12-06TT	MS-68	$525.00
NV	2006-D	10-23-06TT	MS-69	$100.00	AZ	2008-D	11-16-08TT	MS-69	$600.00
VA	2000-P	10-25-0-6TT	MS-68	$110.00	MI	2004-D	10-11-05TT	MS-69	$625.00
CT	1999-P	10-11-06TT	MS-68	$120.00	IN	2002-P	053103Her	MS-69	$690.00
AR	2003-D	11-8-06TT	MS--68	$120.00	NY	2001-P	11-19-06TT	MS-69	$1,050.00
AK	2003-D	11-18-06TT	MS--68	$120.00	WV	2005-D	12-13-06TT	MS-69	$1,600.00
OR	2005-D	022606TT	MS-69	$130.00	WI	2004-D (error)	07-06H	MS-66	$2,530.00

Mint errors in the state quarter series are more than usual. Wrong planchet (quarter design on nickel planchet; dollar planchet) are rare but widely known. Here is general pricing for some errors (misplaced planchets).(Prices courtesy of Fred Weinberg, Fred Weinberg, Inc.). Examine the coins themselves more closely and view a 21.2mm diameter planchet (nickel-sized) versus a 24.3mm quarter-sized planchet. The difference is 3.1mm – or about 0.1168 inches. That silly millimeter longer represents a $1,500 price difference.

State Quarter Errors Prices

State	Ter #	Date	Philadelphia	Denver
DE	1	1999		Nickel $825
PA	2	1999	Sacagewea dollar $4,600	Nickel $995
NJ	3	1999	Nickel $,2000-$2,500	
GA	4	1999	Dollar $13,000	
MA	6	2000	Dollar $13000	
MD	7	2000	Nickel $22,000	Dollar, $8,000
IL	21	2003	Nickel $1,700-$2,500	
FL	27	2004	Nickel $1700-2750	

Error coins among state quarters have a bright future in part because that is a segment of the market that is growing, in part because of incredible eye appeal, and partly because they are scarce. Here are general values for defined errors (Prices courtesy Fred Weinberg, Fred Weinberg, Inc.).

Dbl Struck Reported Struck Twice	Multi-Struck 3-4 Times	Obverse Clad Missing	Reverse Clad Missing	Cud Reverse	Off-Center Minor	Off-Center Major	Rotated Reverse	Clipped
$550	$750	$375	$1,250	NF	$125	$250	$250	$100

Granddaddy of all of the state quarter errors is the $1.25 coin – a state quarter married to a Sacagewea dollar coin. (Some would call this a dollar coin error, but the coin is demonstrably part of the statehood quarter series by virtue of its design). With a state quarter obverse (undated) and a Sacagewea die reverse (also no date), there's no way of telling exactly when it was produced, but the price is well known: $56,300 for an NGC MS-67 version of a golden state quarter obverse, Sacagewea dollar reverse, on a golden dollar planchet in a May 2001 Heritage coin auction

The cataloged sale of the most valuable statehood quarter mint error: a Philadelphia Mint-manufactured 2000-P $1 Sacagewea dollar muled with a state quarter dollar of unknown date in NGC-MS 67. It has an interesting history. It was sold on eBay to collector Jeff Allen for $41,295. Since that time at least six other pieces have come to light (only one of which is equal in grade to the Allen piece). Heritage sold a slightly less prestigious uncirculated example in MS-66 in their 2000 ANA sale at Philadelphia for $31,250.

The mule and its owner, Jeff Allen, were featured on the Discovery Channel's "The Best Kept Secrets of Money," broadcast on March 15, 2001. A muling error on a circulating American coin was unknown until this piece was discovered and, as such, it represents a numismatic discovery of the greatest importance.

"Mules" or "muling errors" of rare patterns and restrikes were produced intentionally during the 19th century and have long been known to exist. Heritage's view as cataloguer and auctioneer:"A mule that combines the obverse and reverse of two different denominations would seem to be the most unusual mistake that can be made in the Mint."

Despite some initial speculation that it may have been intentionally produced by a Mint employee, on June 19, 2001, the U.S. Mint issued a press release acknowledging the Sacagewea Dollar-Washington quarter mule as a legitimate error. Apparently, it was produced when an obverse Sacagewea die cracked, and was accidentally replaced by a quarter obverse die. Upon discovery by Mint employees, several thousand mules were apparently retrieved and destroyed.

There are two varieties of this extremely rare error known. This piece is from the second die pair, which is characterized by a curved die crack on the lower portion of the eagle's left (facing) wing. Two other faint cracks project from the rightmost points of the first two stars just below that same wing. the other die variety (sold at the 2000 ANA Sale) shows a die crack through the "F" in OF down to the eagle's wing.

The coin itself has virtually perfect surfaces that display the lustrous golden color common to Sacagewea dollars with just a hint of rose patina.

Another version is the overstrike, a $3,200 error. Heritage sold one in 2006, also from the Philadelphia Mint, a 2000-P $1 Sacagewea dollar – a double denomination struck on a Maryland quarter – in PCGS MS-67. That coin was described as a lustrous superb gem, beautifully preserved and toned in lovely steel-blue and chestnut colors. Although well struck, traces of the Maryland quarter undertype remain visible. the 2000 date from the undertype is visible beneath the Sacagewea mintmark, and a tree branch from the Maryland design is seen on her shoulder beneath the slumbering baby.

And yet another type is the Sacagewea dollar struck on a state quarter blank planchet– a $2,760 item at a Heritage May, 2007 auction that again came from the Philadelphia Mint: a 2000-P $1 Sacagewa dollar struck on a quarter planchet in NGC-MS-66. The confirming factor is the weight of 5.7 grams, making this an off-metal error that was both well struck and fully lustrous, with a hint of gold toning visits the pristine surfaces. the rims are broad and have a stretched appearance, where metal struggled to reach the collar.

Dennis Baker of NumisMedia, (www.numismedia.com) is a good friend and a true gem uncirculated guy. He searched out and reliably reported prices for state quarters. While the pricing here is no longer unique, it is very, very accurate. He now uses them in NumisMedia's "Wholesale Market Dealer's Price Guide".

Baker provided current fair market values for coins of Philadelphia (P or plain) and Denver (D mintmarks) in superior grades (MS-65 and higher). Fair market value prices listed are for certified coins only (usually PCGS, NGC, or ANACS). Raw coins may bring substantially less. Prices may fluctuate considerably as new issues are brought on the market and certified. As populations increase in a particular grade, coins may be easier to obtain and prices may fall. A comprehensive listing of fair market values of American coins is found on the Web site of NumisMedia, http: //www.numismedia.com.

There are some good investment buys that can be made among state quarters; all that it takes is a little knowledge, and some research, adoption of an approach, and time.

New Plus Grades from PCGS for MS-63+ to MS-65+

Chapter 10

GRADING OF COINS

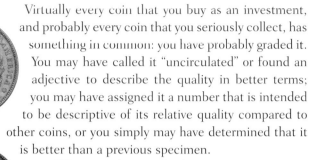

VF-45
Teletrade

Fine-12
Teletrade

Virtually every coin that you buy as an investment, and probably every coin that you seriously collect, has something in common: you have probably graded it. You may have called it "uncirculated" or found an adjective to describe the quality in better terms; you may have assigned it a number that is intended to be descriptive of its relative quality compared to other coins, or you simply may have determined that it is better than a previous specimen.

What exactly is grading?

Grading is an attempt to quantify, and describe, the various states of preservation (or condition) that a coin is in. It is not uniform; whether numerical descriptions or their adjectival counterparts are utilized, they differ from person to person, dealer to dealer, buyer to buyer, and from seller to seller.

Generally speaking, the better the condition of a coin, the more it is worth. A coin may be in poor condition and still be quite valuable; but if the "poor" condition coin is instead in "fine" condition, it will be worth more than its lesser-graded counterpart.

Most of the coins purchased by you for investment will be uncirculated coins, yet widely respected commentators still do not agree on how to describe differing types of uncirculated coins. In Dr. Richard Doty's *The MacMillan Encyclopedic Dictionary of Numismatics* (1982), he refers to "MS-65s, sometimes called 'choice uncirculateds,'... [which] will command much higher prices than MS-60s ..."

In *Penny Whimsy*, (1958) Dr. Sheldon (who invented the numerical grading scale) said, "The MS-65 is a coin that would be a perfect MS-70 except for some small minor blemish. It may lack full mint luster, or some microscopic or almost negligible blemish may be demonstrable. There may be a spot of discoloration, a fingermark or a barely discernible nick."

I have surveyed and read dozens of books that deal with grading in both practical and abstract terms.

Grading differences are perhaps best summed up by Q. David Bowers, a former president of the ANA and also the Professional Numismatists Guild, in his book *Adventures with Rare Coins* (1979):

"Often five different sellers will assign five different grades to the same coin, perhaps differing just slightly but still differing, often with important financial consequences ... ss the evaluation of the grade or condition of a coin is a largely subjective matter, experts can legitimately differ."

How is it that coin grade descriptions, and hence opinions, can differ?

Grading, is inherently subjective and represents one person's view as to its state of preservation, and, if uncirculated, the degree or extent of pleasure (eye appeal) that it beholds to the purveyor.

The principal problem with numerical grading, of course, is that it gives the impression of exactitude and precision and it is, in the final analysis, little more than a subjective view of the cataloger.

Grading is an art and not an exact science. More precisely, grading is a matter of opinion. Differences of opinion may occur among graders as to a particular coin, and any grader could conceivably change his interpretation of the grading standards over the years.

When the *ANA Official Grading Standards for United States Coins* book was published in 1978, it represented a new grading system, previously untried. * * *

The grading standards as enumerated in the book were and are not precise, with the descriptions lending themselves to different interpretations. The market-place composed of collectors and dealers has tightened its interpretation in recent years.

1868 Half Dime
Heritage Rare Coins

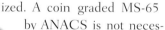

1868 Quarter Reverse
Heritage Rare Coins

Even with the creation of commercial grading services that utilize a "sight unseen" market for purposes of buying, and selling, grading (and pricing) has not standard-ized. A coin graded MS-65 by ANACS is not neces-sarily the same price as a coin graded by PCGS (the Professional Coin Grading Ser-vice), and a PCGS-graded coin may not be the same price as one graded by the Nu-mismatic Certification Institute (NCI) or Numismatic Guaranty Corporation (NGC).

1876 5-Cent Obverse
Heritage Rare Coins

1823 $5
Heritage Rare Coins

Grading of rare coins, even with profes-sional services doing the bulk of the work on ex-pensive, hard-to-grade items, still hasn't solved the issue that the description of a coin remains more of an art than it is a science. (To the extent that 1 to 70 is inadequate to describe a coin, 1 to 100 offers more territory but no more precision).

1916 25-Cent Obverse
Heritage Rare Coins

Excellent text books such as a Jim Halperin's *NCI Grading Guide*, and the *Official PCGS Grading Guide* edited so well by Scott Travers, go a long way toward making the process scientific and actually can teach reliable techniques that collectors, investors and dealers can consistently use.

Respected numismatist, Steve Ivy, conducted a hands-on survey whose purpose was to hire a professional numismatist for his company, Heritage Auctions. World class graders examined a series of coins and placed grades on them.

1921 50-Cent Obverse
Heritage Rare Coins

At issue was their ability to grade to the marketplace. The prize was a job with Heritage, one of the world's largest, and fastest growing coin companies. Across the board there were significant variations of one point, two points or even more on the MS-60 to MS-70 uncirculated grading scale. The world class graders who applied could not agree on a majority of the grades.

A major Court case was decided Jan. 27, 1998, in a ruling by the U.S. Tax Court in Washington on the estate of Ed Trompeter, a well-known collector of proof gold coinage and other rarities.

Trompeter's estate became embroiled in a claim of tax fraud because of allegations that the gold coin collection, part of which was sold by Superior, was deliberately undervalued. A $14.8 million fraud penalty assessed by the IRS was the subject of the dispute.

The court's decision recites that over 180 coins were submitted to PCGS for grading. The conclusion: 69 were Proof-63, 78 were Proof-64 and 12 were Proof-65. (There was just one found to be Proof-66, one Proof-67 and one Proof-69).

Trompeter's gold was then shipped to Numismatic Guaranty Corporation, whose experts had a different view of part of the collection. They agreed that there was one Proof-69, but after that they parted company.

NGC's found five Proof-67, 22 that graded Proof-66, 51 that graded Proof-65, 71 that graded Proof-64, and only 21 that graded proof-63. In contrast to the 15 pieces PCGS found to be 65 or better, NGC ruled 78 to be in that state of preservation.

Tax Court Decision in Trompeter Estate

	PCGS	NGC		PCGS	NGC
Proof 69	1	0	Proof 64	78	71
Proof 67	1	5	Proof 63	69	15
Proof 66	1	22	Total	162	164
Proof 65	12	51			

This is not the end of it, however, for the Tax Court had to decide who was right in the grade. Other experts were provided compliments of both sides in the litigation – the IRS and the Trompeter Estate.

In the final analysis, the court rejected all of the experts save one: the decedent himself, Ed Trompeter, who had placed a value on the coins that Superior sold at auction before his death. Their reasoning: he had predicted within 2 percent the selling prices received at auction.

The standards set out in the ANA guide and its successors are quite vague and leave a great deal of room for interpretation. For example, an MS-65 will have "fewer bag marks than usual," but there is no definition of what is "usual." An MS-60 will have "a moderate number of bag marks." An MS-63 will be somewhere in between. What coin will fit within each level will vary from series to series, from design to design, and, most importantly for the consequences in the marketplace, from grader to grader.

In a case brought by the Federal Trade Commission alleging grading and pricing violations, the Court tried to explain the difference in various grading systems.

"¶19. The value of a rare coin depends on its condition. In evaluating a coin's condition or "grade," a number of factors are considered, including: (1) the coin's overall appearance and eye appeal; (2) the number of marks and scratches it has; (3) its toning, color, and tarnish; and (4) its "strike" or the clarity of the impression made in the minting process. Different grading systems and individual graders may weight these factors differently in grading coins. Thus, for example, some graders may be more strict about overall eye appeal, while others give more emphasis to the amount of rubbing and bag marks.

In the 5th edition of the ANA *Grading Guide*, Q. David Bowers writes in the introduction:

"[i]t is not the slight differences which concern us here; it is serious or major differences. Unfortunately, it is not easy to define what major differences are. The problem is that grading is a matter of opinion, and experts may differ. I cite several examples:

"(1) I have in my office a silver dollar sent to a leading grading service on three different occasions, and it came back with three different grades.

"(2) Barry J. Cutler, formerly of the Federal Trade Commission, told a sym-

| AG3 | Good-4 | Good 6 | VG8 | Fine-12 |
| Heritage (www.HA.Com) | Teletrade | Heritage (www.HA.Com) | Heritage (www.HA.Com) | Teletrade |

posium at the ANA convention in Seattle, August 1990, that he had conducted a blind test of grading accuracy. Although professional graders had claimed before hand that they were so accurate that they could consistently tell the difference between a coin graded MS-63 and one graded "MS-63 plus" (or very slightly better than MS-63; plus marks are not part of the ANA grading system), in a test conducted by Mr. Cutler, expert opinions for the same specimen of a Saint-Gaudens $20 gold piece ranged from AU-58 to MS-64.

"(3) In 1990, I sent an uncirculated 1893-S Morgan dollar, one of the most highly prized varieties in the series, to a leading grading service where it was graded as MS-63. I then sent it to another leading service where it was graded MS-65. At the time the market difference between the MS-63 and MS-65 grade was approximately $100,000!"

Bowers concludes that "most experts can agree with a point or two in the Uncirculated range," but goes on to state that when it is claimed that "a difference of two points, three points or some other difference... indicated overgrading,... the situation is not that simple."

To understand the numerical grading system, it helps to visualize a 12-inch ruler, with the numbers running from left to right. Generically, "good" is at the left end, perhaps at the 1-inch mark, and refers to well-worn coins of the type that had served as pocket change for a substantial period of time. The "fine" coin is in the middle, perhaps at the 6-inch mark; its design elements are all quite clear, but it, too, has been in circulation. The typical so-called uncirculated coin falls at the 10-inch mark and still has its mint sheen, without a lot of contact marks on its surface.

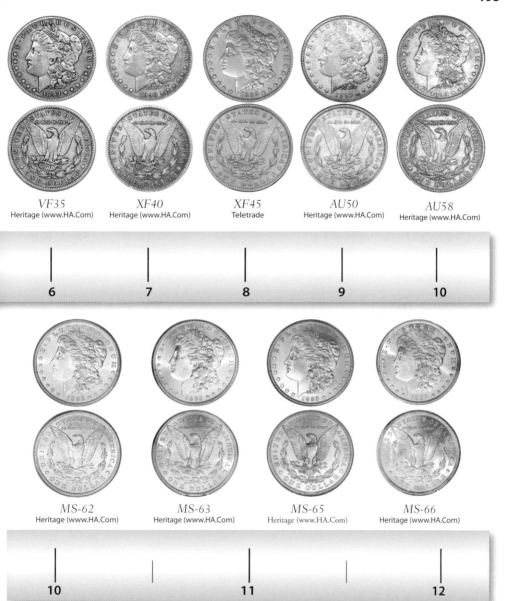

VF35
Heritage (www.HA.Com)

XF40
Heritage (www.HA.Com)

XF45
Teletrade

AU50
Heritage (www.HA.Com)

AU58
Heritage (www.HA.Com)

6   7   8   9   10

MS-62
Heritage (www.HA.Com)

MS-63
Heritage (www.HA.Com)

MS-65
Heritage (www.HA.Com)

MS-66
Heritage (www.HA.Com)

10   11   12

From 10 to 12 inches on the ruler are the other, "better" grades of uncirculated coins.

In 1958, a book entitled *A Guide to the Grading of United States Coins*, by Martin R. Brown and John W. Dunn, revolutionized the field of coin grading. For the first time, it systematized in comprehensive fashion the description of all circulated coins. Another important book on the subject of coin grading was *Photograde*, by James F. Ruddy, which was published in 1970. This book marked the first commercial attempt to systematically photograph each type of coin in all of its varying circulating grades. It also demonstrated that photographs could reveal the differences among coins in various states of grading preservation.

Creation of the American Numismatic Authentication Trust (ANAT), later ANACS (originally the American Numismatic Association Certification Service), was another milestone. This trust was formed by the American Numismatic Association for the purpose of, among other things, funding the writing and publication of a major treatise covering circulated and uncirculated coins. The resulting volume, entitled *Official A.N.A. Grading Standards for United States Coins*, is now in its sixth revised edition (2005) and is notable for the fact that its grading criteria are systematically and explicitly listed in a form that can be utilized by others for both circulated and uncirculated conditions.

There are other grading guides, too (see bibliography) but in terms of significance, the issuance in 1997 of the *Official Guide to Coin Grading and Counterfeit Detection*, a Professional Coin Grading Service publication edited by Scott A. Travers, is a major milestone since it systematically describes coin grading in circulated and uncirculated states of preservation, by series, and explains how a third party grading service functions.

Given the number of organizations that perform grading, it is presently impossible to speak of a "market standard" or of any single standard within the coin industry. A fact of life for investors, coin collectors and buyers is simply that, even today, there are numerous and often inconsistent standards for grading coins. Likewise, there is a broad range of pricing in the rare coin field that can and does differ for identically described coins--even for coins advertised several pages apart in the same periodical.

Here is a non-exclusive list of major coin grading services in 2010 along with their Web sites:

Coin Grading Services

Acronym	Name	Web Site	Location
ACCGS	American Coin Club Grading Service	www.accgs.org	Beverly Hills, CA
ACG	ASA Accugrade, Inc	www.asa-accugrade.com	Melbourne, FL
ANACS	ANACS Certification Service, Inc	www.anacs.com	Austin, TX
DGS	Dominion Grading Service	www.dominiongrading.com	Virginia Beach, VA
HCGS	Hallmark Coin Grading Services	www.hcgshallmark.com	Vancouver, BC, Canada
ICG	Independent Coin Grading Company	www.icgcoin.com	Tampa, FL
NCGS	National Coin Grading Service	www.nationalcoingradingservice.com	Scottsdale, AZ
NGC	Numismatic Guaranty Corporation	www.ngccoin.com	Sarasota, FL
NTC	Numistrust Corporation	www.numistrust.com	Boca Raton, FL
PCGS	Professional Coin Grading Service	www.pcgs.com	Newport Beach, CA
PCI	PCI Inc.	www.pcicoins.com	Rossville. GA
SEGS	Sovereign Entities Grading Service	www.segscoins.com	Chattanooga, TN
SGS	Star Grading Services	www.stargrading.org	Bellville, OH

Coins may be graded using either adjectives, a numerical description, or some combination of the two, and as Dr. Richard Doty notes, "along with rarity and demand, they establish the buying and selling prices for coins, tokens, paper money, etc."

Unlike many other objects d'art, the condition or state of preservation of a coin cannot be improved. Metal cannot be added to or "repaired". It can, of course, worsen with time, which is to say that it can deteriorate, or its grade can worsen.

It can never, however, get better.[16] Despite this, the subjectivity of grading can allow for differing interpretations as to the grade or condition of a coin – so much so that a coin's description can appear to "improve" its grade from one owner to the next.

For many years, an adjectival description was utilized based on the following scale: poor condition, fair condition, good condition, very good condition, fine condition, very fine condition, extremely fine condition, about uncirculated condition, and uncirculated condition. Poor condition is the least impressive state of preservation, and can commonly be referred to as a worn coin, not unlike the buffalo nickels, dateless with little facial or other detail which frequently appeared in pocket change two decades ago. Uncirculated is the best condition, though it is not fully descriptive of what the term actually means.

Technically, the coin cannot be said to be "without any circulation" at all, since it is the act of placing the coin in circulation which removes it from the Mint.

Rather, uncirculated is said to refer to an absence of wear on the metal surface of the coin, and to mean that the coin has not been in general circulation.

Precisely how a coin is described to refer to its grade is the subject of considerable discussion, and debate, though there is less debate over whether a coin is "uncirculated" or "circulated" than with degrees in those various categories.

What, though, about the uncirculated grade and with coins like silver dollars, or others?

Grading, there, is subject to considerable discussion as to how each of these series are to be described. Even seemingly identical numerical descriptions and their adjectival counterparts differ from person to person, dealer to dealer, buyer to buyer, and seller to seller. It differs among experts, and amateurs, experienced and inexperienced collectors. Most disputes and litigation center on grades of MS-63 and above and whether a coin sold as MS-65 is that grade or an MS-64, or lower.

One thing that probably will become apparent: when it comes time to invest in coins, whether for your rare coin retirement or for other purposes, the better the condition you can acquire, the greater the anticipated return is likely to be.

Chapter 11

AFFORDABLE RARE COINS AND CAN'T MISS COINS — THE GROUND RULES

In the introduction, a number of theorems were set forth in the guise of survey results. Many of them have corollaries that lead to sound investment guidelines. Following the logic leads to a better understanding of the marketplace, and a means by which the applied rules can lead your affordable rare coin purchases to become anchors of a successful rare coin retirement.

So here is a summary of key analytical data and points from all the interchange with collecting investors:

• The average collector spends $2,500 annually maintaining and expanding his collection

This is true of the collector, but not necessarily true of the investor. But the important thing to remember is that the investor both buys and sells. If the investor is going to have a buyer when he or she is selling, that buyer is either a) another investor b) a collector or c) a different entity who is acquiring for entirely different reasons.

The higher the price, the fewer collectors and investors there will be to buy the coin on resale. There are more collectors willing to buy affordable rare coins at $2,500 and under than there are to buy rare coins at substantially higher prices.

David Ganz displays a Trade dollar that is still legal tender.
Author's Photo

David L. Ganz

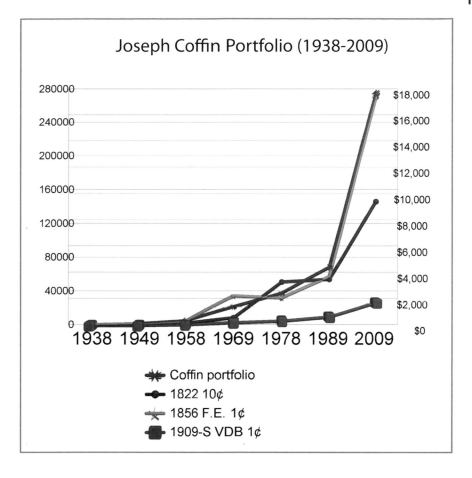

Joseph Coffin Portfolio (1938-2009)

Legend:
- Coffin portfolio
- 1822 10¢
- 1856 F.E. 1¢
- 1909-S VDB 1¢

• More than 40 percent of hobbyists collect modern issues (post 1964). This is significant for world mints and those who service them. It presents unique marketing opportunities, such as a modern gold ducat (Dutch Mint, 1986), as well as investment opportunities (for example, low mintage U.S. commemorative coin issues).

• I have found that if you draw a line in the sand (flexible, to be sure) it can be rewarding. For example, U.S. coins with a mintage of less than 30,000 are rare and collectible (see Chapter 11 on modern U.S. commems for an expanded analysis). I did the same successfully with lower-grade gold mintmarked coins (that means Charlotte, Dahlonega, and so forth) in very good to fine condition. There aren't that many to begin with; they are scarce, collectible, and oh, oh what a glorious chase! Want one example? Compare an 1839-O quarter eagle (mintage around 9,000) with other coins. Very expensive in uncirculated, it's a bargain in fine-12 condition. Another example? Try the 1860-O quarter eagle (mintage about 21,000) which is underappreciated in nicer-looking conditions, and very under-appreciated in better-graded coins.

- Prior to 1999, there were about three million coin collectors in the United States. This is the number that circulated widely. The *Wall Street Journal* quoted it; Congressional hearings utilized the number, the Mint predicated proof set production based on it, and organizations set goals with this number as keystone. The number is probably way off. The number of collectors who bought, sold or invested in coins prior to 1999 was more than likely closer to one million.

- Prior to 1999, there were about 200,000 serious coin collectors in the U.S.

- Post 1999 and the introduction of the state quarter program, the U.S. Mint says that between 120 and 140 million people collect coins (most of them collecting state quarters)

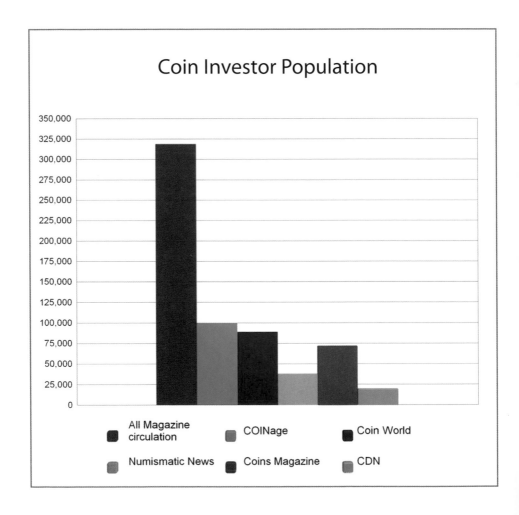

The demographics and economics of numismatic investment

By the numbers:

- Median age of collector: 63 [21]

- Average Investment position: $380,000

- Average Investment position excluding coins: $342,000

- Average value of numismatic collection: $39,100

- Collects popular series such as silver dollars (59%)

- Collects other silver coins (50%)

- Collects gold coins (25%)

- Collects modern U.S. 1964-date (45%)

- Collects bullion coins (39%)

- Collects foreign coins (8%)

- Collects other things: antiques (28%), old books (12%), toys (11%); autographs (5%).

Social and economic:

- Gender - male (92%)

- Married (74%)

- Attended college (70%)

- Own own home (89%)

- Average net worth (about $800,000)

- Average household income exceeds $100,000

The goal of the state quarter program, when it was proposed to the Citizens Coinage Advisory Committee, was to allow people to acquire coins out of circulation and start collecting them again, the old-fashioned way. In this, it has been a dramatic success. It has not led to a new generation of mature coin collectors in large measure because the collectors of the state quarters are collectors of state quarters, not coin collectors per se or coin investors per chance. This turns out to have been a flaw in the model for using state quarters to create a new generation of collectors, nationwide.

• Today there are probably more than 300,000 serious collector-investors, evidenced by hobby periodical circulation reports. It is a thin market, but an active one. It suggests that modern issues with mintages of 400,000 or more may have a practical difficulty in including the model portfolios.

The typical collector's demographics, as published in *Coin World*'s reader survey, is similar to that which I recall from the *Numismatic News* surveys of a generation ago – except that the age of the collector has gone from 55 years old in the mid-1970s to 63 years old today.[20] The ANA found these demographics as well, and found it problematical since the age meant that the average "long term" member was rarely there for many years before they became retired or semi-retired and started paring down assets, rather than acquiring them.

But that also gives you an edge: if the majority of investors are in a disposition mode at a certain age (say normal retirement between 65 and 67 years of age), you can plan your rare coin retirement differently and use the funds you invest to supplement your retirement – or you can use it as an estate planning tool to pass your wealth down another generation.

The marketplace is being constantly replaced and turning over because of the median age.

It is fortunate that the U.S. Mint has taken the time, and the taxpayer's money, to survey its clientele. This has yielded substantial benefit to market analysts trying to ascertain who their customers are; why they buy the coins that they do; how much they spend; what are the economics of the transaction, and whether the consumer believes that they are getting good value for their money.

Of course, the surveys are only as good as the questions and interpretation. In anticipation of the state quarter program, the Mint gave Coopers & Lybrand a contract to study the prospective market and concluded that about 36.8 percent of the American people would collect the coins from circulation.22 That number underestimated by 20 million people the number of people who would be moved by the statehood quarter program.

It is intriguing to look at this data and the demographics. For example, only 25 percent of the surveyed group collects gold coins. That could be a function of relative cost, actual cost, or accessibility. But it pares nicely with the Salomon Brothers tangible asset survey which has no gold coins in it – something that 75 percent of those surveyed have in common with it.

But gold coins are more than adequately covered because they were part of the original $10,000 portfolio and the $100,000 portfolio, and are part of the new method to help you plan our rare coin retirement.

Nearly half of those surveyed collect modern coins (defined as post 1964, when silver was all but removed from circulating American coinage. That is fortuitous, too, since the original portfolio considered and included many modern coin issues. Some of them are foreign and some bullion, which means that selling into that market when you liquidate your holdings to fund your retirement requires advanced thinking.

One thing is clear. The statehood quarters took coin collecting and investing to a whole new level, from about 5 million collectors to over 140 million people. Where it goes from there will be studied for generations to come.

Chapter 12

THE NEW PORTFOLIOS

It's time to put together model portfolios. You've seen the results of the examples used in *Planning Your Rare Coin Retirement* (1998), and the results speak for themselves – a substantial profit with or without gold and platinum coinage. That provided a series of choices and alternatives – and so do these.

Each of the chapters – on modern coins, old-time proof sets, state quarters, American silver eagles, gold eagles and platinum eagles – even American Arts Gold Medallions – are a component part of the portfolios. Chapters on gold, silver and platinum show the role that I believe you can use to find the right way to invest in affordable rare coins right now. Even the Salomon Brothers portfolios offer a choice.

Together, we've looked at the underlying premises, examined hypotheses, looked at theorems and postulates that are essential to a successful investment, right now, in affordable rare coins. We've considered why lower-value rare coins

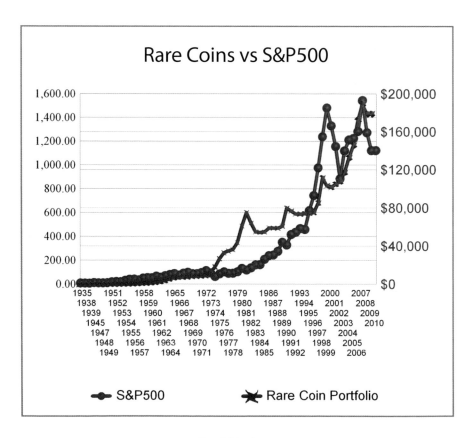

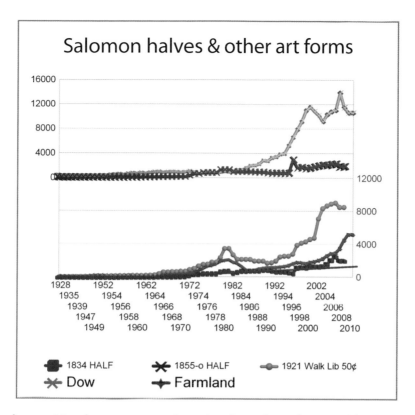

Salomon halves & other art forms

Legend:
- 1834 HALF
- 1855-o HALF
- 1921 Walk Lib 50¢
- Dow
- Farmland

are less exciting, but more rewarding, than big-ticket substitutes like the mega-rarities that most collectors can only dream about.

Then we've taken the relatively common coins in the Salomon Brothers survey of the 1978-1990 era and seen how they grow – and compare– against other assets in the tangible field. Significantly, we have also looked at several collectors from different eras, and have seen how they invested in affordable rare coins and made their rare coin retirement a reality.

In the contemporary period, Reed Hawn has shown that $600 coins can make a 500 percent profit more easily than a $500,000 coin. From Harold Bareford, we've seen that a fine eye and regular purchases in not only gold, but also silver and even English coinage, can turn a good profit. With John Jay Pittman, it's easy to see that grit, determination and a fine eye (coupled with vest pocket dealing) brought together one of the finest collections ever assembled – all the while being a salaryman (chemical engineer) for Eastman Kodak.

And then there's Louis Eliasberg, truly the King of Coins – but, it turns out, even he needed a little help from his friends to get the final coin necessary to complete the collection for his estate.

For convenience, the portfolios can be assembled with a little bit of this and a little bit of that. That is, take an old-time proof set, pick a gold or platinum Eagle, add a state quarter error, and compile a modern commemorative series.

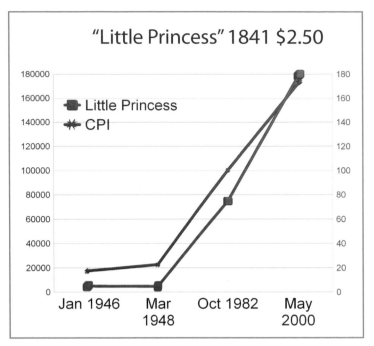

"Little Princess" 1841 $2.50

1982=100 Bureau of Labor Statistics

It's all about choices.

Some people are uncomfortable placing a high percentage of precious metal in their long-term retirement portfolios. Some think modern commemoratives are only a fluke or even a fad that will fade with time. Other people are uncomfortable putting a high percentage of their investment in one or two high priced coins.

Regardless of your position on this, it's clear that a significant body of collectors seek to acquire the coins for collecting purposes – a core reason in the profit motive to make an investment in the class in question. That makes them investable and gives them a forward outlook.

If you look at it as if you were investing in stocks, there are those who are only comfortable buying, for the most part, stocks in the Dow Jones Industrial Average. It gives a level of security that many seek and keeps the buyer away from highly premised (and promised) value. There is some comparable thought that to buy Salomon-like coins is to have that similar level of security.

What that means, by way of example, is that if you wanted an 1876 20-cent piece, its basic characteristics are a mintage of a little over 14,000 and a sale price of around $1,700 in early 2010 in choice uncirculated (MS-63) condition. You could easily expand that to include other similar 20-cent pieces, for example, 1875 in uncirculated, or several where the mintage is higher but it's still hard to get in choice uncirculated like the 1875-CC or 1875-S.

Instead of an 1881 Trade dollar, a proof only issue, there are other proof Trade dollars to choose from. These include, 1879, 1880, 1881, 1882 and 1883.

In the list that follows, a selected coin can be substituted with a similar coin type. Also, where a better condition can be acquired at more or less the same price, that represents better value. An asterisk (*) indicates that the coin is overweight for a portfolio of $100,000 or less and perhaps overweight even in a portfolio of a quarter of a million dollars.

That does not say that it does not have good value; what it says is that the concentration of wealth in a coin valued at $40,000 leaves no margin of error. To put it differently, if your goal is 100 percent increase in seven years (a 10.4 percent compounded rate of return), an 1862 half dime ($258) is more likely to go to $516 than an 1884-S silver dollar is to go to $93,760 from its current $46,000 valuation.

A word further about the substitutes. This is strictly my analysis and is based on mintage, availability, condition and price.

I. Salomon coins ands possible substitutes

Salomon	Salomon substitutes	Overweight	Value
1795 Draped Bust $1	1795-1797 Dollars (all)	*	$47,500
1881 Trade Dollar, proof only	1879-1883 Trade Dollar		$3,310
1862 Half Dime	1860-1873 Half Dimes (all)		$258
1807 Draped Bust 10¢	1798-1807 Dimes (all)		$6,160
1866 Libery Seated 10¢	1861-S,1865-S,1867-S,1870-S,1872-S 10¢		$2,310
1876 20¢	1875 20¢ all dates/mintmarks 1876-P		$1,690
1873 Arrows 25¢	1873-4 25¢ all dates/mintmarks		$1,530
1886 25¢	1875-1891 25¢ all dates/mintmarks		$1,660
1847 $1	1840-50 $1 all dates/mintmarks		$5,940
1884-S $1	1889-CC, 1893-CC, 1895-O Dollar	*	$46,880
1925 Hawaiian 50¢	1921 Missouri Centennial		$3,300
1862 3¢ Silver	1859-1872 3¢ Silver		$330
1916 25¢ Lib Standing	1918/17 25¢, 1927-25¢	*	$17,190
1815 Bust 50¢	1818-1836 50¢		$15,940
1834 Bust 50¢	1834-1836 50¢ (all)		$2,040
1855-O 50¢	1855 50¢ (all), 1854 50¢ all dates/mintmarks 1861-1865 50¢ all dates/mintmarks		$1,780
1921 Walking Lib 50¢	1919-S 50¢ MS-63, 1921-D 50¢ unc., 1917-S 50¢ unc. obv, mintmark		$8,480
1866 5¢ (Rays), proof	1877 proof 5¢, 1878 5¢ proof, 1883 3/2 5¢ proof, 1881 5¢ proof		$1,900

Salomon	Salomon substitutes	Overweight	Value
1794 Half Cent Libery Cap XF	1794 Half Cent (all), 1794 Half Cent (all), 1797 Half Cent (most types)		$5,660
1873 2¢ br proof	1871 2¢, 1872 2¢ proof, 1873 open proof, 1873 closed proof		$3,340
Total			$177,198
Overweight coins			$111,490
No-overweight			$65,708

*Overweight for portfolio if using Salmon-based coins

A final reminder – recall Reed Hawn's admonition: you can make a better return (i.e., make more money) on low value items than on the great rarities. The 1838-O half dollar that increases 50 percent is a six-figure change. By contrast, a $1,000 coin that goes up to $1,750 in the same time frame has made a greater profit.

II. Modern Proof Sets

Here's what I keep from the old portfolio. These are widely collected, and the later dates are so low priced that they can only go up.

Proof sets	2010 price	Proof sets	2010 price
1936	$6,150	1962	$20.00
1937	$3,300	1963	$15.75
1938	$1,510	1964	$15.75
1939	$1,400	1965	None issued
1940	$1,185	1966	None issued
1941	$1,175	1967	None issued
1942-6 piece	$1,125	1968	$5.85
1950	$780.00	1969	$6.75
1951	$670.00	1970	$7.25
1952	$300.00	1971	$5.10
1953	$250.00	1972	$6.15
1954	$118.00	1973	$7.25
1955	$175.00	1974	$7.25
1956	$65.00	1975	$7.75
1957	$29.00	1976	$6.35
1958	$54.00	1977	$6.25
1959	$29.00	1978	$7.50
1960	$29.00	1979	$6.35
1961	$38.00	1980	$5.35

Proof sets	2010 price	Proof sets	2010 price
1981	$6.65	1995	$14.90
1982	$3.52	1996	$13.25
1983	$5.00	1997	$21.50
1984	$5.60	1970 no S mintmark	$950.00
1985	$4.45	1971 no S on 5¢	$1,475.00
1986	$4.45	1983 no S on 10¢	$825.00
1987	$3.75	1990 no s on 1¢	$5,100.00
1988	$5.00	1968 no S on 1¢ *	$12,350.00
1989	$6.50		
1990	$5.25	Total	$39,349.72
1991	$9.65	Overweight	$12,350.00
1992	$4.50	Without overweight	$26,999.72
1993	$8.85		
1994	$8.25	*Overweight	

III. Foreign gold coins

They're hard to get at $100 apiece or less, largely because gold has settled in on a niche of more than $1,000 an ounce; the coins, particularly those dated before 1960, were composed and struck when gold was $35 an ounce, or less. But these coins for the most part are still affordable, most under $400. The coin are all figured at $1,100 an ounce for gold; their troy ounce weight is listed, and the probable (current) selling price is predicted in POG [price of gold] multiplied by 25 percent. If you were to buy them all, it's a $25,000 (gold) portfolio.

Date	Country	Denomination	Troy oz	$1,100.00 Price of gold	POG+25%
1896	Australia	Sovereign	0.2354	$258.94	$323.68
1881	Austria	8 Florin/20 Franc	0.1867	$205.37	$256.71
	Austria	1 Ducat	0.1109	$121.99	$152.49
1915	Austria	1 Ducat (restrike)	0.1109	$121.99	$152.49
1974	Bahamas	$100	0.1609	$176.99	$221.24
1975	Barbados	$100	0.0998	$109.78	$137.23
	Belgium	20 Francs	0.1867	$205.37	$256.71
1981	Belize	$100 national Independence	0.0998	$109.78	$137.23
1981	Belize	$50	0.0541	$59.51	$74.39
1985	Belize	$100	0.0988	$108.68	$135.85
1975	Bermuda	$100	0.2034	$223.74	$279.68
1977	Bermuda	$50	0.1172	$128.92	$161.15

Date	Country	Denomination	Troy oz	$1,100.00 Price of gold	POG+25%
1952	Bolivia	7 Gramos	0.2251	$247.61	$309.51
1981	Brit. Virgin Islands	$50	0.043	$47.30	$59.13
1975	Brit. Virgin Islands	$100	0.2054	$225.94	$282.43
1894	Bulgaria	10 Leva	0.2443	$268.73	$335.91
	Canada	1/15 oz Maple Leaf	0.07	$73.33	$91.67
	Canada	1/10 oz Platinum Maple Leaf	0.1	$110.00	$137.50
1987	Canada	Olympic $100 proof	0.25	$275.00	$343.75
1995	Canada	1/10 oz Platinum Lynx	0.1	$110.00	$137.50
1989	Canada	Indian	0.25	$275.00	$343.75
1976	Canada	Olympic $100 unc	0.25	$275.00	$343.75
1997	Canada	Maple leaf 1/4 oz	0.25	$275.00	$343.75
1990	Cayman Islands	$25	0.1008	$110.88	$138.60
1913	Columbia	5 Pesos	0.1177	$129.47	$161.84
1976	Comoros	10,000 Francs	0.0888	$97.68	$122.10
1975	Cook Islands	$100	0.2778	$305.58	$381.98
1988	Cook Islands	Bison	0.1	$258.94	$323.68
1916	Cuba	2 Peso	0.0968	$106.48	$133.10
1930	Egypt	100 Piastres	0.2391	$263.01	$328.76
1971	El Salvador	50 Colones	0.1701	$187.11	$233.89
1971	El Salvador	25 Colones	0.085	$93.50	$116.88
1970	Equatorial Guinea	250 Pesetas	0.1018	$111.98	$139.98
1882	Finland	100 Maarka	0.25	$275.00	$343.75
1801	France	(AN 12A) 20 Francs	0.1867	$205.37	$256.71
1815	France	20 Fr Bordeaux Louis XVIII	0.1867	$205.37	$256.71
1814	France	20 Francs	0.1867	$205.37	$256.71
1886	France	20 Francs (3d Republic)	0.1867	$205.37	$256.71
	France	20 Francs	0.1867	$205.37	$256.71
	France	20 Franc Rooster (1899-1914)	0.1867	$205.37	$256.71
1856	France	A 5 Francs	0.0467	$51.37	$64.21
	Germany	10 Marks	0.1152	$126.72	$158.40
	Germany	20 mark	0.2354	$258.94	$323.68
1997	Gibralter	Classical heads (set of 4)	0.2354	$258.94	$323.68
	Great Britain	Sovereign Eliz II	0.2354	$258.94	$323.68
	Great Britain	Sovereign Old Style	0.2354	$258.94	$323.68

Date	Country	Denomination	Troy oz	$1,100.00 Price of gold	POG+25%
1989	Great Britain	Sovereign	0.2354	$258.94	$323.68
1986	Great Britain	½ Sovereign	0.1177	$129.47	$161.84
1981	Guernsey	£1	0.2354	$258.94	$323.68
1970	Guinea	1000 Francs	0.1157	$127.27	$159.09
1976	Guyana	$100	0.0923	$101.53	$126.91
1973	Haiti	200 Gourdes	0.5715	$628.65	$785.81
1973	Haiti	100 Gourdes	0.3427	$376.97	$471.21
1885	Hungary	20 Fr/8 Florin	0.3427	$376.97	$471.21
1918	India	Sovereign	0.2354	$258.94	$323.68
AH1322	Iran	5000 Dinars	0.0406	$44.66	$55.83
1342	Iran	AH ½ Toman	0.04	$44.66	$55.83
1971	Iran	500 Rials (Fr 109)	0.1883	$207.13	$258.91
	Italy	20 Lire	0.1867	$205.37	$256.71
1975	Jamaica	$100	0.2265	$249.15	$311.44
1835	Japan	2 Shu	0.0965	$106.15	$132.69
1977	Liberia	$100	0.3163	$347.93	$434.91
1953	Luxembourg	20 Francs (KM #1M)	0.1867	$205.37	$256.71
1976	Malaysia	200 Ringgit	0.215	$236.50	$295.63
1974	Malta	20 Pounds	0.3534	$388.74	$485.93
1974	Malta	10 Pounds	0.1767	$194.37	$242.96
	Mexico	2 Pesos	0.0482	$53.02	$66.28
1906	Mexico	5 Pesos	0.1206	$132.66	$165.83
1946	Mexico	2½ Pesos	0.0603	$66.33	$82.91
1905	Mexico	10 Pesos	0.2411	$265.21	$331.51
	Mexico	5 Pesos	0.1206	$132.66	$165.83
	Mexico	10 Pesos	0.2411	$265.21	$331.51
	Mexico	2½ pesos	0.0603	$66.33	$82.91
1985	Mexico	250 Pesos	0.25	$275.00	$343.75
	Netherlands	10 Guilder	0.1947	$214.17	$267.71
1988	Netherlands	2 Ducats	0.1104	$121.44	$151.80
1975	Netherlands	1 Ducat	0.0552	$60.72	$75.90
1979	Netherlands Antilles	50 Gulden	0.0972	$106.92	$133.65
1975	Panama	100 Balboas	0.2361	$259.71	$324.64
1975	Papua New Guinea	100 Kina	0.2769	$304.59	$380.74

Date	Country	Denomination	Troy oz	$1,100.00 Price of gold	POG+25%
1965	Peru	10 Soles	0.0677	$74.47	$93.09
	Russia	5 Roubles Nicholas II	0.1867	$205.37	$256.71
1964	S. Africa	Proof Set	$0.00	$0.00	
	South Africa	2 Rands (1961-83) 1/4 oz	0.2354	$258.94	$323.68
1894	South Africa	½ Pond	0.1177	$129.47	$161.84
1982	South Africa	Krugerrand 1/10 oz	0.1	$110.00	$137.50
1878	Spain	Alfonso XII (Fr 343R) 20 Pesetas	0.1867	$205.37	$256.71
1978	Sudan	25 pounds (Fr 4)	0.2432	$267.52	$334.40
	Switzerland	20 Francs	0.1867	$205.37	$256.71
	Switzerland	10 Francs	0.09335	$102.69	$128.36
1969	Turkey	500 Kurish	0.2358	$259.38	$324.23
1976	Turks & Caicos	50 Crowns	0.1447	$159.17	$198.96
1981	Turks & Caicos	100 Crowns	0.2	$220.00	$275.00
1976	Turks & Caicos	25 Crowns	0.0723	$79.53	$99.41
1987	USA	Constitution $5 commemorative	0.241875	$266.06	$332.58
1997	USA	Gold 1/10 oz Eagle	0.1	$110.00	$137.50
1997	USA	Gold 1/4 oz Eagle	0.25	$275.00	$343.75
1988	USA	Olympic $5	0.241875	$266.06	$332.58
	USA	$1 Type 1 (1849-1854)	0.0967	$106.37	$132.96
	USA	$1 Type 3 (1856-1889)	0.0967	$106.37	$132.96
	USA	$2½ Indian (1908-1929)	0.241875	$266.06	$332.58
1905	Venezuela	20 Bolivares (Fr 6)	0.1867	$205.37	$256.71
1789	Venice	Zecchino (Fr. 1445)	0.1109	$121.99	$152.49
1982	Yugoslavia	5000 Dinara	0.2315	$254.65	$318.31
Total				$19,726.57	$24,658.21

IV. Selected gold coins from the Eliasberg Collection

As fabulous as the Eliasberg collection was, its principal deficiency was that Louis Eliasberg increased the scope of his holdings by buying out interests of others. You can find this in the material that has since found a new home. On these four dozen plus pieces, consider the grade catalogued (1982) Eliasberg and that in 2008 by Scotsman, a well-known coin dealer.

Once again, where the coin tabulates poorly, there is no necessity of acquiring it. An asterisk (*) says that the 2008 Scotsman price shows overweight to the coin and column and is predicated on several price sources (principally its auction on Oct. 17, 2008). NGC was kind in its grading opportunities and the coins are probably looking at the grade a quarter century later.

Eliasberg Gold Coins

Date	Denomination	Scotsman Catalogue Condition	Eliasberg Grade	Eliasberg Oct. 1982	Scotsman sale Oct 17 2008
1855-O	$1	NGC AU-58	XF-45	$1,000	$4,100
1857-C	$1	NGC AU-58	XF-40	$700	$5,250
1857-S	$1	NGC AU-55	XF-40	$900	$1,500
1860-S	$1	NGC AU-58	XF-40	$750	$1,400
1862*	$1	NGC PF-67 Ultra Cameo	PF-67	$8,000	$45,000
1840-O (large O)	$2.50	NGC AU 58	AU-55	$1,000	$4,500
1842-O (large O)	$2.50	NGC AU-55	VF-30	$550	$3,300
1843-O small date	$2.50	NGC AU-58	AU-50	$750	$1,300
1847	$2.50	NGC AU-58	VF-30	$425	$1,350
1848-C	$2.50	NGC AU-58	XF-45	$1,000	$5,500
1850-C	$2.5	NGC AU-58	XF-40	$750	$8,750
1850-O, Breen-1	$2.50	NCS scratched cleaned	XF-45	$525	$650
1851*	$2.50	NGC MS-67	MS-67	$6,750	$25,000
1852-C	$2.50	NGC AU-58	XF-40	$950	$7,000
1855	$2.50	NGC MS-62	MS-60/63	$550	$1,050
1856-S	$2.50	NGC MS-61	AU-55	$500	$4,400
1859-S	$2.50	NGC AU-58	XF-45/AU-50	$450	$4,750
1865-S	$2.50	NCS cleaned	AU50/60	$750	$1,450
1867-S	$2.50	NGC MS-61	AU50/55	$850	$3,750
1877-S	$2.50	NCS polished, AU Details	XF-45	$500	$300
1925-D Indian Head $2.50	$2.50	NGC MS-64	BU-65/60	$600	$2,500
1927 Indian Head $2.50	$2.50	NGC MS-63	MS-60	$350	$825
1928 Indian Head $2.50	$2.50	NGC MS-63	AU-55	$550	$925
1929 Indian Head $2.50	$2.50	NGC MS-64	MS-65rx60	$750	$1,500

Eliasberg Gold Coins

Date	Denomination	Scotsman Catalogue Condition	Eliasberg Grade	Eliasberg Oct. 1982	Scotsman sale Oct 17 2008
1880 $4 Flowing Hair*	$2.50	NGC PF-66	PF-67	$50,000	$430,000
1808 (normal date, wide 5 D)*	$5		XF-40	$2,600	$440,000
1847-C	$5		VF-30	$550	$4,000
1855-C	$5		XF-45	$850	$5,250
1857-S	$5		VF-30	$1,400	$850
1858-C	$5			$850	$500
1866-S	$5	No Motto.	NGC VF-25	$750	$2,100
1870-S	$5		VF-30	$800	$6,750
1872-S	$5		VF-20	$400	$350
1874-S	$5		VG-8	$300	$600
1876-S	$5		VG-30	$950	$950
1879-S	$5		AU-58	$450	$450
1881-CC	$5		AU-53	$450	$450
1881-S	$5		XF-45	$850	$850
1883-CC	$5		Cleaned	$550	$1,950
1883-S	$5		XF-45	$350	$390
1884-CC	$5		XF-45	$850	$10,000
1884-S	$5			$550	$500
1888-S	$5			$550	$425
1909-D Indian Head	$5	NGC MS-62	AU-55	$800	$650
1911-S Indian Head	$5	NGC AU-58	AU-50/55	$700	$650
1914-S Indian Head	$5	NGC XF-45		$400	$360
1842 (large date)	$10			$650	$675
1850 small date	$10			$500	$3,000
Total				$97,000	$1,047,750
Overweight coins					$940,000
Net					$107,750

This is a virtual $100,000 portfolio on its own.

There are other portfolios that can be suggested by Eliasberg:

Power of an Eliasberg Sale

Coin	Condition	Sale	Eliasberg	Current	Gain
1904-O 25¢	NGC MS-66	Aug 7, 2009	$4,630.00	$5,290.00	1.03%
1850-O $1	PCGS AU-53	Aug 7, 2009	$1,320.00	$3,832.95	8.55%
1859-S	PCGS AU-50	Aug 7, 2009	$2,310.00	$2,853.15	1.64%
1870 $1	PCGS PF-64	Aug 7, 2009	$3,520.00	$6,049.00	4.25%
1875-Cc Trade $1	PCGS PF-64	Aug 7, 2009	$5,930.00	$10,638.65	4.60%
1833 50¢	PCGS MS-66	April 2009	$3,410.00	$9,200.00	7.93%
1952 25¢	PCGS MS-66	Jan 8, 2007	n/a	$345.00	n/a
1861 25¢	PCGS PR-62	Oct 24 ,2009	880	$891.25	0.10%

Annual Date	Denomination	Condition	Collection	Date	Price Realized	Gain/Loss
1860-S	$1 gold	XF	Dunham	1941	$10	
1860-S	$1 gold	XF-40	Eliasberg	1982	$750	740%
1860-S	$1 gold	AU-58	Scotsman	2008	$1,400	86.67%

V. Silver eagles

Proof silver eagles offer an exciting opportunity by focusing on mintage and collectability. It is shown side-by-side by year and then sorted by mintage.

Silver Eagle Proofs Sorted by Date			Silver Eagle Proofs Sorted by Mintage		
Date	Mintage	Value	Date	Mintage	Value
1986	1,446,778	$59.95	1986	1,446,778	$59.95
1987	997,732	$59.95	2006	1,043,602	$59.95
1988	557,370	$59.95	1987	997,732	$59.95
1989	617,694	$59.95	2007	827,106	$59.95
1990	695,510	$59.95	2004	801,602	$59.95
1991	511,925	$59.95	2003	747,831	$59.95
1992	498,654	$59.95	2001	746,398	$59.95
1993	405,913	$109.50	2005	701,606	$59.95
1994	372,168	$149.50	1990	695,510	$59.95
1995	438,511	$139.50	2002	647,342	$59.95
1996	500,000	$79.50	1989	617,694	$59.95
1997	435,368	$89.50	2000	600,000	$59.95
1998	450,000	$59.95	1988	557,370	$59.95
1999	549,769	$59.95	1999	549,769	$59.95
2000	600,000	$59.95	2008	546,765	$99.00
2001	746,398	$59.95	1991	511,925	$59.95
2002	647,342	$59.95	1996	500,000	$79.50
2003	747,831	$59.95	1992	498,654	$59.95

Silver Eagle Proofs Sorted by Date

Date	Mintage	Value
2004	801,602	$59.95
2005	701,606	$59.95
2006	1,043,602	$59.95
2007	827,106	$59.95
2008	546,765	$99.00
2009	0	None
Total	15,139,644	$1,685.65

Silver Eagle Proofs Sorted by Mintage

Date	Mintage	Value
1998	450,000	$59.95
1995	438,511	$139.50
1997	435,368	$89.50
1993	405,913	$109.50
1994	372,168	$149.50
2009	0	None

Gold proof eagles also represent good value:

Gold Eagle Proof Coins Sorted by Date

Date	1OZ	½ OZ	1/4OZ	1/10 OZ
1986	446,290	N/A	N/A	N/A
1987	147,498	143,398	N/A	N/A
1988	87,133	76,528	98,028	143,881
1989	54,570	44,798	54,170	84,647
1990	62,401	51,636	62,674	99,349
1991	50,411	53,125	50,839	70,334
1992	44,826	40,976	46,269	64,874
1993	34,369	43,819	46,464	58,649
1994	46,674	44,584	48,172	62,849
1995	46,368	45,388	47,526	62,667
1996	36,153	35,058	38,219	57,047
1997	32,999	26,344	29,805	34,977
1998	25,886	25,374	29,503	39,395
1999	31,427	30,427	34,417	48,428
2000	33,007	32,028	36,036	49,971
2001	24,555	23,240	25,613	37,530
2002	27,499	26,646	29,242	40,864
2003	28,344	28,270	30,292	40,027
2004	28,215	27,330	28,839	35,131
2005	35,246	34,311	37,207	49,265
2006	47,096	34,322	36,127	47,277
2007	51,810	44,025	46,189	58,553
2008	30,237	22,602	18,877	28,116

The rule of thumb that I would use on acquiring proof eagles is to focus on those at 35,000 or fewer mintage (more or less):

Gold Eagle Proof Coins Sorted by Mintage

Date	1 OZ	Date	½ OZ	Date	1/4 OZ	Date	1/10 OZ
2001	24,555	1986	N/A	1986	N/A	1986	N/A
1998	25,886	2008	22,602	1987	N/A	1987	N/A
2002	27,499	2001	23,240	2008	18,877	2008	28,116
2004	28,215	1998	25,374	2001	25,613	1997	34,977
2003	28,344	1997	26,344	2004	28,839	2004	35,131
2008	30,237	2002	26,646	2002	29,242	2001	37,530
1999	31,427	2004	27,330	1998	29,503	1998	39,395
1997	32,999	2003	28,270	1997	29,805	2003	40,027
2000	33,007	1999	30,427	2003	30,292	2002	40,864
1993	34,369	2000	32,028	1999	34,417	2006	47,277
2005	35,246	2005	34,311	2000	36,036	1999	48,428
1996	36,153	2006	34,322	2006	36,127	2005	49,265
1992	44,826	1996	35,058	2005	37,207	2000	49,971
1995	46,368	1992	40,976	1996	38,219	1996	57,047
1994	46,674	1993	43,819	2007	46,189	2007	58,553
2006	47,096	2007	44,025	1992	46,269	1993	58,649
1991	50,411	1994	44,584	1993	46,464	1995	62,667
2007	51,810	1989	44,798	1995	47,526	1994	62,849
1989	54,570	1995	45,388	1994	48,172	1992	64,874
1990	62,401	1990	51,636	1991	50,839	1991	70,334
1988	87,133	1991	53,125	1989	54,170	1989	84,647
1987	147,498	1988	76,528	1990	62,674	1990	99,349
1986	446,290	1987	143,398	1988	98,028	1988	143,881

That means that there are 11 one ounce pieces within those guidelines, 12 half ounce pieces, eight quarter ounce pieces and 3 tenth of an ounce coins.

VI. American Arts Gold Medallions

	Design	Mintage	
1984	John Steinbeck	32,572	½ oz
1984	Helen Hayes	33,546	1 oz
1983	Alexander Calder	74,571	½ oz
1981	Willa Cather	97,331	½ oz
1981	Mark Twain	116,371	1 oz
1980	Marian Anderson	281,624	½ oz
1980	Grant Wood	312,709	1 oz
1982	Frank Lloyd Wright	348,305	½ oz
1983	Robert Frost	390,669	1 oz
1982	Louis Armstrong	409,098	1 oz
Total		2,096,796	

The favorites in this series are 1984 (Steinbeck, Helen Hayes) and this belongs in a precious metal retirement account

VII. Platinum:

Platinum's rendevous with destiny again has me playing a bit part while representing the Platinum Guild.

	1 Ounce	½ Ounce	¼ Ounce	¹⁄₁₀ Ounce
1997	56,000.	20,500	27,100	70,250
1998	133,002	32,419	38,887	39,525
1999	56,707.	32,309	39,734	55,955
2000	10,003.	18,892	20,054	34,027
2001	14,070	12,815	21,815	52,017
2002	11,502	24,005	27,405	23,005
2003	8,007	17,409	25,207	22,007
2004	7,500	13,236	18,010	15,010
2005	6,310	9,013	12,013	14,013
2006	7,000	6,600	7,800	13,000
2007	7,202	7,001	8,402	13,003
2008	21,800	14,000	22,800	17,000
Total ounces	339,108	208,199	269,227	368,812

VIII. State quarters

Here's where I see the market. You can use this as guidance, but my view is that any state quarter in MS-68, MS-69 or that rare MS-70 belongs in a long term portfolio – and will be an affordable coin investment that you can make right now.

State Quarter High Prices

State	Date	Auction	Grade	Price
AL	2003-P	11-28-06TT	MS-68	$90
AK	2003-D	11-18-06TT	MS-68	$120
AZ	2008-D	11-16-08TT	MS69	$600
AR	2003-D	11-8-06TT	MS-68	$120
CA	2005-D	11-3-06TT	MS-69	$300
CO	2006-D	10-3-06TT	MS-69	$45
CT	1999-P	10-11-06TT	MS-68	$120
DE	1999-D	10-23-06TT	MS-67	$260
FL	2004-P	5-09-05TT	MS-69	$320
GA	1999-P	10-9-06TT	MS-67	$280
HI	2008-P	11-30-08TT	MS-69	$275
ID	2007-D	02-08-08TT	MS-69	$50
IL	2003-D	12-18-06TT	MS-68	$475
IN	2002-P	5-31-03Her	MS-69	$690
IA	2004-D	10-18-06TT	MS-69	$130
KS	2005-P	8-28-06TT	ANACS-65	$70
KY	2001-D	5-15-05TT	MS-68	$210
LA	2002-P	12-09-03H	MS-69	$346
ME	2003-P	11-12-06TT	MS-68	$525
MD	2000-D	11-19-06TT	MS-68	$260
MA	2000-D	5-15-05TT	MS-68	$140
MI	2004-D	10-11-05TT	MS-69	$625
MN	2005-D	9-13-06TT	MS-69	$200
MS	2002-D	12-3-06TT	MS-68	$33
MO	2003-D	10-11-06TT	MS-68	$360
MT	2007-P	5-07TT	MS-67	$55
NE	2006-D	9-24-06TT	MS-69	$60
NV	2006-D	10-23-06TT	MS-69	$100
NH	2000-P	10-11-06TT	MS-68	$210
NJ	1999-D	10-11-06TT	MS-67	$425
NM	2008-P	9-25-08TT	MS-67	$75
NY	2001-P	11-19-06TT	MS-69	$1,050
NC	2001-D	11-26-06TT	MS-68	$320
ND	2006-D	10-23-06TT	MS-69	$65
OH	2002-P	5-31-03H	MS-69	$494
OK	2008-P/D	10-05-08TT	MS-69	$360
OR	2005-D	2-26-06TT	MS-69	$130
PA	1999-D	11-19-06TT	MS-67	$340

State Quarter High Prices

State	Date	Auction	Grade	Price
RI	2001-D	12-11-06TT	MS-68	$525
SC	2000P	10-23-06TT	MS-67	$70
SD	2006-P	11-29-06TT	MS-69	$70
TN	02d	11-02-05TT	MS-68	$140
TX	04p	10-11-06TT	MS-68	$50
UT	07P	73008TT	MS-69	$80
VT	01-d	11-19-06TT	MS-68	$70
VA	00-p	10-25-0-6TT	MS-68	$110
WA	07D	+2-17-08TT	MS-67	$28
WV	05-d	12-13-06TT	MS-69	$1,600
WI	04-d (error)	07-06h	MS-66	$2,530
WY	07D	072708TT	MS-65	$85
DC	09D	7-20-09TT	MS-67	$60
PR	09D	72009 TT	MS--67	$60
Guam	09	7-20-09TT	MS-60	$36
AM Samoa	09P	01-27-20TT	MS-(pf) 65	$45
V ISLANDS	09P	112809TT	MS-68	$60
Mariana	NONE	None Posted		$45
Total				$15,686
Average				$314

TT=Teletrade; H=Heritage

The key to studying the above chart is to see how the value of a coin can go from $28 to over $2,500.

My picks for uncirculated coinage from change are the state territories issues of 2009, all of which are low mintage:

Low Mintage State Territory Unc

Territory	Mintmark	Date	Price
Mariana	P	2009	35,200,000
Mariana	D	2009	37,600,000
Amer Samoa	D	2009	39,600,000
Virgin Islands	D	2009	41,000,000
Virgin Islands	P	2009	41,000,000
Guam	D	2009	42,600,000
Amer Somoa	P	2009	42,600,000
Guam	P	2009	45,000,000
Puerto Rico	P	2009	53,200,000
DC	P	2009	83,600,000
Puerto Rico	D	2009	86,000,000
DC	D	2009	88,800,000

VI. Some old favorites from 1997 *Rare Coin Retirement*

Date	Mintmark	Type	Condition	2010 Value
1881	S	Morgan $	MS-63	$138
1878	CC	Morgan $	MS-63	$318
1879	CC	Morgan $	VF	$306
1880	CC	Morgan $	MS-60	$526
1881	CC	Morgan $	MS-60	$490
1882	CC	Morgan $	MS-64	$263
1883	CC	Morgan $	MS-64	$244
1884	CC	Morgan $	MS-64	$210
1885	CC	Morgan $	AU-50	$570
1965	to date	Wash set	BU & Pf	$185
1941	to 1964	Wash set	BU	$675
1979	to 1981	Anthony $1	BU	$285
1981	P	Anthony $1	BU	$18
1981	D	Anthony $1	BU	$15.60
1981	S	Anthony $1	BU	$31
1971	to 1978	Ike dollars	BU & Pf	$175
1938	to 1965	Jeff. 5¢ set	BU	$290
1934	to 1958	Lincoln set	BU	$280
1959	to 1997	Lincoln set	BU & Pf	$135
1904	O	Morgan $	MS-65	$140
1904	P	Indian cent	MS-65	$440
1904	P	Indian cent	Pf-64	$280
1946	to 1965	FDR Set	BU	$180
1901	P	Indian cent	MS-65	$440
1902	P	Indian cent	MS-65	$440
1903	P	Indian cent	MS-65	$440
1905	P	Indian cent	MS-65	$440
1906	P	Indian cent	MS-65	$440
1907	P	Indian cent	MS-65	$440
1908	P	Indian cent	MS-65	$440
1909	P	Indian cent	MS-65	$440
1900	P	Indian cent	Pf-64	$280

Date	Mintmark	Type	Condition	2010 Value
1901	P	Indian cent	Pf-64	$280
1902	P	Indian cent	Pf-64	$280
1903	P	Indian cent	Pf-64	$280
1905	P	Indian cent	Pf-64	$280
1906	P	Indian cent	Pf-64	$280
1907	P	Indian cent	Pf-64	$280
1908	P	Indian cent	Pf-64	$280

VIII. Old time proof sets

It is probably an acceptable risk to have $10,000 or under invested in a single old-time proof set. You may feel differently, but there are 13 different sets that in January 2010 sold for under $10,000 at the Florida FUN show auction conducted by Heritage. The sets below are presented by date, but the limit that this book suggests may vary according to your willingness to concentrate your capital:

Proof Sets Sold at FUN 2010

Date	Price	Date	Price
1856	$69,000	1878	$23,000
1857	$43,125	1879	$13,225
1858	$37,375	1880	$18,400
1859	$18,400	1881	$13,800
1860	$25,300	1882	$15,065
1861	$27,600	1883	$25,300
1862	$17,250	1884	$11,500
1863	$17,250	1885	$9,775
1864	$18,400	1886	$9,775
1865	$17,250	1887	$10,925
1866	$37,375	1888	$16,100
1867	$17,250	1889	$9,488
1868	$9,488	1890	$138,000
1869	$19,550	1891	$13,800
1870	$16,675	1892	$12,133
1871	$18,400	1893	$23,000
1872	$18,400	1894	$17,250
1873	$37,375	1895	$86,250
1874	$12,650	1896	$10,925
1875	$11,500	1897	$14,950
1876	$19,550	1898	$19,550
1877	$25,300	1899	$11,500

Date	Price	Date	Price
1900	$8,338	1908	$7,475
1901	$14,950	1909	$21,850
1902	$8,085	1910	$7,475
1903	$10,350	1911	$8,625
1904	$9,200	1912	$5,750
1905	$27,600	1913	$14,950
1906	$8,625	1914	$12,368
1907	$12,075	1915	$9,775

For your convenience, below appear a listing of sets as sold at the 2010 FUN auction for under $20,000:

Proof Sets Sold at FUN 2010 for Under $20,000

Date	Price	Date	Price
1912	$5,750	1879	$13,225
1910	$7,475	1881	$13,800
1908	$7,475	1891	$13,800
1902	$8,085	1897	$14,950
1900	$8,338	1913	$14,950
1906	$8,625	1901	$14,950
1911	$8,625	1882	$15,065
1904	$9,200	1888	$16,100
1868	$9,488	1870	$16,675
1889	$9,488	1894	$17,250
1885	$9,775	1867	$17,250
1915	$9,775	1862	$17,250
1886	$9,775	1863	$17,250
1903	$10,350	1865	$17,250
1887	$10,925	1871	$18,400
1896	$10,925	1872	$18,400
1875	$11,500	1859	$18,400
1884	$11,500	1864	$18,400
1899	$11,500	1880	$18,400
1907	$12,075	1869	$19,550
1892	$12,133	1898	$19,550
1914	$12,368	1876	$19,550
1874	$12,650		

Some additional favorites recommended in *Planning Your Rare Coin Retirement* (1997) and recommended again at current market prices:

- Peace Dollar (MS-65)
- Barber Dime (MS-63)
- 1991 1/4 oz. $10 American Eagle (gold) (Unc.)
- 1970-D Kennedy Half Dollar (Unc.)
- 1970-S Kennedy Half Dollar (Proof)
- Complete Set of Kennedy Half Dollars
- 1989-D Congressional Half Dollar (Unc.)
- 1993 Madison 50-cent Commemorative (lettered edge) (Unc.)
- 100 Foreign Gold Coins Under $100 [separate chart] summarized in the whole.
- Vietnam War Memorial Commemorative $1 (Unc.)
- Thomas Jefferson Commemorative $1 (Unc.)
- 1995 Double Die Lincoln Cent (MS-65)
- 1988W Olympic $5 Gold (BU)
- 1903-O Morgan Silver Dollar (MS-60)
- U.S. Proof Set Collection 1950-1997 (complete) [separate chart summarized in the whole]
- 1997 Platinum 1/10th Ounce Bullion Coin
- 1881-S Morgan Silver Dollar (MS-65)
- 1994 ANA Commemorative Platinum Coin (Turks & Caicos)
- Roosevelt Dime Set 19946 - 1997 (Unc. and Proof)
- Indian Head Cents 1900-1909 (MS-65 and Proof-64)
- 1904-O Silver Dollar (MS-65)
- Lincoln Memorial Cent 1959 - 1997 (Proof) Including S-Mint Proofs
- Lincoln Cent 1934-1958 (Unc.)
- Jefferson Nickel 1938-1965 (Unc. set)
- Roosevelt Dimes 1965-1997 (Unc. and Proof)
- Eisenhower Dollars 1971-1978 (Unc. and Proof)
- Susan B. Anthony Dollar Set 1979-1981 PDS (Unc. and Proof)
- Washington Quarter Sets 1941-1964
- Washington Quarters 1965-1997 ((Unc. and Proof)
- Carson City Silver Dollar Set (Various)
- Silver Eagle Sets 1986-1996 (Gem Proof)
- Isle of Man 1/25 oz. Gold
- $5 Gold Pieces (about One Dozen Half Eagles)
- Modern Commemorative Coinage

IX. Modern Commemoratives

It's a fair bet that modern commemoratives have a stronger future, but the key is to identify low mintages (which are mostly, but not exclusively, uncirculated coins rather than the proofs. The chart below shows overall mintages (not a bad way to start) that go from a low of under 30,000 (combined) for Jackie Robinson $5 gold to over 7.8 million for the Statue of Liberty 50 cents.

But you have to look deeper; on Jackie Robinson $5 for example, the real value is in 5,202 (uncirculated), not that 24,000 proofs (only) is not an impressive number. First, the overall modern commemorative package sorting by gross mintage:

Modern Commemoratives Listed by Mintage

Date and Type	Face Value	Total Mintage	Proof	% Proof	Unc	% Unc
1997 Jackie Robinson 50th Anniv	$5	29,748	24,546	82.51%	5,202	17.49%
1996 Smithsonian 150th Anniv	$5	30,840	21,772	70.60%	9,068	29.40%
2003 First Flight	$10	31,975	21,846	68.32%	10,129	31.68%
2000 Library of Congress gold/pt	$10	33,850	27,167	80.26%	6,683	19.74%
1997 Franklin D. Roosevelt	$5	41,368	29,474	71.25%	11,894	28.75%
1996 Olympics Flag Bearers	$5	42,060	32,886	78.19%	9,174	21.81%
2002 Salt Lake City Olympics	$5	42,523	32,351	76.08%	10,172	23.92%
1996 Olympics Cauldron/Flame	$5	47,765	38,555	80.72%	9,210	19.28%
2006 San Francisco	$5	51,200	35,841	70.00%	15,359	30.00%
1995 Olympics Stadium	$5	53,703	43,124	80.30%	10,579	19.70%
1999 George Washington	$5	55,038	35,656	64.78%	19,382	35.22%
2007 Jamestown	$5	60,805	43,609	71.72%	17,196	28.28%
2001 Capitol Visitor's Center	$5	65,669	27,652	42.11%	38,017	57.89%
1995 Civil War Battle	$5	67,981	55,246	81.27%	12,735	18.73%
1995 Olympics Runner	$5	72,117	57,442	79.65%	14,675	20.35%

Date and Type	Face Value	Total Mintage	Proof	% Proof	Unc	% Unc
2000 Leif Erikson	$1	86,762	58,612	67.55%	28,150	32.45%
1994 WWII	$5	90,434	66,837	73.91%	23,597	26.09%
1996 Paralympics Wheelchair	$1	98,777	84,280	85.32%	14,497	14.68%
1995 Civil War Battle	$1	101,112	55,246	54.64%	45,866	45.36%
1993 Madison	$5	101,928	78,654	77.17%	23,274	22.83%
1992 Columbus	$5	104,065	79,734	76.62%	24,331	23.38%
1992 Olympics	$5	104,214	76,499	73.41%	27,715	26.59%
1996 Olympics Tennis	$1	107,999	92,016	85.20%	15,983	14.80%
1994 World Cup	$5	112,066	89,614	79.97%	22,447	20.03%
1998 Black Patriots	$1	112,280	75,070	66.86%	37,210	33.14%
1996 Nat'l Community Service	$1	125,043	101,543	81.21%	23,500	18.79%
2007 Little Rock	$1	127,698	89,742	70.28%	37,956	29.72%
2006 Ben Franklin 300 Youth	$1	130,000	85,000	65.38%	45,000	34.62%
2006 Ben Franklin Old	$1	130,000	85,00	65.38%	45,000	34.62%
1995 Olympics Cycling	$1	138,457	118,795	85.80%	19,662	14.20%
1997 National Law Enf. Mem.	$1	139,003	110,428	79.44%	28,575	20.56%
1996 Olympics High Jump	$1	140,199	124,502	88.80%	15,697	11.20%
1997 Jackie Robinson	$1	140,502	110,495	78.64%	30,007	21.36%
1991 Mount Rushmore	$5	143,950	111,991	77.80%	31,959	22.20%
1999 Yellowstone	$1	152,260	128,646	84.49%	23,614	15.51%
1996 Smithsonian 150th Anniv.	$1	160,382	129,152	80.53%	31,230	19.47%
1995 Olympics Track & Field	$1	161,731	136,935	84.67%	24,796	15.33%
1996 Olympic Swimming	$0.50	163,848	114,315	69.77%	49,533	30.23%
1995 Olympics Paralympics	$1	166,986	138,337	82.84%	28,649	17.16%
1996 Olympics Rowing	$1	168,148	151,890	90.33%	16,258	9.67%
2003 First Flight Centennial	$0.50	169,295	111,569	65.90%	57,726	34.10%
1996 Olympics Soccer	$0.50	175,248	122,412	69.85%	52,836	30.15%
2001 Capitol Visitor Center	$0.50	177,119	77,962	44.02%	99,157	55.98%
2001 Capitol Visitor Center	1	179,173	143,793	80.25%	35,380	19.75%
2005 Ch Justice Marshall	$1	180,407	133,368	73.93%	47,039	26.07%
1999 DolleyMadison	$1	181,195	158,247	87.34%	22,948	12.66%
2002 Salt Lake City Olympics	$1	202,986	163,773	80.68%	39,213	19.32%
1998 Robert F. Kennedy	$1	205,442	99,020	48.20%	106,422	51.80%

Date and Type	Face Value	Total Mintage	Proof	% Proof	Unc	% Unc
1989 Congress	$5	211,589	164,690	77.83%	46,899	22.17%
1995 Olympics Gymnastics	$1	225,173	182,676	81.13%	42,497	18.87%
2006 San Francisco Mint	$1	227,970	160,870	70.57%	67,100	29.43%
2003 First Flight Centennial	$1	246,847	193,086	78.22%	53,761	21.78%
2000 Library of Cngress	$1	249,671	196,900	78.86%	52,771	21.14%
2004 Edison	$1	253,518	194,189	76.60%	59,329	23.40%
1994 Women in Military	$1	259,100	207,200	79.97%	51,900	20.03%
1994 POW	$1	267,800	213,900	79.87%	53,900	20.13%
1994 Vietnam	$1	275,800	219,300	79.51%	56,500	20.49%
1995 Olympics Baseball	$0.50	282,692	118,087	41.77%	164,605	58.23%
2007 Jamestown 400th	$1	289,880	213,065	73.50%	76,815	26.50%
1994 Capitol Bic	$1	304,421	243,597	80.02%	60,824	19.98%
2004 Lewis & Clark	$1	314,342	234,541	74.61%	79,801	25.39%
1995 Olympics Basketball	$0.5	340,656	169,655	49.80%	171,001	50.20%
2002 West Point Military Bicen	$1	363,852	267,184	73.43%	96,668	26.57%
1988 Olympics	$5	413,055	281,465	68.14%	131,590	31.86%
1995 Civil War	$0.50	434,789	322,245	74.12%	112,544	25.88%
1995 Special Olympics	$1	441,065	351,764	79.75%	89,301	20.25%
1994 World War II	$1	445,667	339,358	76.15%	106,309	23.85%
1991 USO	$1	446,233	321,275	72.00%	124,958	28.00%
1992 Columbus	$1	492,252	385,290	78.27%	106,962	21.73%
1992 White House	$1	498,753	375,154	75.22%	123,599	24.78%
1986 Statue of Liberty	$5	499,261	404,013	80.92%	95,248	19.08%
2005 Marines 230th anniv.	$1	500,000	370,000	74.00%	130,000	26.00%
2001 American Buffalo/Indian	$1	500,000	272,869	54.57%	227,131	45.43%
1994 WWII	$0.50	512,759	313,801	61.20%	198,958	38.80%
1992 Columbus	$0.50	525,973	390,255	74.20%	135,718	25.80%
1984 Olympic	$10	573,364	497,478	86.76%	75,886	13.24%
1994 Jefferson	$1	599,844	332,890	55.50%	266,954	44.50%
1993 Madison	$1	627,995	532,747	84.83%	95,248	15.17%
1994 World Cup	$1	656,567	577,090	87.73%	81,524	12.27%
1992 Olympic	$0.50	678,484	517,318	76.25%	161,166	23.75%
1992 OLY $1	$1	688,842	503,239	73.06%	185,603	26.94%

Date and Type	Face Value	Total Mintage	Proof	% Proof	Unc	% Unc
1993 Madison	$0.50	775,287	584,350	75.37%	190,937	24.63%
1994 World Cup	$0.50	776,851	609,354	78.20%	168,208	21.80%
1991 Korea	$1	831,537	618,488	74.38%	213,049	25.62%
1987 Constitution	$5	865,884	651,659	75.26%	214,225	24.74%
1991 Mount Rushmore	$1	871,558	738,419	84.72%	133,139	15.28%
1989 Congress Bicentennial	$0.50	897,401	762,198	84.93%	135,203	15.07%
1991 Mount Rushmore	$0.50	926,011	753,257	81.34%	172,754	18.66%
1989 Congress	$1	931,650	767,897	82.42%	163,753	17.58%
1990 Eisenhower	$1	1,386,130	1,144,461	82.57%	241,669	17.43%
1988 Olympics	$1	1,550,734	1,359,366	87.66%	191,368	12.34%
1983 Olympics	$1	2,219,596	1,577,025	71.05%	642,571	28.95%
1984 Olympics	$1	2,252,514	1,801,210	79.96%	451,304	20.04%
1987 Constitution	$1	3,198,745	2,747,116	85.88%	451,629	14.12%
1982 Washington	$0.50	7,104,502	4,894,044	68.89%	2,210,458	31.11%
1986 Statue of Liberty	$1	7,138,273	6,414,638	89.86%	723,635	10.14%
1986 Statue of Liberty	$0.50	7,853,635	6,925,627	88.18%	928,008	11.82%

To make it easier, here is a re-sort of the data with uncirculated mintage coins of under 30,000; the proof data for the same and total mintage is a bonus:

Modern Commemorative Unc with Mintages Under 30,000

Date and Type	Face Value	Total Mintage	Proof	% Proof	Unc	% Unc
1997 Jackie Robinson 50th Anniv	$5	29,748	24,546	82.51%	5,202	17.49%
2000 Library of Congress gold/pt	$10	33,850	27,167	80.26%	6,683	19.74%
1996 Smithsonian 150th Anniv	$5	30,840	21,772	70.60%	9,068	29.40%
1996 Olympics Flag Bearers	$5	42,060	32,886	78.19%	9,174	21.81%
1996 Olympics Cauldron/Flame	$5	47,765	38,555	80.72%	9,210	19.28%
2003 First Flight	$10	31,975	21,846	68.32%	10,129	31.68%
2002 Salt Lake City Olympics	$5	42,523	32,351	76.08%	10,172	23.92%
1995 Olympics Stadium	$5	53,703	43,124	80.30%	10,579	19.70%
1997 Franklin D. Roosevelt	$5	41,368	29,474	71.25%	11,894	28.75%
1995 Civil War Battle	$5	67,981	55,246	81.27%	12,735	18.73%
1996 Paralympics Wheelchair	$1	98,777	84,280	85.32%	14,497	14.68%
1995 Olympics Runner	$5	72,117	57,442	79.65%	14,675	20.35%

Date and Type	Face Value	Total Mintage	Proof	% Proof	Unc	% Unc
2006 San Francisco	$5	51,200	35,841	70.00%	15,359	30.00%
1996 Olympics High Jump	$1	140,199	124,502	88.80%	15,697	11.20%
1996 Olympics Tennis	$1	107,999	92,016	85.20%	15,983	14.80%
1996 Olympics Rowing	$1	168,148	151,890	90.33%	16,258	9.67%
2007 Jamestown	$5	60,805	43,609	71.72%	17,196	28.28%
1999 George Washington	$5	55,038	35,656	64.78%	19,382	35.22%
1995 Olympics Cycling	$1	138,457	118,795	85.80%	19,662	14.20%
1994 World Cup	$5	112,066	89,614	79.97%	22,447	20.03%
1999 Dolley Madison	$1	181,195	158,247	87.34%	22,948	12.66%
1993 Madison	$5	101,928	78,654	77.17%	23,274	22.83%
1996 National Community	$1	125,043	101,543	81.21%	23,500	18.79%
1994 WWII	$5	90,434	66,837	73.91%	23,597	26.09%
1999 Yellowstone	$1	152,260	128,646	84.49%	23,614	15.51%
1992 Columbus	$5	104,065	79,734	76.62%	24,331	23.38%
1995 Olympics Track and Field	$1	161,731	136,935	84.67%	24,796	15.33%
1992 Olympics	$5	104,214	76,499	73.41%	27,715	26.59%
2000 Leif Erlkson	$1	86,762	58,612	67.55%	28,150	32.45%
1997 National Law Enf. Memo	$1	139,003	110,428	79.44%	28,575	20.56%
1995 Olympics Paralympics	$1	166,986	138,337	82.84%	28,649	17.16%
1997 Jackie Robinson	$1	140,502	110,495	78.64%	30,007	21.36%

STEPS TOWARD FINANCIAL FREEDOM IN YOUR RARE COIN RETIREMENT

"Taxes are what we pay for civilized society."

— Oliver Wendell Holmes, Associate Justice of the United States Supreme Court
dissenting, (Brandeis, J., concurring), in Compania General de Tabacos de Filipinas v.
Collector of Internal Revenue 275 U.S. 87, 100 (1927)

The hardest decision for the new investor in rare coins is deciding what to do with the tangible investment itself, for unlike stock certificates or bond coupons, rare coins have a beauty all their own that commands attention and may demand that its owner put it in a display. Even if that's not your intention, how and where you store your investment becomes important. Just how you create and maintain a record of their holdings, and ultimately how to maintain the investment, or if it is large enough, the collection itself becomes important. But eventually, it becomes clear that, similar to a Patek Philippe watch, you are merely a custodian for the next generation, and the issue arises as to how to either pass the collection on to another generation, or dispose of it with grace.

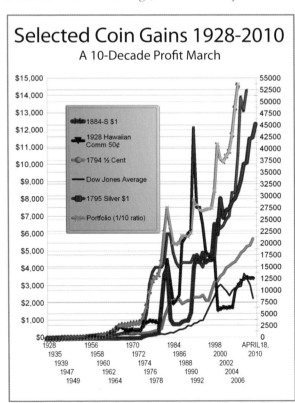

Of some 300 million Americans, nearly a third of whom are over age 50, there is now a steadily graying population. Longevity is increasing, with 13 percent of the population now over age 65, and, for the first time, a significant population—

David L. Ganz

3.6 million—over the age of 85. Asset management for those unable to financially handle all of their own affairs, as well as the subsequent Estates, or assets of the deceased, is a growing industry, and a growing problem.

Lifetime Management and Planning

For the collector who buys, sells, and acquires a coin collection over a lifetime, and for the investor who acquires an investment in rare coins over a shorter period of time, it is important to take steps during your lifetime to minimize your estate taxes and maximize your profits and capital gains—or to allow your heirs to do at least some post-mortem estate planning.

Even if you haven't made effective plans for your rare coin retirement, there are several highly effective post-mortem estate planning techniques that permit you, as the living beneficiary or successor, to make plans for the decedent.

You can effectively plan to lower or eliminate estate taxes on your collection; you can also create a trust, and a will, that gives your executor and to your trustee the broad powers necessary to take steps that will reduce what you pay to the tax man.

Every action that you take will, and should, be legal. Each step of the process can be done so that it is part of an overall plan designed to postpone, minimize or eliminate the tax bite that those who don't take the time to plan must pay.

Ten Steps to (Estate) Financial Freedom

Here's a summary of 10 key steps that you can take to facilitate handling of your numismatic estate.

1. Consider placing your coin investment into corporate ownership. You can also do this with a coin collection. You issue "A" and "B" shares, voting and non-voting, and retain voting control for as long as you need to. This allows for making gifts to your heirs, and also allows for income shifting; significantly, it can also create significant valuation changes to lower overall taxes. I've recommended this to clients for years. Ownership becomes shares of stock instead of outright ownership of coins, but it facilitates disposition, transfer and even valuation.

2. Make a comprehensive listing of your coin investment, complete with an expanded description of what each item is, the acquisition costs, and if the coins (in whole or part) constitute a collection that is esoteric, give your your best estimate of the value, and explain why you are valuing it that way.

It's amazing how often this is neglected. Don't depend on your friends from the coin club to guide your family; don't depend on a local dealer or even a nationally recognized expert (unless you are incapable of describing it yourself). Don't even depend on your attorney, accountant or bank advisor. You should know your own investment in rare coins, so do this work yourself!

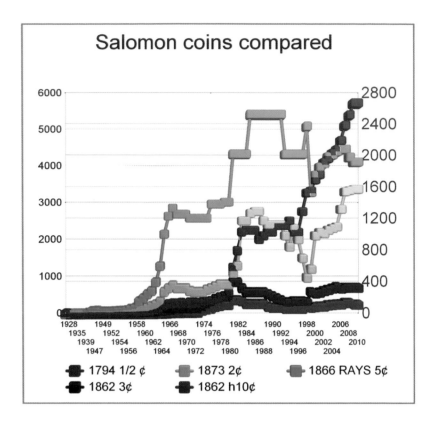

Salomon coins compared

Legend:
- 1794 1/2 ¢
- 1862 3¢
- 1873 2¢
- 1862 h10¢
- 1866 RAYS 5¢

A major Tax Court case on this very topic (*Matter of Trompeter*) was decided Jan. 27, 1998. The rare coin investor was a well-known collector of proof gold coinage and other rarities.– and he left behind a multi-million dollar estate. After his death, the heirs, executors, and the Internal Revenue Service became embroiled in a claim of tax fraud because of allegations that the gold coin collection, part of which was sold by Superior Coin Galleries of Beverly Hills, was deliberately undervalued. A $14.8 million fraud penalty assessed by the IRS was the subject of the dispute.

At the heart of the matter was over 180 coins were submitted to the Professional Coin Grading Service (PCGS) for grading. The conclusion: 69 coins were proof-63, 78 were proof-64 and 12 were proof-65. (There was just one found to be proof-66, one proof-67 and one proof-69).

Trompeter's gold was then shipped to Numismatic Guaranty Corporation (NGC), whose experts had a different view of part of the collection. They agreed that there was one proof-69, but after that they parted company. NGC's findings: there were 5 proof-67s, 22 that graded proof-66, 51 that graded proof-65, 71 that graded proof-64, and only 21 that graded proof-63.

In contrast to the 15 pieces PCGS found to be 65 or better, NGC ruled 78 to be in that state of preservation (MS or Proof-65).

This is not the end of the story, however, for the Tax Court had to decide whose view of the grade – which ultimately determined value – was correct. Other experts were provided, hired with the expensive compliments of both sides in the litigation – the IRS and the Trompeter Estate.

Maurice Rosen, a well known writer, and investment counselor, was one expert that was engaged. His finding as a reported by the Court: "he graded 61 percent of the coins the same as a PCGS, 26 percent of the coins lower than PCGS, and 13 percent of the coins higher than PCGS."

There were other experts also involved, but they focused on the worth of the coins -- which is after all what grading really is: a short-hand for the value of the coin.

In the final analysis, the Court rejected all of the experts save one: the decedent himself, Ed Trompeter, who had placed a value on the coins that Superior sold at auction before his death. Their reasoning: he had predicted within 2 percent the selling prices received at auction.

3. Maintaining good records of your coin investment.

You should maintain an inventory record of your rare coin investment. It will assist in the process of eventually liquidating your investment for top dollar and will also be helpful to an executor, or to your attorney-in-fact (someone who is not a lawyer but has a power of attorney from you). It should have a list that contains at least the following information:

• What the specific item is (list its date, markings that are special, type if applicable and catalogue number.

• Grade or condition. If an item should be graded by a particular grading, certification or authentication service in your opinion, you should note this factor.

• Purveyor or dealer or collector you purchased from. This may not be obvious, but some vendors are known for particular types of coins. The identically-described coin sold by a non-specialist may be worth less than from a specialist.

• Cost of the item.

• Who you believe might be the best person or firm to handle disposition (can be done by classes of items or individually)

• What you believe "current" value is; you should put down a valuation at the time that the list is compiled, and periodically update it. If for any reason you can't do it periodically or regularly, be sure to list the last time that you did it.

• If you have a friend or colleague who can assist the executor as to pricing and valuation, give a name and address.

• Besides executors, powers of attorney (with a clause that permits them to continue in the disability of the principal) are very useful. They can be general and broad (a short form power of attorney for all purposes) or very limited (a power to dispose of a coin collection).

4. Begin a pattern of lifetime giving of appreciated property to charitable institutions; the effect on your estate taxes can be considerable. This is under-appreciated, but obvious. You buy, hold, donate at the appreciated value, take the tax deduction and save on your taxes.

You could, if it seemed appropriate as part of an overall estate plan (designed to save taxes) give a bequest to an organization. It's best to use appreciated property for this, since it avoids the capital gain, but allows a full deduction for the fair market value of the items donated.

A typical clause might read: *I hereby give, devise and bequeath a portion of my coin collection, consisting of Indian Head Cents, to the American Numismatic Society of New York, N.Y..*

What's also important to any executor or other person who is charged with disposing of your collection for you is what your original value is or was on any coin.

This is vital for compiling tax records (since any tax that might be due is calculated on the gain, not merely on the purchase price).

5. If you've come into a numismatic estate, hire a skilled appraiser—someone who is sensitive not only to the value of individual items, but also to the way in which stock can be valued to lower your estate tax. Ignore the appraiser who offers to do it for a percentage of the finalized value; skilled appraisers will work on an hourly basis, or for a fixed fee. That's to your benefit.

6. Watch the rates of taxation, and work them into your coin investment, your coin hobby, and your business life. Individual rates of taxation, the capital gains rate, and estate tax rates aren't the same; if you can shift what tax has to be paid to a lower rate, you're way ahead. This is true now, it was true years ago, and will be true in the future. If the capital gains rate shifts on collectibles, again, be prepared to move. Your investment in rare coins is a collectible thanks to section 408(ms

7. Don't be afraid to take a loss on an item; you can offset against capital gains, and, to a limited extent, against ordinary income. ($3,000 of a capital loss can be used to offset ordinary income)

8. Take the time to have a will prepared—one designed to minimize the total taxes that you, your spouse and heirs will pay. Sometimes it means paying a little more now for a lot less, later. A postscript: don't be afraid to revise it as often as necessary. You can do it by a codicil or have a new document prepared in its entirety. This is cheap insurance.

9. Consider, if you live in a jurisdiction where probate is time consuming or expensive (Florida is notorious for this), the option of a living trust for your collection and perhaps other assets.

10. Have a power of attorney prepared—with a springing power, or with one in which your attorney-in-fact can act through your disability, and beyond, as a way to take prompt action when it is most needed.

11. Coin collectors and investors who are concerned about their estate planning, about reporting requirements on buys and sales, and on creating a safe and secure

environment for their numismatic holdings ought to consider forming a small, personal corporation.

There are a number of reasons why a small business – even a hobby business – and individual investors ought to consider incorporating today. Privacy heads the list. But so do a number of other requirements for modern living, and the need to protect your assets from suit and seizure. There is also the deductibility of various expenses that are permitted in corporate businesses, but not individually.

Corporations are the preferred method of doing business in the United States. That's true whether you are a large corporation such as AT&T or General Motors or the newest company that has started in your basement, fulfilling orders and trying to make a go of it.

The Internal Revenue Code tends to issue regulations that cover all corporations and treats them the same – except for those corporations that are Sub-Chapter "S" corporations, meaning that the corporation pays no income tax. (That election allows the income to be taxed directly to the shareholders).

Almost anyone can form a corporation today—the real question is why do it in the first place, and then, what's the best state to choose as a business situs (you don't have to do it in the state where you live).

Corporations—even small ones—have at least five strong points that every investor (and even a more than casual collector) ought to carefully examine before deciding whether or not they are ripe for this method of asset protection. There are other minor ones which also make it worthwhile for the more than casual coin investor interested in their rare coin retirement, as well as ordinary coin buyers and sellers to consider, even if you have another job and are an employee of a company.

• Corporations traditionally have perpetual existence, though you can limit its life by so stating in its charter. Since a corporation never dies, it has no estate tax return to fill out, though it has income tax to pay, just as you do.

• Safe deposit boxes can be held in a corporate name. This is a smart way to go. When you die, your personal box may be sealed under your state law; but your corporate box remains open to any authorized signatory, including corporate officers (who may be a spouse or trusted friend). This avoids a lengthy wait to dispose of assets such as double eagles or encapsulated coins which may require prompt sale in a changing marketplace.

• All corporations, large and small, are exempt from the reporting requirements under Section 6045 of the Internal Revenue Code. This means that while an individual who sells certain coins or bullion may be subject to reporting and back-up withholding, it is inapplicable to a corporation. The exemption is written right into IRS regulations.

• If you purchase stock through a corporation, there is a 70% dividend exclusion from taxable income as long as the stock is held for more than 45 days. If you are at the maximum federal rate of individual taxation that savings is almost 10%.

• Corporations can have a health and medical expense plan paid for by the corporation, and deductible by the corporation – rights no longer fully and completely available to individuals or partnerships.

• Particularly in urban areas, corporate employees (you) can exclude a portion from gross income for employer-provided transit passes or an even higher sum for employer-provided qualified parking expenses.

• The corporation can have its required meeting of the board of directors anywhere. Not just in your state. But anywhere. Perhaps in a nice place such as Puerto Rico or San Diego. Just make sure that you stick to the formalities.

To form a corporation, you can go to a lawyer or an accountant and spend up to $1,500 or more-- or you can find a service that will do it for you for a fifth of that price, or less. One that many investors and collectors have found impressive is Inc. Plan U.S.A., located in Delaware. Their address:

Inc. Plan (USA)

818 Washington Street, Wilmington, DE 19801, Tel. (800)462-4633

Fax (302)428-1274.

For around $300, Inc. Plan USA create your corporation the same day and let you start on your path to financial freedom.

Mention this book and Inc. Plan USA will give you a whole year's service of acting as statutory agent for the corporation—a $100 value—for free.

12. Don't be afraid to pay some tax. If you make a gift, payment of a tax starts the running of the statute of limitations on challenging it; if you pay estate taxes, or capital gains taxes, the income has been declared, and unless fraudulent is likely to remain unchallenged. It makes sense to pay tax that is due; get the statute of limitations started early, and let it be complete.

Why to Plan Now

It's best to prepare now, because disposition of a collection can be difficult even under the best of circumstances. And at an emotional time, such as in the event of a death, it's best to have pre-set instructions that a loved one or an executor can follow. The reason for this is clear: you can minimize the amount of taxes that have to be paid, maximize the value of the collection, and dispose of it in accordance with your wishes, not those of individuals who may not care about the collection the way you do.

Today, with many people living longer, but becoming disabled, it is also important to consider what you might want done in the event that you become too disabled to assist in the disposition of your collection. This could be due to Alzheimer's disease (formerly called "senility" by many), a catastrophic illness or a disabling stroke or other event that leaves you with no capacity to complete disposal of the collection.

If you have a strong preference as to how you wish your collection to be handled, you can note it in a precatory (advisory) letter to your executor, and then have your will merely remark that such a side letter exists.

Dispose By Letter, Not By Will

If a will states "I give my $250,000 coin collection to my friend, Bill," it is likely to trigger interest from tax authorities, and others. There's a better approach: a letter of instruction over the disposition. A typical will clause that can accomplish this easily, without undue publicity, and in close to anonymous fashion, might read as follows (the bracketed portion can be omitted if it is known by your heirs that you have a collection):

All of my personal property, [including my coin collection if still in my possession at the time of my death], should be disposed of by my executor in accordance with the instructions that I have left in a written letter that is kept in my safe deposit box.

If you change your mind about the disposition, you can change the letter easily. How you dispose of it is up to you, but there are some general guidelines. First, unless you have a long and established relationship with someone in the field, if an outright purchase is contemplated, you should require three separate bids to be prepared. This avoids the possibility of collusion, and more importantly, increases the possibility of receiving the maximum value for the collection.

If you decide to have the collection auctioned, it is not necessary to have all of it sold by the same auctioneer. Not all auctioneers specialize in the same areas. Some, for example, are more competent in ancient coins than they are in modern foreign issues. Some auction houses are excellent with the Old Masters but less than adequate for newer material.

As a collector, and a purchaser of a collectible, you know this inherently. But your heirs won't unless you tell them. So do that in a letter to the executor or side letter to someone who has a power of attorney to act on your behalf.

Typically, the letter might read "I direct that my collection of Byzantine gold coins be sold by Heritage Numismatic Auctions, Dallas, Texas," or that "I direct my collection of U.S. coins be sold by this year's official ANA auctioneer," if location rather than auctioneer is important.

In summary, investing in rare coins and planning a rare coin retirement affords an opportunity and the opportunity for gain. It encourages you to acquire for investment affordable rare coins right now, and to use the laws and regulations that affect all businesses, and investments, to help you plan for your financial tomorrow.

Chapter 14

PLANNING YOUR RARE COIN RETIREMENT AND GRADUATION DAY: ESTATE PLANNING FOR COIN COLLECTORS AND INVESTORS

Birth, death and taxes are the only three certainties in life, and with astute planning, you can minimize or almost eliminate the death taxes that are typically conclude the life of many unprepared collectors. You also can use the opportunity as you plan for your rare coin retirement to do estate planning while you are alive (and set the stage for post-mortem estate planning, as necessary and conssient with your goals).

Both rare coin retirement and estate planning have some things in common. One is the "death tax" imposed several years ago. It expired on Dec.31, 2009,

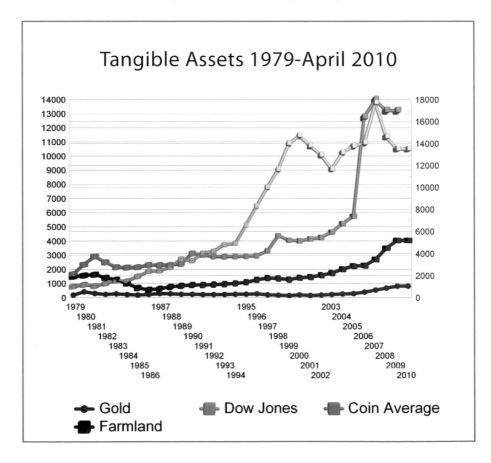

(not in effect in 2010) – but is on schedule to go back into effect at a steep 55 percent in 2011. It's a gamble as of this writing as to whether or not Congress will impose a lower rate, stay with the program at a lower rate, by legislation in 2010, or recognize that the "death tax" was so political unpopular that it's best to eliminate it entirely. In this fiscal climate, my guess is that it will be extended at a lower rate, but that's still something tangible that everyone who collects or invests in numismatic items or precious metals ought to consider.

This is not necessarily a pleasant matter, but for the collector who buys, sells, and acquires a coin collection over a lifetime, it is important to take steps to allow you to minimize your estate taxes, maximize your profits and capital gains during your lifetime and either pass on the benefit to your heirs, or as you best feel your estate should be distributed.

Back in 1997, I wrote the prequel to this book which had the neat title, "Planning Your Rare Coin Retirement." Demographics show that many collectors start (or return to) their hobby in middle-age and pursue it avidly until their retirement, when they begin to scale back. This means that they have a collection from childhood that has appreciated substantially in value, or are in the process

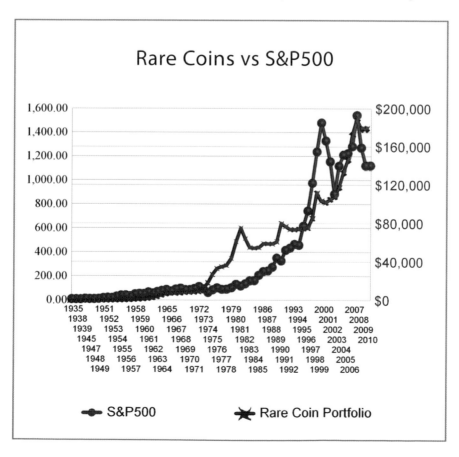

of trying to do the same in a shorter period of time.

Eventually, they are faced with a dilemma: Do they continue actively participating in a hobby that their spouse or children (or both) do not appreciate? If they do decide to reduce their involvement, what becomes of the collection that they have spent years acquiring. If they don't decide to reduce their involvement, what then?

Worse still, what if the collection actually has substantial value — where a miscue could easily result in a substantial tax burden on an estate.

Many simply do nothing and take the position of "que sera, sera" — what will be will be. They are actually immobilized with fear of what to do, or what not to do during their lifetimes.

Fortunately, even if your haven't made effective plans during your rare coin retirement, there are several highly effective post-mortem estate planning techniques -- that let the living successor (usually a spouse, sometimes a child, infrequently someone else), make plans for the decedent long after they are gone.

As a vibrant, living collector, you can plan effectively to lower or eliminate estate taxes on your collection; you can also create a trust, and will, that give your executor and trustee broad powers necessary to take steps that will reduce what you pay to the tax man. Every action that you take will be legal. That is essential in any advice that I would give, or offer.

After nearly a quarter century of practicing law, I have often been called on to offer advice, and to give assurance that it both minimizes taxes and complies with the law. Some look to cheat the tax man; they don't remain my clients for long, for the methodology that I recommend is within the letter and intent of the law. In fact, let me warn you right now: if you want to work outside the boundaries of what the law allows, the odds favor that you will be found out – or worse, your family will be discovered in a scandal after you are gone and can't explain it – and not only will your plans come to naught, but you may lose every advantage and dollar you thought that you saved and watch it disintegrate in interest and penalties.

Each step of the process can be done so that it is part of an overall plan that is designed to postpone, minimize or eliminate the tax bite that those who don't take the time to plan must pay.

Here's a handy summary of key steps that you can take in your rare coin retirement -- a guaranteed way to reduce the amount that your estate will pay to the federal and state tax authorities, and a way to facilitate handling of your numismatic estate.

• Consider placing your coin collection into two parts: the fun part that you collect for shear enjoyment, and that which you are looking for substantial value change. As to the former, which might be presidential inaugural medals or state quarters, or similar, do what you want with them but leave clear instructions how to value them.

As to the areas where you anticipate growth, consider making a changeover into corporate ownership. This allows for gifting, income shifting, and valuation changes to lower overall taxes.

Here's an added bonus of running your rare coin retirement as a business corporation: corporations that are in the business of buying and selling rare coins don't have sales tax -- because they are buying for resale – though there may be other taxes that are owing from time to time. Saving eight percent or more on your investment coins intended for buy and sell and trade, anyway, can be substantial.

This works most easily when you start collecting this way — from the beginning — but corporate ownerships can be, and are, useful in dividing interests and allowing a shift in value appreciation to move down a whole generation, given passage of time.

Just by way of example, suppose Joe Collector forms a corporation with his spouse, Harriet, and children little Ricky and Lucy as shareholders.

Joe funds the corporation with his collection; the voting shares are owned by Joe and Harriet. Little Ricky and Lucy own non-voting shares that share in the appreciated value, which perhaps will be realized when they, themselves, are adults.

Eventually, little Ricky and Lucy will purchase Joe and Harriet's shares — or perhaps their yet unborn children will. Joe Collector will have a capital gain, but the real appreciation is that the asset has been seamlessly moved down one or more generations.

• Have a comprehensive list of your collection made, complete with acquisition costs, and (if esoteric) your best estimate of the value.

This is perhaps the most important thing that any collector can do. You know your own collection best of all. If you have an odd die variety, your spouse will never know it. Speaking from experience, the more detailed the list, the better chance of realizing what the collection is worth when it is eventually sold or liquidated.

• Begin a pattern of lifetime giving of appreciated property to charitable institutions. The effect on your estate taxes can be considerable. Suppose that you bought a 1927-D Peace dollar in MS-65 from Heritage in 1987 for $520 at one of their auction sales. In January 2008, Heritage sold a PCGS-graded MS-65 for $5,750. The appreciation in value, if the coin is given to a recognized charity, goes to the charity; the fat tax deduction is yours.

You could, if it seemed appropriate as part of an overall estate plan (designed to save taxes) give a bequest to an organization. It's best to use appreciated property for this, since it avoids the capital gain, but allows a full deduction for the fair market value of the items donated.

A typical clause might read:

I hereby give, devise and bequeath a portion of my coin collection to the Ameri-

can Numismatic Society of New York, New York.

What's also important to any executor or other person who is charged with disposing of your collection for you is what your original value is or was on any coin.

This is vital for compiling tax records (since any tax that might be due is calculated on the gain, not merely on the purchase price).

• If you've come into a numismatic estate, hire a skilled appraiser — someone who is sensitive to not only the value of individual items, but also the way in which stock can be valued to lower your estate tax.

There are multiple ways that coins (and other collectibles) can be valued. The liquidation value differs from the long-term disposal valuation. The IRS will allow various techniques to be used; you can pick the one that works best for your own situation.

Valuation differences

Valuations can be done in several ways. First, the pieces can be valued at their liquidation value, or the price they would likely bring in a "fire sale" where the buyer didn't really have to buy, but the seller was forced to sell. Or the coins could be valued at their fair market value, or the price a reasonable seller would ask and a reasonable buyer would pay.

Or there might be a valuation on a more esoteric basis, as where two or more interested buyers sought the identical piece from the same seller; the free market would determine who would offer the higher price.

Problems of valuation are commonly encountered in connection with the insuring of coins, paying insurance proceeds in the event of their loss, valuing collateral for loan purposes, selling collateral in liquidation of loans, bankruptcy situations, and ascertaining the losses (or gains) of someone complaining about a wrong alleged to have been committed as the result of a coin purchase, sale, or trade. It can also take place in estate proceedings.

If there is a large quantity of coins, either of the same type or simply in volume, a "blockage" discount might be appropriate. Two examples explain the concept. An 1856 flying eagle cent is rare, and one example in fine condition might sell for $4,000 or more. When the John Beck collection was sold, there were 531 pieces of 1856 flying eagle cents that had to be valued. It would not have made sense to do a unit price multiplied by the number of coins because placing that many identical rarities on the market at the same time would depress the marketplace.

The valuation of a coin collection is usually likely to differ depending on the purpose for which the appraisal is made. It stands to reason, for example, that an appraisal based on the price that a dealer would pay for a coin will be substantially lower than one based on the price–the so-called replacement cost--that a person would have to pay in order to buy the item on the open market; the dealer is purchasing with the expectation of reselling at a profit. In general, the only time that a valuation by a dealer in preparing to make a purchase bid is involved is when the bid itself gives rise to litigation.

By contrast, an appraisal based on replacement cost is the most likely method of valuation to be encountered and is usually involved when, for example, insurance questions arise concerning coins that have been lost, stolen, damaged, or destroyed. Even though lost, stolen, or destroyed coins may not be physically available for examination, they can nonetheless be appraised if they have been encapsulated by a grading service such as ANACS, PCGS, or the Numismatic Guaranty Corporation (NGC), certified, or otherwise photographed.

Alternatively, value can often be determined by examining invoices that reflect the grade and the original acquisition costs.

A third basis of valuation is the fair market value, or the price a coin would bring if the holder sold it to a willing buyer. Typically, in the absence of extreme rarity or some other highly unusual factor, the fair market value will be less than or equal to the replacement cost.

Appraisal at fair market value is generally done when valuing a coin collection in connection with a decedent's estate or when a coin or coin collection is donated to a tax-exempt organization for income tax purposes.

Fair market value also comes into play when a collector seeks to exchange coins of like kind with another collector, a trade which typically does not have tax consequences under section 1031 of the Internal Revenue Code. Fair market value is not explicitly defined in the Internal Revenue Code, but the judicial standard for determining fair market value is the price at which the property will change hands between a willing buyer and a willing seller, with neither being under any compulsion to buy or sell and with both having reasonable knowledge of the facts.

There are other methods of valuation that can be defined by contract, such as rare coin inventories valued at liquidation market value and variations on that theme including appraisals of condition only, where the lender does the pricing based on the condition of coins proffered. There is also the difference between wholesale and retail prices to consider in any appraisal.

Even assuming that there's agreement on appraisal and valuation methodology, that does not preclude litigation, even when payment exceeds the appraised amount. It may also be necessary to provide an increase or decrease in value based on blockage, the size of the collection, and its importance in or to the marketplace.

Here are some other tips:

• Consider placing gold, silver or platinum eagles that you intended to purchase anyway in a Roth IRA. A Roth IRA (named after Delaware Sen. William Roth, who originated the concept) is funded with post-tax income, but the gains are not taxable. Withdrawals of earnings are tax-free if you're over age 59½ and at least five years have expired since you established your Roth IRA.

Effect of Modified AGI on Roth IRA Contributions[23]

This table shows whether your contribution to a Roth IRA is affected by the amount of your modified Adjusted Gross Income as computed for Roth IRA purposes.

If you have taxable compensation and your filing status is	And your modified AGI is	Then
married filing jointly or **qualifying widow(er)**	Less than $167,000	you can contribute up to the limit
	at least $167,000 but less than $177,000	the amount you can contribute is reduced
	$177,000 or more	you cannot contribute to a Roth IRA
married filing separately and you lived with your spouse at any time during the year	zero (-0)	you can contribute up to the limit
	more than zero (-0-) but less than $10,000	the amount you can contribute is reduced
	$10,000 or more	you cannot contribute to a Roth IRA
single, head of household, or **married filing separately** and you did not live with your spouse at any time during the year	less than $105,000	you can contribute up to the limit
	at least $105,000 but less than $120,000	the amount you can contribute is reduced
	$120,000 or more	you cannot contribute to a Roth IRA

The IRS says that if you are 50 years of age or older before 2010: The maximum annual contribution that can be made to a traditional or Roth IRA is the smaller of $6,000 or the amount of your taxable compensation for 2009.

This limit can be split between a traditional IRA and a Roth IRA but the combined limit is $6,000. The maximum deductible contribution to a traditional IRA and the maximum contribution to a Roth IRA may be reduced depending on your modified adjusted gross income

If you are married, filing jointly, you may contribute if your adjusted gross income is less than $176,000. If you are single, head of household, or married filing separately and you did not live with your spouse at any time during the year, and your modified adjusted gross income is less than $120,000, you may contribute to a Roth IRA.

Some additional tips:

• Be certain that your collection is held in a safety deposit box, and that the safety deposit box is not in your individual name.

Individual boxes are frequently sealed at the time of the death of a box holder. Corporate boxes (like corporations themselves) are "forever."

• Watch the rates of taxation, and work them into your hobby, and your business life. Individual rates of taxation, the capital gains rate, and estate tax rates aren't the same; if you can shift what tax has to be paid to a lower rate, you're way ahead.

• Don't be afraid to take a loss on an item; you can offset against capital gains, and (to a limited extent) against ordinary income.

The late Bob Medlar, a San Antonio coin dealer and member of the ANA Board of Governors, once told me that the hardest lesson he ever learned was that he had to sell off the "bad" buys that he had made — pieces that didn't quite make the grade. But those losses ultimately became, and can become, big gains if you capitalize on your mistake and buy what you wanted in the first place.

• Take the time to have a will prepared — one that is designed to minimize the total taxes that you, your spouse, and heirs will pay. Sometimes it means paying a little more now for a lot less, later. Make sure your counsel is well-versed in how your hobby and investments are linked, and is familiar with estate law concerns.

• Consider if you live in a jurisdiction where probate is time consuming or expensive the option of a living trust for your collection, and perhaps other assets. Or, transferring your collectible assets into a corporate ownership.

• Have a power of attorney prepared — with a "springing power," or with one in which your attorney-in-fact can act through your disability, and beyond, as a way to take prompt action when it is most needed.

• Don't be afraid to pay some tax. If you make a gift, payment of a tax starts the statute of limitations on challenging it; if you pay estate taxes, or capital gains taxes, the income has been declared and (unless fraudulent) is likely to remain unchallenged.

Why to Plan Now

It's best to prepare for that now, because disposition of a collection can be difficult even under the best of circumstances. And, at an emotional time (typically in the event of a death), it's best to have pre-set instructions that a loved one, or an executor can follow.

Reason for this is clear: you can minimize the amount of taxes that have to be paid, maximize the value of the collection, and dispose of it in accordance with your wishes— not those of individuals who may not care about the collection the way you do.

Today, with many people living longer, but becoming disabled, it is also important to consider what you might want done in the event that you become too disabled to assist in the disposition of your collection.

This could be in the form of Alzheimer disease (formerly called senility by many), or even something more serious such as a catastrophic illness, or perhaps even a disabling stroke or other event that leaves you with no capacity to complete disposal of the collection.

If you have a strong preference as to how you wish your collection to be handled, you can place it in a precatory (advisory) letter to your executor, and then have your will merely remark that such a side letter exists.

This is merely precatory, or advisory, but your heirs are most likely to follow your advice about something you know far more about than they do.

Dispose by Letter, Not by Will

If a will states, "I give my $250,000 coin collection to my friend, Bill," it is likely to create interest from tax authorities, and others. There's a better approach — a letter of disposition.

A typical will clause that will accomplish this, easily, and without undue publicity, and in close to anonymous fashion, might read as follows:

All of my personal property, including my coin collection, should be disposed of by my executor in accordance with the instructions that I have left in a written letter that is kept in my safe deposit box.

If you change your mind about the disposition, you can change the letter easily.

How you wish to dispose of it is up to you, but there are some general guidelines. First, unless you have a long and established relationship with someone in the field, if an outright purchase is contemplated, you should require three separate bids to be prepared.

This avoids the possibility of collusion, and more importantly also tends to maximize the possibility of receiving the most value for the collection.

If you decide to have the collection auctioned, it is not necessary to have all of it sold by the same auctioneer. Not all auctioneers specialize in the same areas. Some, for example, are more competent in ancient coins than they are in modern foreign issues. Some auction houses are excellent with the Old

Masters but less than adequate for newer material.

As a collector, and a purchaser of a collectible, you know this inherently. But your heirs won't unless you tell them. So do that in a letter to the executor or side letter to someone who has a power of attorney to act on your behalf.

Typically, the letter might read "I direct that my collection of Byzantine gold coins be sold by Sotheby's, London," or that "I direct my collection of U.S. coins be sold by this year's official ANA auctioneer," if location rather than auctioneer is important.

Or you may believe that a specific auctioneer whose promotional abilities are well known could work in your favor. You can even negotiate estate commissions — in advance — while you are alive.

One thing is clear. It's hard to imagine a more satisfying result to a life of collecting and investing than to be able to pass the fruits of your labor down one generation, two generations or more. It is the ultimate culmination of planning your rare coin retirement.

GLOSSARY

1964 Peace dollar — Struck on LBJ's orders, recalled and eliminated by Congress.

3 Roubles — Russian platinum coin of the mid-19th century; also 6 and 12 roubles.

ACCGS — American Coin Club Grading Service

ASA — Accugrade, Inc

Adams, Eva B. — Director of the Mint, 1961-1969. Later a member of the ANA Board of Governors.

Adams-Woodin — HA book (1913) on pattern coins that precedes Judd (1959). William Woodin has the added distinction of being FDR's first Secretary of the Treasury.

Akers — David W. Akers (coin dealer). Cataloguer of the John Jay Pittman Collection. An expert on gold coins (and author of a six volume auction history of America's gold coins, Akers first worked for Paramount and also headed up their international coin marketing efforts. His career would make for the subject of a fascinating biography.

American Arts Medallion — Authorized by Congress before gold coin ownership was allowed by the government (1979-1984)

ANA — American Numismatic Association. Largest educational, non-profit organization of coin collectors in the world. Founded 1891, chartered by Congress 1912 (50 years) and for perpetuity (1962). The author was the 48th president of the ANA from 1993-1995.

ANACS — ANACS Certification Service, Inc

Assay — The process of melting and testing a coin, lode, rock or placer for its metal content or fineness.

Atwater — William Cutler Atwater, a collector. B. Max Mehl's Atwater sale, 1946. Contains many famous rarities.

Auction — A method of sales in which a middleman (auctioneer) offers an item for sale and receives steadily upward bids until the last bid standing is declared the winner. A preferred way too sell coins.

Avoirdupois — Method of measure. 16 avoirdupois ounces in a pound. Not used in measuring precious metal. See troy ounce.

Avoirdupois ounce — Traditional method of weights and means (16 ounces per pound); not used to measure precious metals (see troy ounce).

B.U. — Brilliant uncirculated condition (from MS-60 upward).

Ballerina — Russian bullion coin.

Barber — Chief Engravers of the United States (father and son) William Barber and Charles Barber. Barber dimes, quarters and half dollars refer to Charles Barber's designs which entered circulation (1892) serving until 1916.

Bareford — Harold S. Bareford. N.Y. attorney with a fine eye for rare coins. (1894-1978) stack's sold his collection in 1978 and 1982.

Bland Allison — Congressional Act (1878) that passed over veto of President Hayes, causing the government to buy silver, coin it (principally Morgan dollars) and recoin old silver.

Bland-Allison Act — Passed by Congress (1878) over the veto of President Rutherford B. Hayes, this led to the Morgan silver dollar. The veto was one of 12 of the Hayes presidency and the only one overridden by Congress. In the history of the United States, there have been over 2,500 vetoes; only 110, including this one, were overridden.

Brand, Virgil — Chicago 'Twenties beer baron (d. 1926) who was also a coin collector. His collection was still being sold into the 21st century.

Bryan, William Jennings — Three time Democratic presidential nominee, pro-silver ("shall not crucify mankiund upon a cross of gold"). Famous in later years as WIlson's Secretary of State and, of course, the Scopes ("Monkey" Trial).

Buffalo — Image by James Earl Fraser on reverse of the nickel (1913-1938) and more recently on a one ounce gold coin 24k fineness.

Bullion — Raw or refined precious metal, traded in defined units on commodity exchanges; some bullion items cast into ingots or bars are collected in their own right.

Bullion-like — Semi-numismatic, an ingot or a coin that has nominal numismatic value and is intended for use other than as a coin.

Byzantine — Coinage of Constantinople (the Eastern Roman Empire). Also politics in the ANA.

Casa de Moneda — The Mint (Mexico)

Charles Jay — Collection sold by Stack's October 1967

Citizens Commemorative Coin Advisory Committee — Congressionally mandated committee to assist in commemorative coin design and mintages, succeed by the Citizens Coin Advisory Committee.

Clad coinage — Current US dime, quarter and half dollar, nickel-copper outer sandwich, copper inner core. Process is a DuPont patent.

Coinage Act of 1873 — Sometimes referred to as the "Crime of '73", this remodification of the minting and coinage law took away a privilege of converting silver into coin (based on weight) for a nominal service charge, preventing "cheap" money from inflating the country after vast quantities were discovered at the Comstock Lode.

Commemorative — Coins designed to honor a person or event. Some circulate, some do not.

Common date — Coins whose date and mintmark are seen frequently compared to scarce coins.

Comstock Lode — The mother of all silver discoveries, in Nevada.

Copper nickel — Composition of some modern coins, and older ones such as Indian head cents (1859-1864)

Copper nickel half dollar — Clad commemorative half.

Croesus — King Croesus (d. 546 B.C.) is widely credited with creating the first gold (electrum) coinage; his name was a symbol of wealth in the ancient world ("as rich as Croesus").

Date Freeze — When the 1964 date was frozen on U.S. coins by order of Congress; it turned out coin collectors were not the root cause of the nation's coin shortage.

Demonetize — Takes away legal tender property of a coin. Money of the 3rd french republic was demonetized.

Devaluation — Altering the value of a foreign or domestic currency in the international arena. U.S. has done it in 1934, 1971 and 1972 by changing the official value of gold from $20.67 to $35, then $42.2.2 (official price in 2010).

DGS — Dominion Grading Service

Dollars — Universal currency and symbol ($) of the United States

Ducat — Trade coin of the Austro-Hungarian Empire, Netherlands, and others, struck in gold.

Eagle — Statutorily found on reverse of all U.S. subsidiary coinage above a dime; the name of the gold, silver ands platinum precious metal coins.

Eliasberg — Louis Eliasberg who had acquired and displayed a complete set of U.S. coins, half cent through double eagle (including the 1933 $20, which he returned when controversy was raise). His collection was sold by Stacks (H.R. Lee, 1947) and Bowers & Ruddy (1996-1997).

Euros — The Euro [€] is the currency of the old "Common Market". Now the expanded European Union. It is used in 16 of the 27 Member States. The states, known collectively as the Eurozone, are Austria, Belgium, Cyprus, Finland, France, Germany, Greece, Ireland, Italy, Luxembourg, Malta, the Netherlands, Portugal, Slovakia, Slovenia and Spain.

Fabrication — Minting term: the process of making coin or bullion products.

Farouk — Last King of Egypt and a significant coin collector. "The Palace Collection" acquired by the Egyptian government in the coup d'etat that overthrew him, was sold in Cairo in 1954. John Jay Pittman was one of the buyers.

FDR — 32nd American President, nationalized gold (1933) and silver (1934). Portrait found on the dime (1946-date).

Franc — The currency of France and several French-speaking countries. Among gold coins, 20 franc equals .1867 troy ounces of gold.

Friedberg numbering — System of numbering devised in Gold Coins of the World (1957), currently found in 8th edition by Arthur Friedberg and his brother, Ira Friedberg. (Also seen as F., or F-, followed by a number which is that assigned by the book's editor to the catalogue, usually in chronological date/denomination order).

FTC — The Federal Trade Commission. A government watchdog agency known in the numismatic field for their aggressive actions against firms who over graded, overpriced, and over represented the truth about rare coin investment. Their "jawboning" on Salomon Brothers caused the "white shoe" firm to discontinue tracking rare coins against other assets, including stocks and bonds.

Grams — Method of measure (metric). There are 31.1035 grams in a troy ounce.

Grinnell — Albert Grinnell, currency collector. Collection sold over 7 auctions, 1944-1946. Catalogued by Barney Bluestone.

Guidebook of United States Coins — The "Red Book," by R.S. Yeoman (now edited by Kenneth E. Bressett). First published in 1947.,

Guilder — Dutch national currency prior to the Euro.

Hawn, Reed — Texas collector (b. 1950) whose six "name" sales with Stack's (1973-1993) have set the standard of a fine sale. Owner of major rarities including the 1804 silvee dollar, 1913 Liberty nickel, 1838-o half dollar, others

HCGS — Hallmark Coin Grading Services

Howard, Leland — "Doc" Howard, one time acting mint director, longtime head of ODGSO. Also involved with 1933 $20.

Hunt — Hunt Brothers Bunker and William, active in the silver market (1980) and also in ancient coins (Sotheby's sale, 1990), Numismatic Fine Arts (1993).

ICG — Independent Coin Grading Company

ICTA — Industry Council for Tangible Assets, a Washington-basd lobbying organization, founded 1983. The author is a founding member of the board of directors.

INCO — International Nickel Company (major platinum producer)

IRA —Individual Retirement Accounts. Most coins prohibited in self-directed IRAs, except for American Eagles.

Keogh — Retirement account named for Congressman Eugene Keogh

Kilogram — Metric weight equal to about 2.2 avoirdupois pounds.

KM— Krause-Mishler numbering system (world coins)

Koala — Australian bullion coinage

Krugerrand — South African gold coin .917 fine (22k). The original "gold standard" of modern non-circulating bullion coins. The name has taken on a secondary meaning for purity of gold and weight (1 troy ounce of gold).

Liberty — A U.S. Liberty head $20 gold piece

Loupe — Eyepiece (magnifier)

Lydia — Part of western Turkey where coinage first began circa 750 B.C.

Maple leaf — Canadian bullion coin

MS-60 (to MS-70) — Grading system for uncirculated coins, only, Mint State 60 to Mint State 70.

NCGS — National Coin Grading Service

NGC — Numismatic Guaranty Corporation

Norweb — The family who collected coins from Cleveland. Very advanced collectors. Ambassador & Mrs. Norweb were patrons of the American Numismatic Society and the Smithsonian and the ANA.

NTC — Numistrust Corporation

Obverse — Front or face of the coin.

ODGSO — Office of Domestic Gold & Silver Operations. U.S. Treasury Department agency (circa 1934-1975) that regulated gold and silver.

Palladium — Precious metal in the platinum group.

Pandas — Chinese Bullion Coin

PCGS — Professional Coin Grading Service

PCI — PCI Inc.

Philadelphia Mint — Home of several US Mints since 1792, the "P" mint began when the City was the nation's Capital.

Pillar Dollars — The coin which, when sliced and divided like a pie, had the components known as "pieces of eight". These coins whose pillars make them stand out were legal tender in the United States until 1857.

Pittman — John Jay Pittman, who 1971-1973 was president of the ANA, the Canadian Numismatic Association, and honorary president of the Sociedad Numismatica de Mexico (1913-1996). His collection was sold by Akers following his death.

Platinum — Precious metal.

PNG — The Professional Numismatists Guild, Inc. Founded in 1955, a prestige dealer's organization. The author has been an affiliated member for many years and served as general counsel 1981-1993.

Portfolio — In this book, it represents the 19 coins in the Salomon Brothers survey picked by Stack's and identified by Hans M.F. Schulman and Neil S. Berman as the basis for the underlying review of rare coin investments. No gold coins are included.

Prooflike — Coins that are made similar to proofs (or specimen) but which are not

Recoinage — Coin of the realm returned to the mint, melted, and turned into coinage.

Restrike — Coin produced by a government mint or with their authorization from original government dies using the same design, old date, and precious metal content. In silver, one of the most famous is the Maria Theresa Thaler (an Austrian coin dated 1780), still struck today by the Austrian Mint in Vienna. Gold coins include the 1915 Austrian 1 ducat coin,

Restrike — A copy of the original coin, usually by an authorized Mint, using original or copied dies.

Reverse — Back of the coin

Rim — A coin's third surface (after obverse and reverse)

Rooster — French 20 franc coin.

Saint — A US $20 gold piece designed by Augustus St. Gaudens, struck 1907-1933.

Salomon Brothers — A Wall Street investment banking firm (since merged with Smith Barney, now part of Citicorp group, who first charted coins and compared them with other tangible assets.

SEGS — Sovereign Entities Grading Service

Self-directed — Retirement account that permits the depositor to direct how assets will be held, and which ones.

SGS — Star Grading Services

Shillings — Part of the British Pound. £1=20 shillings.

Sovereign — British gold coin weighing .2354 troy oz.

Stillwater — America's platinum mine (located in Columbus, Montana). In 2009, it produced 63,000 ounces of platinum during the first three-quarters of the tear at a cost of $349 an ounce (selling for on average $1,089 an ounce).

Troy ounce — Method used to weigh precious metals. 31.1035 grams = 1 troy ounce. There are 12 troy ounces to the troy pound.

Uncirculated or Unc — A coin that has not entered general circulation. Mint state (MS-60 or better)

VF — very fine (a coin grade)

VG — very good. Another coin grade not so very good.

XF or EF — extremely fine (a coin grade)

SELECTED BIBLIOGRAPHY

David Akers, *U.S. Gold Coins An Analysis of Auction Records* (6 vols)

Joseph Coffin, *The Complete Book of Coin Collecting*, and in the revised third edition (1959)

R.S. Yeoman, *A Guidebook of United States Coins* (Whitman Publishing), 1st ed. 1947 (63rd ed. 2010) (various).

Jeff Garrett and John Dannreuther, *The Official Red Book of Auction Records* (Gold, silver and copper coins) (2 vols.)

Donald O. Case, *Serial Collecting as Leisure, and Coin Collecting in Particular*, Library Trends , vol. 57 No. 4 (Spring 2009)

The Louis Eliasberg Sr. Collection (Bowers & Merena, 1997)

The Louis Eliasberg S.r Collection (Bowers & Merena in cooperation with Stack's, May 1996)

The John Jay Pittman Collection (David Akers Numismatics, Inc., 1997-1998).

Auction Prices Realized (Krause Publications, 1982-2002)

The Reed Hawn Collection of U.S. Coins, Stack's, Aug 1973

The Reed Hawn Collection of U.S. Coins, Stack's,, Oct. 1993

U.S. Gold, Silver & Copper Coins (including the Reed Hawn Collection of Massachusetts Silver), Stack's, May 1998

68th Anniversary Sale (featuring selections from the Reed HawnCollection), Stack's, October 2003.

The W.F. Dunham Collection (Mehl, 1941)

Louis Eliasberg King of Coins (Bowers & Merena, 1996)

The United States Gold Coin Collection [Eliasberg], (Bowers & Merena, 1982)

The King of Siam Sale (Bowers & Merena, October, 1982)

John Kamin's *The Forecaster* (various)

The Wall Street Journal (Internet site)

Federal Reserve Bank of St. Louis (Web site)

Neil S. Berman & Hans M.F. Schulman, *The Investors Guide to United States Coins* (1987)

Neil S. Berman & Silvano DiGenova, *The Investor's Guide to United States Coins* (2007)

"Salomon Brothers Report," by R. Salomon (various)

CPM Gold Yearbook (various years)

CPM Silver Yeaarook (various)

CPM Platinum Yearbook (various)

Numismatic Scrapbook (1935-1976) various

"Under the Glass" column, *Numismatic News*, 1969-date (various)

Arthur & Ira Friedberg, *Gold Coins of the World* (7th ed. 2003); 8th ed. 2009.

Annual Report of the Director of the Mint (various 1867-1981)

The Numismatist (monthly publication of the American Numismatic Association, 1944-1955)

Abe Kosoff, *Kosoff Remembers*

Ganz, "Valuation of Coin Collection," American Jurisprudence 2d Proof of Facts Series (1989)

Ganz, "Proof of Value of Coin Collection," American Jurisprudence 2d Proof of Facts Series (2007)

Interviews

Neil S. Berman (2009)

Reed Hawn (2010)

Professor Michael Duffy, Univ. Of Iowa (2008-2010)

John Jay Pittman (various)

ACKNOWLEDGMENTS

Debbie Bradley, my editor and for this book, guiding light. We planned this at Florida FUN (2009) in the Beeline Diner at the Peabody Orlando. Her belief in the project is what made it a reality.

Harvey G. Stack, for the anecdotes shared

Q. David Bowers, for the repository of his knowledge on many subjects

My longtime friend, dealer and author Scott A. Travers

David Harper, my editor at *Numismatic News*, for his encouragement

My wife, Kathy, for being understanding, and for substantive suggestions in discussing some of the issues, and people, that she knew well from her days as executive assistant to ANA executive director Bob Leuver.

Four cats: Habibi, Mimi, Bizi and Mistletoe, for dropping by as if to help with the typing

David Fanning, David Sklow, George Frederick Kolbe, Bryce Brown, Karl Moulton, and those who collect older public auction sales and old coin books, which are part of my library

Jim Halperin, co-chair of Heritage, in appreciation of allowing use of photos, auction data

Neil S. Berman, a friend of more than 30 years, for sharing his recollections of "topping off" the Eliasberg Gold Coin Collection.

Professor Michael Duffy, University of Iowa for "Farmland" pricing, current and historical

William Bareford

Arthur Friedberg, a longtime friend, for his gold coin research

Grant Marylander, Esq., whose enthusiasm for the FDR gold seizure orders made me look deeper;

Several ICTA directors or regulars at their meetings where some of the issues in this book were raised and discussed first, including Mark Albanian (Goldline), Mike Fuljenz (Universal), Terry Hanlon, Paul Montgomery; Eloise Bredder; Diane Piret

Several well-known dealers and auction firms who lent their expertise and auction records and photos

Christine Karstedt (Stack's)

Ira Goldberg and Larry Goldberg

John Feigenbaum (David Lawrence Rare Coins)

Steve Ivy

For production assistance:

Rob Pantina

Cynthia L. Carter

My law partners Jeri Hollinger and Teri Noel Towe

For information acknowledged previously on Salomon Brothers Survey

Julian Leidman

Stack's Rare Coins
Fred Weinberg
Dennis Baker
Numismedia
Professional Coin Grading Service (PCGS)
Numismatic Guaranty Corp. (NGC)
David W. Akers
The late John Jay Pittman
Lansend (Ashwin Pai), my firm's I-T department
The intensive care facilities, and staff at the CCU Unit of Valley Hospital, Ridgewood, NJ, where this was proofed during my mother's recent illness, and hospital president Audrey Meyers, for her kindness.
Dr. Donald Kagin, longtime friend and colleague
Sue and John Albanese
Donna Mummery (Love those charts!)
Bob and Hilda Leuver
Chris Karlstadt (Stack's)
Clifford Mishler
Chet Krause
Margaret and Dr. Donald E. Herdeck (bicentennial coinage)
Commission of Fine Arts
Charles Atherton
Thomas Wolfe, ODGSO director
Jay Johnson, for his gracious introduction
Jean Gentry, U.S. Mint legal counsel
Sue Kohler, Fine Arts Commission
Bergen County Cooperative Library System (BCCLS) for use of *New York Times* archives
Fair Lawn, N.J., Maurice Pine Public Library, Tim Murphy, Director, for expediting BCCLS use with my library card
Grover C. Criswell Jr.
Paul R. Whitnah, whose M&M Travel in Arlington, Texas, planned every trip made necessary by this book.

ABOUT THE AUTHOR

DAVID L. GANZ, 58, (b 1951) has been a writer in the numismatic field since 1965, when he began writing the column "Under the Glass" for *The Coin Shopper*. He subsequently wrote the same-named column for *The Coin Collector*, Anamosa, Iowa, from 1967-68, *The Coin Collector & Shopper* for Krause Publications in 1968-9, and starting in 1969, for *Numismatic News* where the column is still published today. He authored *A Beginners Guide to Better Coins* in 1965 and has since written more than 20 other books or book-length works.

While attending Georgetown University in Washington, D.C. (1969-1973), he was Washington correspondent for Numismatic News Weekly, and was the first hobby publication writer to be admitted to the Periodical Press Gallery of the U.S. Senate (93rd Congress), representing Numismatic News Weekly.

After graduation from Georgetown (1973), he went to work in Iola, Wis., as assistant editor of *Numismatic News*, and remained there until he started law school at St. John's University School of Law, Jamaica, N.Y. , in February 1974. He graduated in 2-1/2 years in 1976, having spent a semester abroad studying international law in Rome, while also working for the Food & Agriculture Organization of the United Nations. He was then admitted to the New York bar in March 1977. He has since been admitted to practice in the District of Columbia (1980) and New Jersey (1985), and is admitted to practice before the U.S. Tax Court, federal district courts, and multiple circuits courts of appeal. He was admitted to practice before the U.S. Supreme Court, having appeared in person and having been sworn in by Chief Justice Warren Burger in 1980.

David L. Ganz
Steven Stack-Visual Impressions

He joined the American Numismatic Association in 1967, became Life Member 1072 in 1972, and worked on convention committees from 1970 to 1980. In 1978 he was appointed legislative counsel, a post he held until 1996, and in 1985 he was elected to the ANA Board of Governors. He served for 10 years on the ANA Board, culminating with his service as 48th President (1993-1996).

He is a recipient of the Glenn Smedley Memorial Medal from the ANA (1995); the Medal of Merit (1997) from the Token & Medal Society of which he served as 29th president (2004-2006); the Numismatic Literary Guild's highest honor, the Clement F. Bailey Memorial Award (1991) and was awarded the Order of St. Agatha (Commander) by the Republic of San Marino, July, 1994. He received the James U. Blanchard Lifetime Achievement Award, Industry Council for Tangible Assets, 2009.

In his private practice as a lawyer, he has represented the Canadian Olympic Coin Program; the Statue of Liberty Commemorative Coin Program through the Foundation that managed restoration; the 1980 Olympic Coin Program; The Memorial Hospital-Billy Graham Congressional Gold Medal program, and a number of other marketing ventures into the coin field. As ANA president, he chaired the World Mint Council from 1993-1995. In 1995, more than 24 nations ministers attended Council meetings in Anaheim. Ganz addressed the nations in consecutive speeches in French, German, Russian, Spanish and English. He is fluent in Spanish after having lived for two summers as an exchange student in Mexico more than 45 years ago.

Dedicated to public service, he served as a consultant to the Money Office of the Food & Agriculture Organization of the United Nations (Rome) for more than 25 years. He was appointed by President Richard Nixon to the 1974 Annual Assay Commission, and from 1993-1996 served as a charter member of the Citizens Commemorative Coin Advisory Committee, a Clinton Administration appointment by Treasury Secretary Lloyd Bentsen. As a committee member, he was a major advocate for circulating commemorative coins and the state quarter program. Then-U.S. Mint director Philip N. Diehl wrote in 1998, "From my vantage point, the lion's share of the credit for making the 50 State program a reality goes to David Ganz, for his persistence as an advocate ..."

Mint Director Jay Johnson refers to Ganz as the "father of the 50 state quarter program." The program has returned over $5-billion to the American taxpayer since its inception which has been used to lower the interest paid on the national debt.

He served for 10 years as a member of his community's zoning board of adjustment, including four years as chairman, and was then elected councilman in Fair Lawn, N.J. in 1998. He became Mayor in 1999 and served for seven years. He is currently in his third three-year term as a county freeholder (or supervisor) of Bergen County, N.J., where he has chaired the finance committee and has had charge over a $600 million budgetthe past eight years.

He is also managing partner and principal litigator in the law firm of Ganz & Sivin, L.L.P. of Fair Lawn, N.J. and Ganz & Hollinger, P.C. in New York City, and has a law practice that is focused on litigation, guardianship, real estate, land use, and general corporate work in New York and New Jersey.

He has three adult children; Scott is presently in the military, and Elyse and Pam are both graduates (2009) of Florida Atlantic University in Boca Raton. He and his wife, the former Kathleen Gotsch, live in Fair Lawn with their four cats, Mimi, Bizi, Habibi, and Mistletoe.

Books and major articles by David L. Ganz
(A selected Bibliography)

1973   *A Critical Guide to Anthologies of African Literature* (African Studies Ass'n, 1973)

1976   *14 Bits: A Legal & Legislative History of 31 USC 324d-i* (1976)

1977   *Toward a Revision of the Minting & Coinage Law of the United States*, 26 Cleveland State Law Review 177-257 (1977),

1977   *The U.N. and the Law of the Sea*, 26 International & Comparative Law Quarterly 1-53 (1977)

1978   *Probative Value of Currently Dating for Income in Respect of a Decedent*, 51 N.Y.S. Bar Journal 487-491 (1978).

1980   *The World of Coins & Coin Collecting* (first published in 1980, 3d revised edition, 1998)

1989   *Valuation of Coin Collection*, 5 Proof of Facts 3rd 577-655 (1989)

1990   *Legal Ethics: When A Lawyer's Obligation Begins (and Ends)*, 125 N.J. Law J. 1742 (June 28, 1990), reprinted in Lawyer's Liability Rev. Q.J. 3-6 (April, 1991)

1990   *Drop dollar bills; we need $1 coins*, USA Today, May 23, 1990, p. 10A (Guest Columnist, Face-Off).

1991   *America's Coinage Laws (1792-1894)* (ed. David L. Ganz, Bowers & Merena, 1991).

1993   *Foreclosure* in McGraw-Hill Real Estate Handbook 563-582 (1993);
1996   *The 90 Second Lawyer* (Wiley, 1996) (Robert Irwin, co-author)

1997   *How to get an Instant Mortgage* (Wiley, 1997) (Robert Irwin, co-author)

1997   *The 90 Second Lawyer Guide to Buying Real Estate* (Wiley, 1997) (Robert Irwin, co-author)

1998   *Planning Your Rare Coin Retirement* (Bonus Books, 1998)

1999   *The Official Guide to Commemorative Coins* (Bonus, 1999)

2000   *The Official Guidebook to America's State Quarters*, a Random House Fall, 2000

2007   *Proof of Value of Coin Collection*, 95 Proof of Facts 3d 155-465 (2007)

2007   *Wrongful Death in Claims Against Emergency Service Workers*, 101 Proof of Facts 3d pages 1-283 (2008)

2008   *America's State Quarters* (Random House, 2008)

2008   *Profitable Coin Collecting* (Krause Publications, 2008)

2008   *The Smithsonian Guide to Coin Collecting* (Harper Collins, 2008)

2008   *Wrongful Death in Claims Against Emergency Service Workers*, 101 Proof of Facts 3d 1-283 (2008)

2009   *Rent Control: Proof of Tenant's Entitlement to Benefits and Landlord's Right to Terminate*, 108 POF3d (2009)

2010   *Proof of Liability for Police Actions resulting in claims of serious personal injury or wrongful death.* 113 pof3d 305-638 (2010)

2010   *A Critical Guide to Anthologies of African Literature*, revised 2nd edition

Footnotes

[1]David L. Ganz, Smithsonian Guide to Coin Collecting, p. 71 (Harper Collins, 2008)

[2]The section in the CCCAC Annual Report to Congress which advocated circulating commemoratives, and which ultimately became the state quarter program, was drafted by me as a committee member. I so testified before the U.S. House of Representatives subcommittee dealing with coinage matters in July, 1995.

[3]Sadly, bet for a swell meal was forgotten in the excitement. I'm still waiting. The anecdote was previously published in Bowers, Commemorative Coins of the United States, A Complete Encyclopedia, p. 508 (Bowers & Merena, 1991).

[4]R.S. Yeoman, *A Guide Book of United States Coins* (*14th ed.*) P. 81 (Whitman Publishing, 1960).

[5]If you're interested in those and other rare coins, see David L. Ganz, *Profitable Coin Collecting* (Krause Publications, 2008), a Numismatic Literary Guild award-winning book.

[6]Before the issuance of state quarters.

[7]The Annual Report of the Director of the Mint for the fiscal year ended Sept. 30, 1990, p. 9, says there are 147 million casual collectors".

[8]Donald O. Case, Serial Collecting as Leisure, and Coin Collecting in Particular, Library Trends , vol. 57 No. 4 (Spring 2009), quoting from Bacon's 2008 Magazine Directory.

[9]Coin World reader demographics (2006). Collection and investment data drawn from 2006 datum published on the internet (viewed July 5, 2008) Reader profile conducted by Readex, Stillwater, MN (March 28, 2006).

[10]This has a significant bearing on successful investment choices.

[11]Chart adopted from data presented in Joseph Coffin, "The Complete Book of Coin Collecting", 3rd rev. ed. 1959), pages 198-199. Additional data (post-1958) based on author's research.

[12]W.H. Woodin, The Commercial Element in Numismatics", 24 The Numismatist 169-171 (May, 1911).

[13]The formula in Quattro pro for windows or Excel uses the cited variables and is @rate(2008 price realized,1982 price realized, 26), where "26" is the number of years between sales.

[14]See, 49 Fed. Reg. 645, 647 (Jan. 5, 1984). Treas. Reg. §1.6045-1(a)(5) (ii)(D).

[15]The formula used is @rate(future value, initial cost, number of years) in Excel or Quattro Pro for Windows. (page 162

[16]Conservation efforts can, however, improve the appearance of a coin.

[17]Donald O. Case, Serial Collecting as Leisure, and Coin Collecting in Particular, Library Trends , vol. 57 No. 4 (Spring 2009), quoting from Bacon's 2008 Magazine Directory.

[18]The Annual Report of the Director of the Mint for the fiscal year ended Sept. 30, 2008 says (p.9): "demographic trends tell us that our typical retail customer base is shrinking. Our core numismatic customer tends to be an older white male in the upper middle class, college educated, and often retired."

[19]Coin World reader demographics (2006). Collection and investment data drawn from 2006 datum published on the internet (viewed July 5, 2008) Reader profile conducted by Readex, Stillwater, MN (March 28, 2006).

[20]50 State Commemorative Coin Program Study [for the U.S. Mint] (Coopers & Lybrand, 1997) p. 31.

[21]http://www.irs.gov/retirement/participant/article/0,,id=188238,00.html

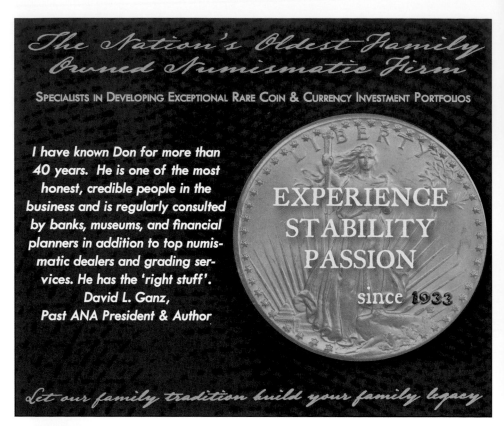

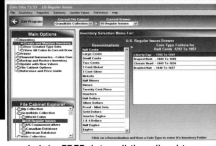

FOR ALL OF YOUR LEGAL NEEDS

GANZ & HOLLINGER
A PROFESSIONAL CORPORATION
ATTORNEYS-AT-LAW
SINCE 1980

DAVID L. GANZ*
JERRIETTA R. HOLLINGER**
MEMBERS OF THE FIRM
●
TERI NOEL TOWE***
OF COUNSEL

*ADMITTED IN NEW YORK, NEW JERSEY &
    DISTRICT OF COLUMBIA
  EMAIL ADDRESS: DavidLGanz@GanzHollinger.com
**ADMITTED IN NEW YORK AND MARYLAND
  EMAIL ADDRESS: JRHollinger@Juno.Com
***ADMITTED IN NEW YORK AND CONNECTICUT
  EMAIL ADDRESS: TeriNoelTowe@Aol.Com

1394 THIRD AVENUE, NEW YORK CITY @ 79TH STREET, NEW YORK 10075
TELEPHONE (212) 517-5500 FAX (212) 772-2720
WEB SITE: www.GanzHollinger.com

OUR AFFILIATED FIRM:
GANZ & SIVIN, LLP
A LIMITED LIABILITY PARTNERSHIP
FAIR LAWN, NEW JERSEY 07410
TELEPHONE (201) 703-0300
FAX (201) 703-0337
www.GanzSivin.com

HOURS BY APPOINTMENT
MAJOR CREDIT CARDS ACCEPTED

DAVID L. GANZ IS A LIFE FELLOW OF THE AMERICAN NUMISMATIC SOCIETY, A LIFE MEMBER (#1072) & PAST PRESIDENT OF THE AMERICAN NUMISMATIC ASSOCIATION, AN AFFILIATED MEMBER (#436) OF THE PROFESSIONAL NUMISMATISTS GUILD AND A FOUNDING BOARD MEMBER OF THE INDUSTRY COUNCIL FOR TANGIBLE ASSETS

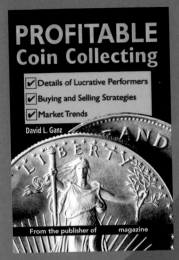

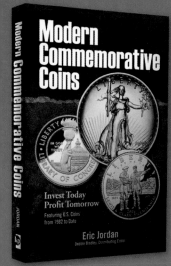
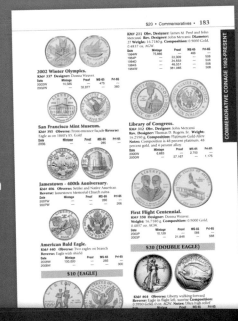

CAC races on, closing in on the $150,000,000 milestone

CAC is about to pass another impressive milestone, soon to purchase more than $150 million of CAC verified coins from the dealer community. That is amazing considering CAC only entered the market a few years ago. But in that short time, CAC has become a powerful market maker for CAC verified coins, strongly backing those sporting the "green bean" as an active bidder in the market.

It's no wonder CAC confidently purchases stickered coins. If you want to easily identify and have confidence that a coin is solid for the grade - look for the CAC verification sticker.

"Because Confidence is Priceless"

www.caccoin.com